L'Ordre du monde

In French, the word *ordre* comes from the Latin *ordo*, and means both "an arrangement of things in which one thing follows another" and "the condition in which everything has its proper place and function". Associated with the word Monde (world), as in the title of this book, it reflects a will to organize (that of God, Fate, Nature, matter).

The expression *L'Ordre du monde* takes on so much spiritual and philosophical signification that it is impossible to translate without betraying the spirit.

That is why Sujata has preferred to leave the title in French; also a homage to the land she has been living in for twenty years.

Sujata Bajaj

L'Ordre du monde

Texts by *Jean-Claude Carrière* and *Lorette Nobécourt*

Albin Michel

In homage to *Baba,* my father.
To *Ma,* my mother.

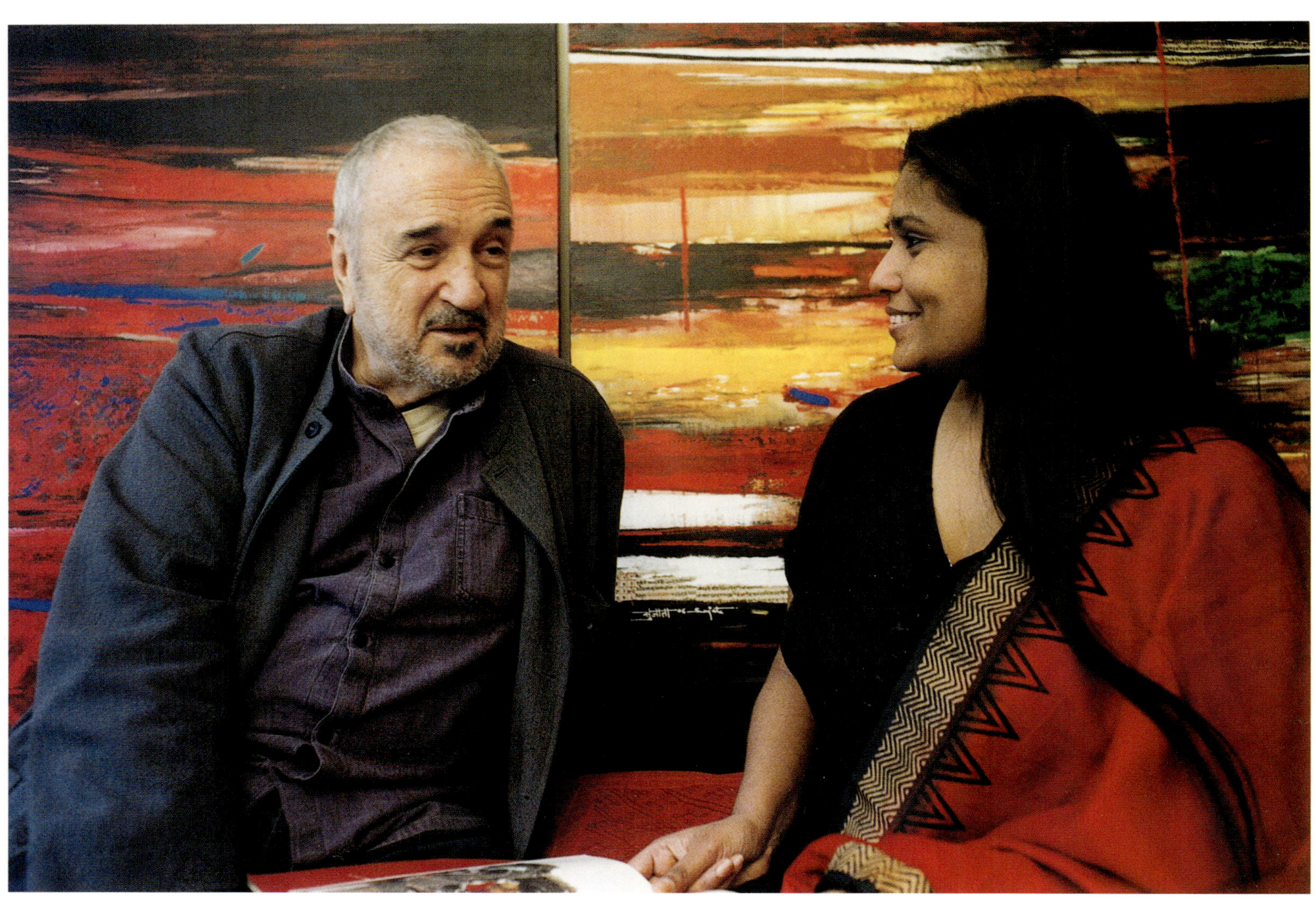

In innumerable villages of India, the woman steps out of her house in the morning to make a pattern on the ground in front of the main door. She draws with her fingers using coloured powder. Often geometric in shape, the design could be called non-figurative, in other words symbolic and allegorical. This is an auspicious pattern that changes with the days, adapts to the seasons, the weather, to the overall condition of the family, the sentiments of the woman that morning and the divinity that should be worshipped. It is a design meant to harmonise the vast sky with her little corner of the earth.

In other words, visually, through a *sign*, things can, indeed, interconnect. Howsoever different they may otherwise be, they can still hold together in a proper order and not sink into chaos.

The order can be maintained by other means as well. The song and the word in the guise of *mantras* also play a propitiatory role. The various rituals, which are our means of defence, are a way of telling the cosmos (or the Gods) that we know what it all means, that we have done whatever is necessary, that we have nothing to reproach ourselves. In return, we wait for external forces to recognise these signals and, in the chaotic march of time, to spare us, to leave us in peace, at least for that one day.

This truly artistic attitude where art is the supreme link, the only way to uncover the secrets of the universe, is the constant, omnipresent manifestation of the Indian notion of *dharma* which is both the cosmic order regulating the movements of the stars and the atoms, and the particular path that each one of us must unfailingly follow. Our path, if you prefer.

The Indian idea, the purely and strictly Indian idea, is that there exists a fundamental solidarity between the individual *dharma* and the cosmic *dharma*. That the proper movement of the cosmic *dharma* depends on how well the individual *dharma* is observed.

All this is by way of understanding how Sujata's work should be seen. We should, if possible, approach it with our eyes wide open, for her compositions are not made to please or amuse. Rather, they are the fruit of a much larger work springing from a long tradition which can and should be preserved. It is the very *dharma* of painters to have no other objective than to put us in harmony and peace with the universe.

Since it burst upon the scene a hundred years ago, non-figurative painting has, by and large, been confined to the expression of an ego that is furtive, dark or shining. We can appreciate this style of painting or reject it, depending on the special resonances it evokes, our state of mind, our tastes and our passing fears. At times we recognise ourselves in it. But more often than not, we move rapidly past the canvases. They say nothing to us and are quickly forgotten.

In some instances, and for reasons we cannot explain, this kind of painting, apparently without a subject, grows in such a way that it touches what is known in India as the "universal form", the kind Krishna assumed in the *Bhagavad Gita* to comfort and convince his friend Arjuna.

A form that contains all forms, a form beyond description or representation.

No figurative painting, necessarily limited by its "subject" could attain this universality. And when such so-called *abstract* painting (a word like any other) comes even imperceptibly close to the universal, not only does it hold the eye, it also calls forth words that stem from the same desire and the same need, and which dance around forms, embrace them and penetrate them as if to reassure us and guide us in this confusing world.

Jean-Claude Carrière

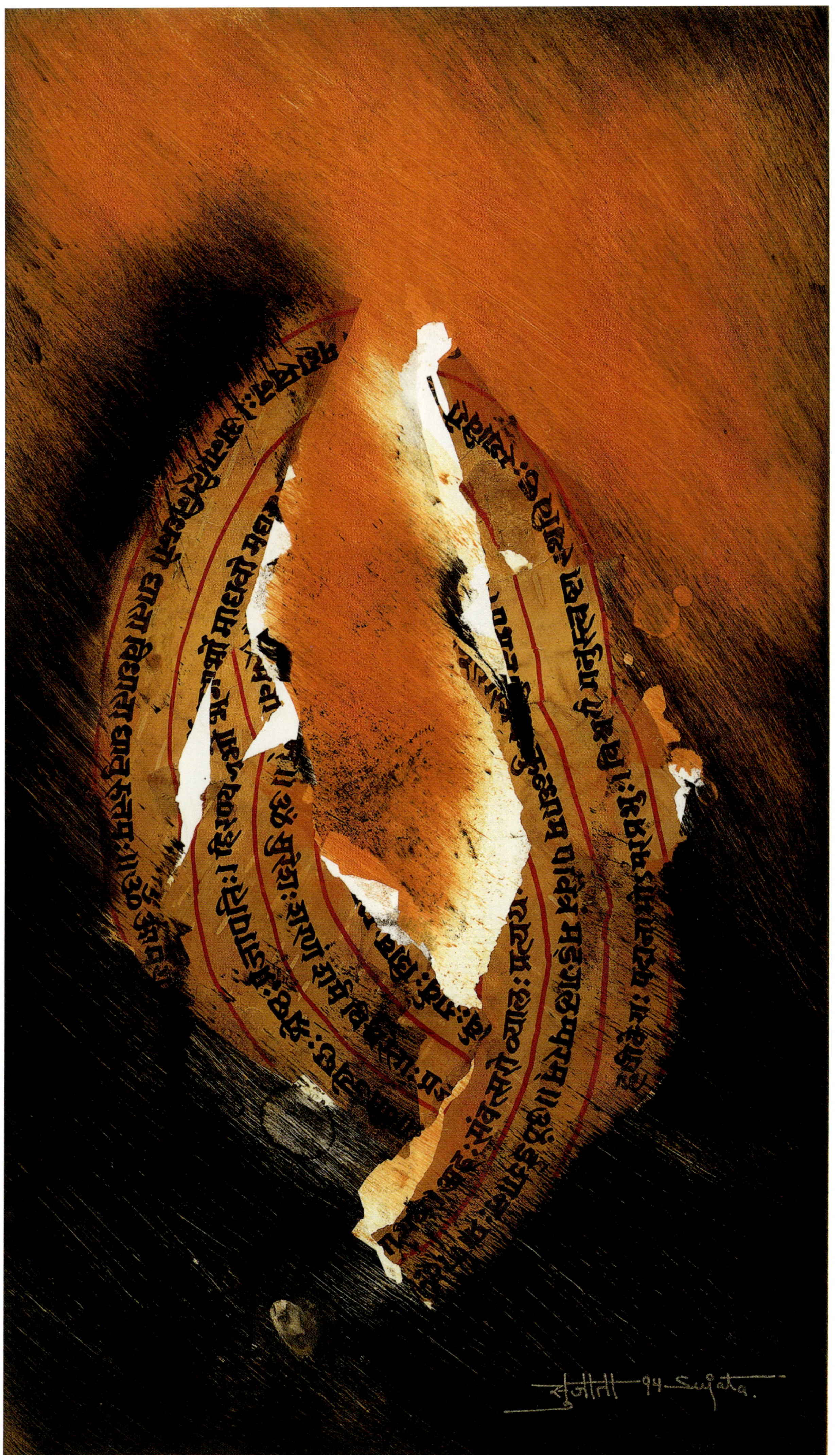
सुजाता 94 Sujata.

Sujata Bajaj, The *Dharma* of a Painter

by *Jean-Claude Carrière*

I have known her for close to twenty years, ever since she held her first exhibition in Paris. I believe, as she sometimes reminds me, that I may have been the first person in France to acquire her paintings. It was a time when I had just emerged, dazed, from a long spell of work with Peter Brook on the *Mahabharata,* and I found in young Sujata the vibrant echoes of that great epic in which India has always sought, and often found, herself.

I couldn't help noting the innumerable resonances the two works stirred in me – the ancient work and the new, the written and the painted, both born of the same soil.

At that moment, it was obviously I who saw and heard these resonances. In the epic, these resonances are violent, even bloody, yet they are also strangely harmonious (or, if you will, harmoniously disquieting).

And so it is in every relationship with a work of art. My impressions as I set my eyes on the paintings of Sujata (who was born in Jaipur in Rajasthan) were inspired by eleven years of work and sojourns in India, of countless encounters, improvisations, conversations, of a profusion of images, stories, colours, movement, even smells, which we had patiently amassed for our production.

In this large river in whose waters I still immerse myself in order to satisfy my curiosity, I found it impossible to *discern* the place Sujata had carved for herself in the painting of her time. I perceived in her early monotypes – quite apart from a special technique which, it seems, we owe to Degas – a juvenile energy, come from afar and unique, somehow connected to the cosmos.

a juvenile energy, come from afar and unique

In India, however, everything is cosmic. Regardless of what we think, no gesture here is merely human, no word stands alone. Unknown to us, the fundamental notion of *dharma* knits all our thoughts and actions into the entire universe. And whether or not the universe moves along the right path depends first and foremost on us.

This is especially true if we are artists, spokesmen, mediators. The crucial mission of establishing such a link is central to all of Sujata's work, the key to her approach, and the reason why this book is entitled *L'Ordre du monde.*

It's a strange order, unfamiliar, hidden, that reveals itself slowly through the pathways of chaos, an order that is neither geometric nor balanced, nor even set to a certain motion in time, an order made up of contrasts, of clashes and unexpected echoes, but an order nonetheless.

Real order, perhaps, disguised as disorder, the only one we can claim to approach with the help of certain signposts.

In the work of the young artist I couldn't help noticing – since it leapt up at the most undiscerning eye – a repeated use of archaic Indian writing, as though we had been sent paper messages through cracks in the sky. That was what struck me. Not that I sought to understand their meaning. What intrigued me was their presence, their placement, their arrangement.

I had just learned that according to the most ancient Indian tradition, the first manifestations of what we call life, and which are inextricably linked to language, emerged from the slow movements of an as-yet unformed cosmos; a cosmos that looked for its form and substance in vaguely musical vibrations. Little by little, and in deference to unknown forces, these vibrations were transformed and reorganised into a secret order, giving birth to sounds, then to vowels and words, and finally to the *Vedas.*

These gradual revelations and modifications place the early texts beyond the pale of any argument, for they are the works of the universe itself.

The first words of the world.

And I was astonished to see that a young artist was suddenly opening doors, and bringing us closer – in however small a way – to the mystery of the world's origins.

This is what I wrote about her at that time: "There is in the work of Sujata Bajaj an obvious search for structure; for a solid, balanced form in the design and colour. But without her knowing it, fragments of another world – images and writings resembling the remains of a tattered memory – slide into her own."

I so liked this "invasion" that I offered no resistance as it seeped into me. I knew other Indian painters (truth to tell, only a handful, Raza among them), all very different from her. Yet I could never have imagined then that I was gazing at the first steps of a pioneer.

a strange order, unfamiliar, hidden, that reveals itself slowly through the pathways of chaos

I found it impossible to link Sujata to a "movement" or a "school". I saw her as an exception, a woman moreover, and an Indian. I felt that through her I loved India, that I was, once again, letting myself be seduced by this flexible and infinite, undulating and unpredictable, particularly secretive country in whose web I had been well and truly caught.
Since this first encounter, contemporary Indian painting has taken flight. Collectors from all over the world, discouraged by the stagnation in Europe and even America, have been heading for Mumbai and Delhi. Publications have multiplied, the value of art works is being assessed, prices are shooting up and museums are opening.
In this changed landscape which is of interest to an increasing number of Indian patrons (with every indication that it will last), Sujata ranks among the frontrunners. Norway, for example, with its chilling mists, long nights and clinging whiteness, has been won over by the zeal in her canvases. And Norway is not the only country clamouring for more. New York, Paris and Mumbai are waiting in line. The pioneer has been transformed into a classic.

the pioneer has been transformed into a classic

Something similar also happened in the cinema. Years ago, we in Europe believed that the cinema we loved, arthouse cinema, the cinema of ambition, beauty and research would disappear definitively under the sustained barrage from Hollywood, where films are regarded as little more than simple products.
We began to despair, to tell ourselves that through the hundred years of its turbulent existence, cinema had come full circle. Now, it could only degenerate and disappear.
That is when Asian filmmakers from Iran, China, Korea, India, Taiwan and Hong Kong came to our rescue and gave us courage. They were taking the same path as we had taken, they liked the same cinema as we did, and they seemed to be saying: "Don't hang your head in despair, don't look so glum, for the cinema is still alive."
Of course they were right. And they convinced us. It was easy.
Something similar is happening in the more fragmented and elusive province of painting. We seem to be caught up in it bit by bit, wholly overpowered by the

pressure of market ratings, by the cult of "record prices in public auctions", by the pirouettes of an art called "contemporary" (meaning, if words still have a meaning, an art that will not last for long); we feel threatened by the same commercial wave that consigned a large part of American cinema to a public of teenagers – ignorant and proud of it – as painters from other parts of the world, and mainly from Asia, arrive on the scene.

Real painters. Painters who paint.

Real painters. Painters who paint. It suffices it to look at their work honestly, simply, almost naively, to understand that here, we are dealing with a struggle against futility, the hopelessness of painting that leads to emptiness and disdain, the two major temptations of the "contemporary" artist.

It is not because we are assailed every day, every hour, under a heap of images that cinema and painting are dead. Quite the contrary. Although it is more difficult today than ever before (and this is true for photographers as well) to make an image, when it comes alive, this image has greater force and a greater possibility of survival. Plagued by a multitude of impressions, we have become formidable image-sorting machines, in other words, image-forgetting machines. Banal images auto-destruct, passing before our eyes and disappearing even as they are born.

We cannot even discard them, because they discard themselves.

We haven't even seen them. Invisible by definition, lost in an ever-growing and invasive mass – for the real grows more and more banal every day – these images were prevented from existing the very moment they appeared.

A few centuries ago, when we hung four or five engravings on our walls, representing – more or less sucessfully – the earth and the sky (and gods and saints and angels), we retained perhaps one image in five. Today we retain one in a million.

Our sensory limits – those antennae of the brain – force us to choose. But how do we choose? And according to what criteria? The most readily available criterion, the infallible guide, is obviously money. It is supposed never to go wrong, although history, even the history of painting, proves just the opposite. For the past sixty years, money has enacted its own laws, nourished its own references, and never needed another judge. In all domains, money is both judge and accused. Every year for reasons of its own, it creates its own market and fights to keep up the prices – in short, it maintains itself.

When it makes a mistake, it tries to deny it for as long as it can. Thereafter, when there is nothing left to defend any more, it turns its back on its favourites, and dryly and forever drops the individual whose value it had earlier decreed.

Apart from money – the great ringleader in the market – all that remains, then, is this secret, indescribable emotion we feel when we look at a painting, or a series of paintings; a kind of coherence, a vision controlled by a technique, a visible, perceptible, indisputable opening that leads us, despite ourselves, to the beyond, sweeping us into a second world and then into a third.

Seen thus, the progress of Sujata Bajaj, whose work I have been faithfully following for twenty years, is, in my view, exemplary. She has maintained her vision while expanding it. And her technique has followed this growth. After the early monotypes that she discovered with Claude Visieux, she moved on to mixed techniques, making collages out of paper, silk, bits of rope and burnt cardboard to which she added wax, chalk, gouache, ink – in short, everything that her hand or eye came across.

This took her towards unexpected forms where uncertain fragments seemed, every now and again, to break out of the frame as though they were asking themselves: What am I doing in this painting? Who put me here? What if I escaped? Where would I go?

Every time we see her work, characterised as it is by a mix of dash and control, we feel it transmits an energy that is akin to a sense of well-being. Contrary to so many exhibitions which harp on the murky, the arid and on a monotonous pathos, we leave this exhibition feeling cheerful. We needed to see it.

We needed to see it because of its predilection for a fragmented message; a message written in an ancient language, coming to us from God knows where, bringing us words that are certainly essential – since they are all about the order of the universe – but which we are unable to decipher.

It is, however, good to know that the words are there, within reach, within one's range of vision.

With her fondness for enigma, for mystery, for beauty as enigma, Sujata poses questions without asking us for an answer.

And she doesn't provide the answers either.

she invented the colour red.
Or even, shades of red.

This colour springs from her as if by surprise. It is her need, her necessity, her deepest nature. It also springs, less overtly, from her native land. When I look upon some of her works, I feel she invented the colour red. Or even, shades of red.

And then we have these sudden, inexplicable yet essential spots and white shafts piercing a mass of dark, tangled matter which, until that moment, appeared to be looking for light.

Her unmistakable concern is not to make something new but to make something come alive.

Her preference for openings and plunges, downwards, even upwards (for the direction of movements depends upon us), for other dimensions, perspectives, sensations, for worlds rushing precipitately towards one another, worlds that move, telescope, mingle, disappear and sometimes forget one another.

What we have here are intimate upheavals: inconclusive battles between earth and sky, the ruins of stars, imperfect circles floating in space as if uncaged, and a few promises – even stealthy ones – of brilliance, of calm, of radiance.

And, to continue with India, we could also evoke the stubborn effort to break through the famous *maya* – that tissue of illusions which covers our life and deceives us – and try to reach the beyond. But the web is tight, so finely woven, that I will not hazard my way there for fear of losing myself.

her unmistakable concern is not to make something new but to make something come alive.

Today, without abandoning her other techniques (mixed media, torn paper glued on to the support then painted), Sujata has reached the stage of painting with acrylic medium directly onto the canvas, using only the paint itself. We see highly developed horizontal or vertical structures that appear to call for a formal composition, immediately belied, disrupted, by irruptions, flaws, debris and precipices.

Her motto could read: Leave from someplace to arrive elsewhere.

She is both spontaneous and methodical. She does not make any rough sketches or meticulous preparations for her projects. Neither does she prepare herself.

She does not seek multiplication in her work. On the contrary, the more she is in demand, the more slowly she works. She says she would like to be able to see each of her canvases ten or twenty years on without ever having to deny them.

She is a painter – this much is certain. She has not erred on her *dharma*. Before every empty canvas she waits, watchful, for something irresistible to beckon her.

If it is true that we are made up of millions of atoms, more than the unimaginable numbers of stars in the sky, Sujata's journey is far from over.

For, awaiting her are other abysses, other ascents, other breakthroughs and other infinities.

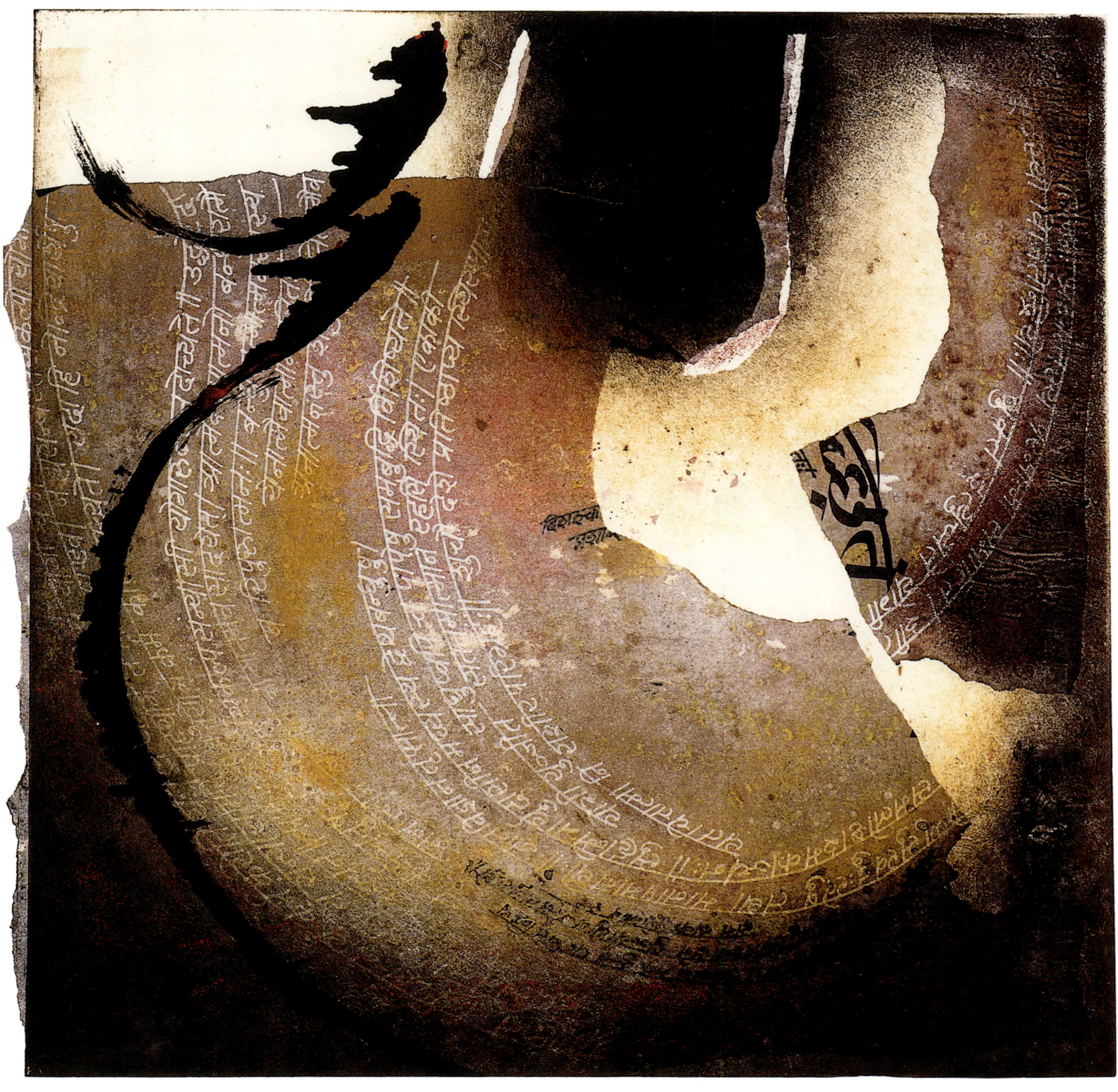

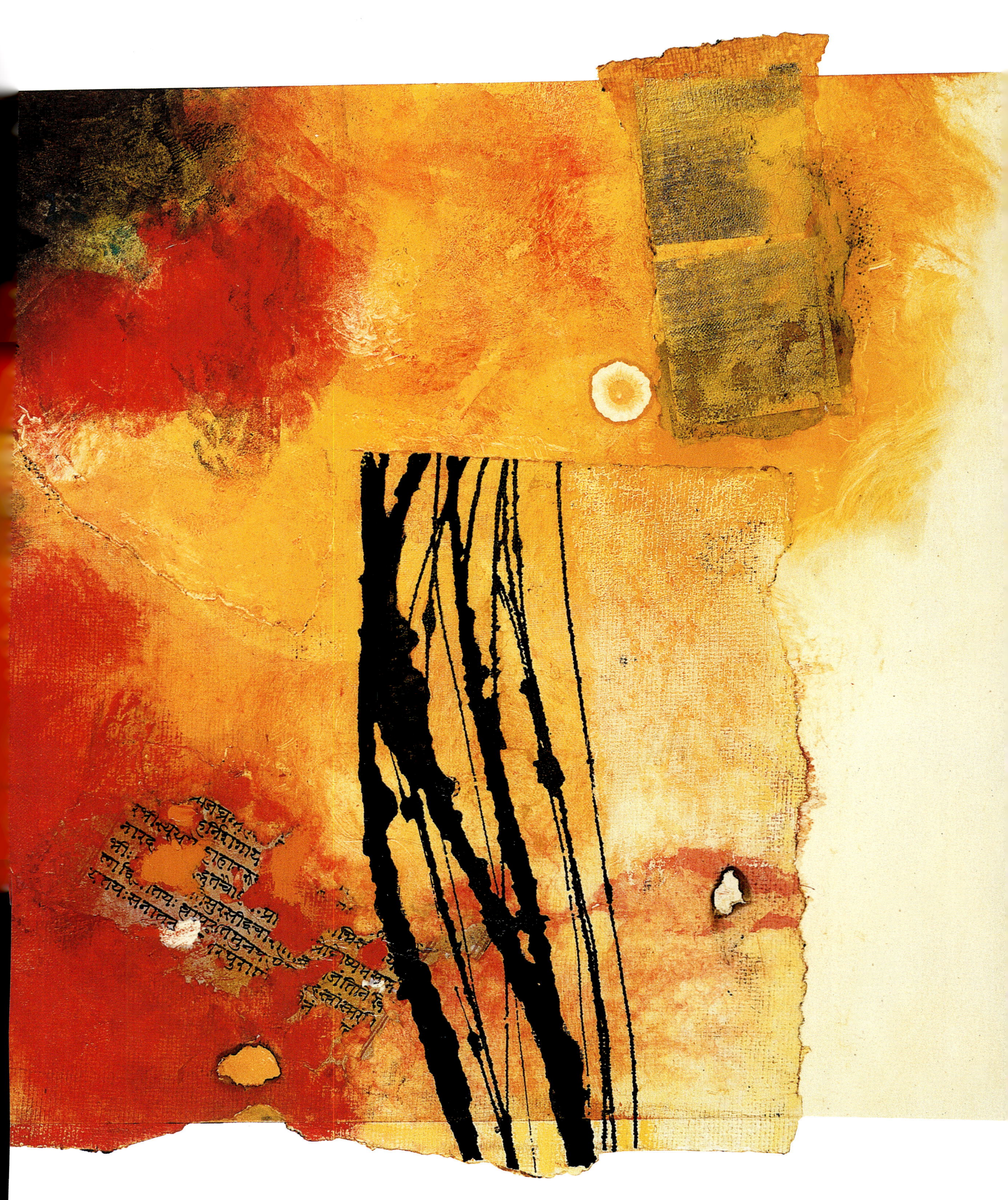

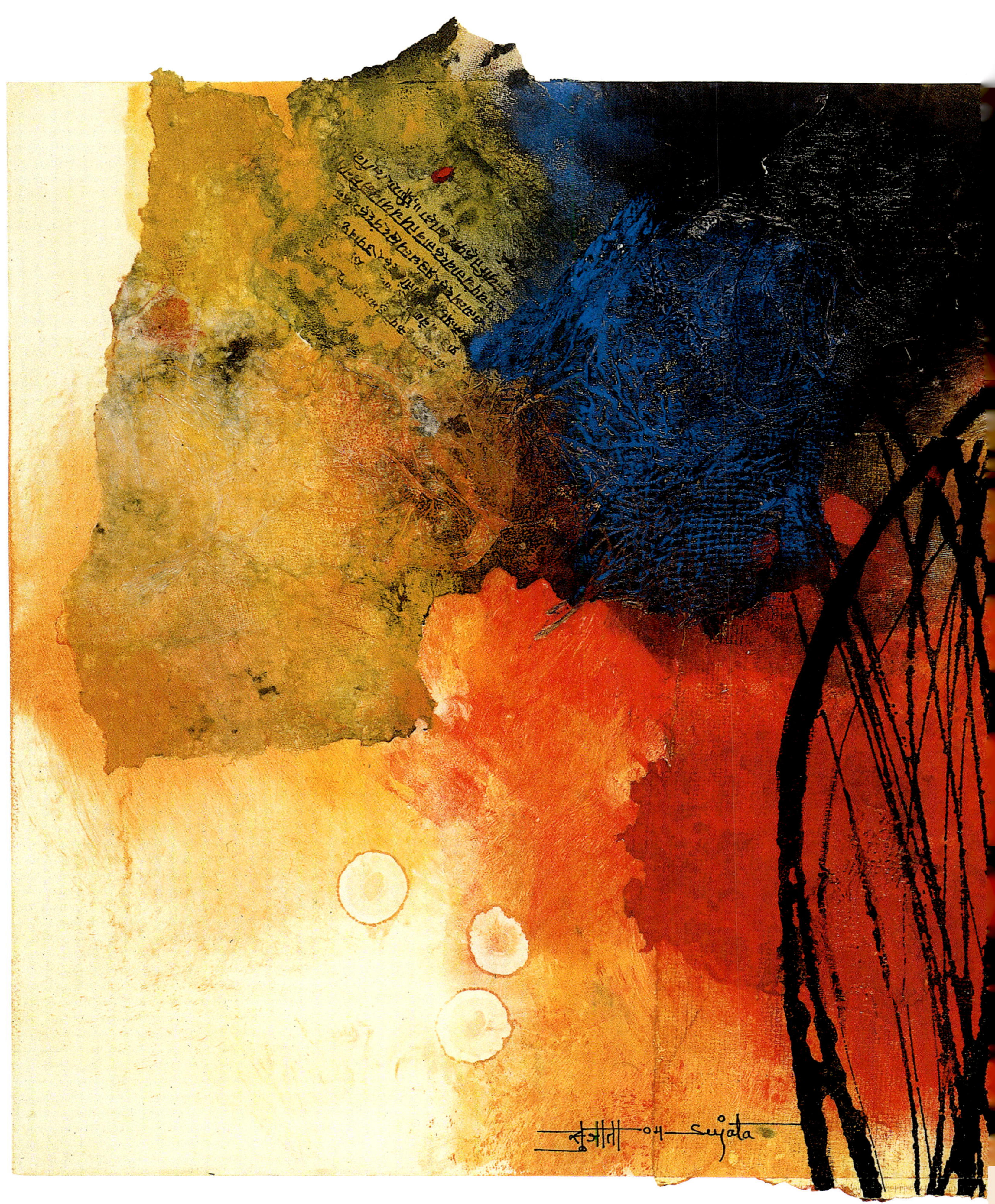
सुजाता 04 Sujata

Mixed media

Techniques mixtes

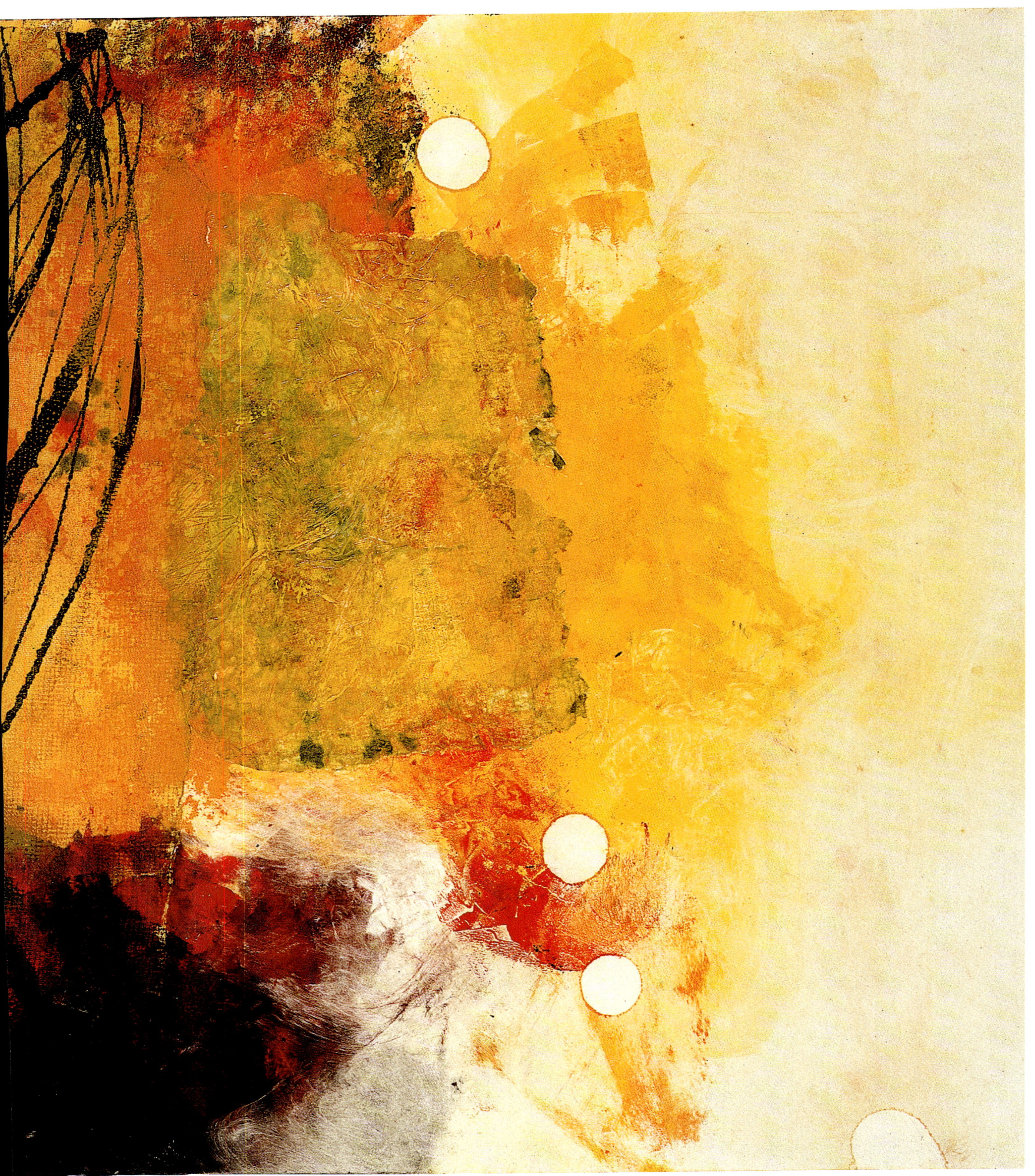

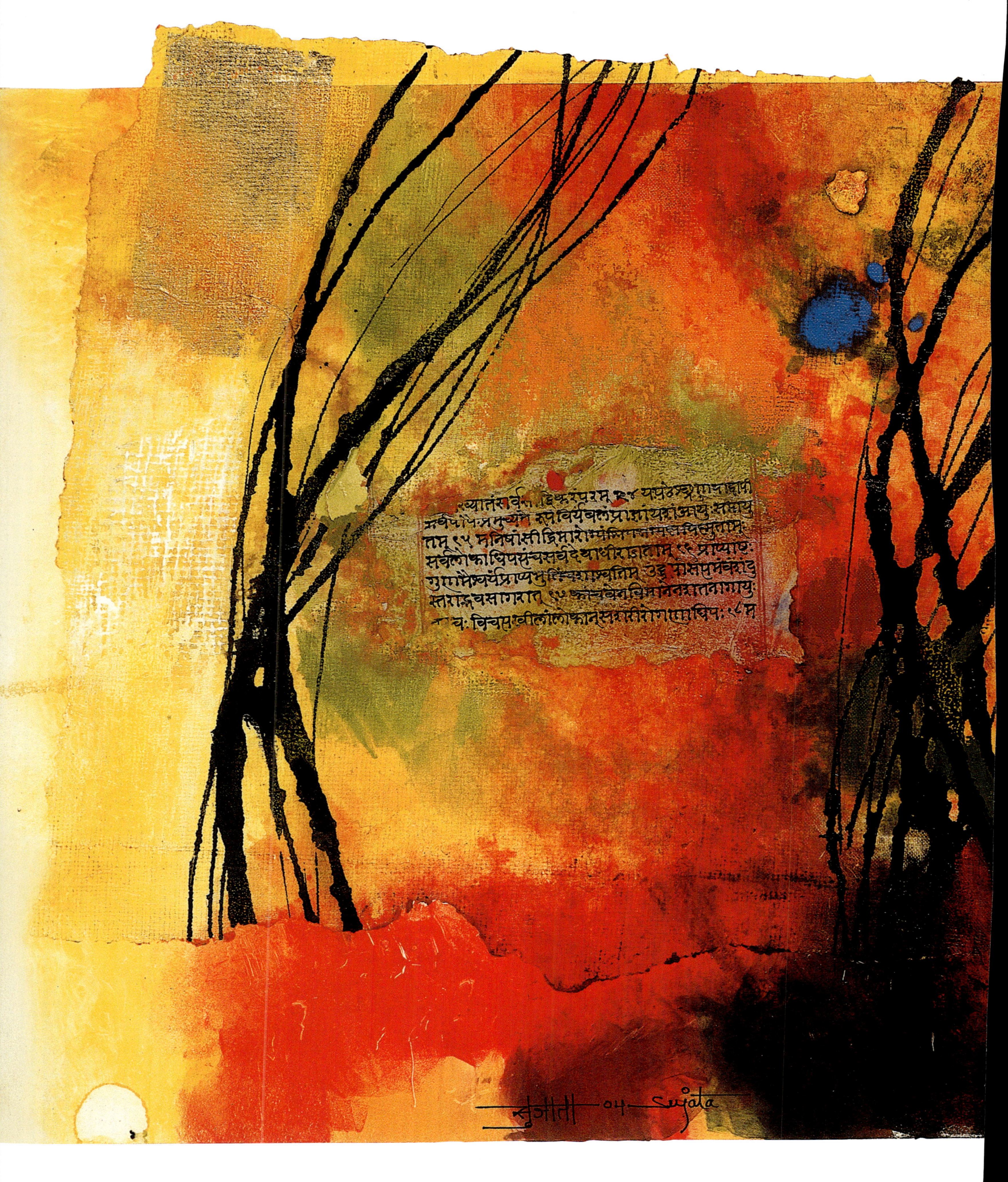
सुजाता 04 Sujata

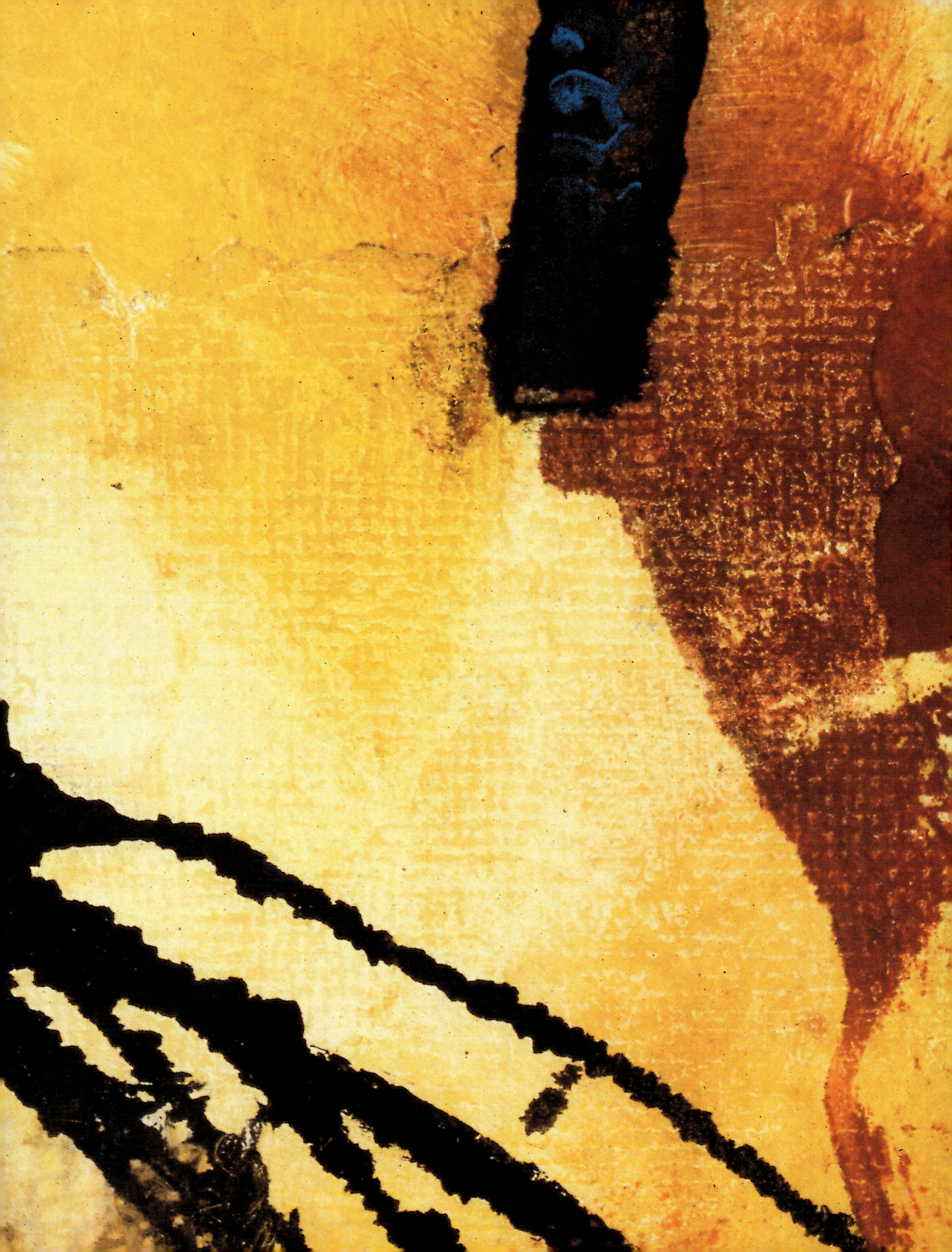

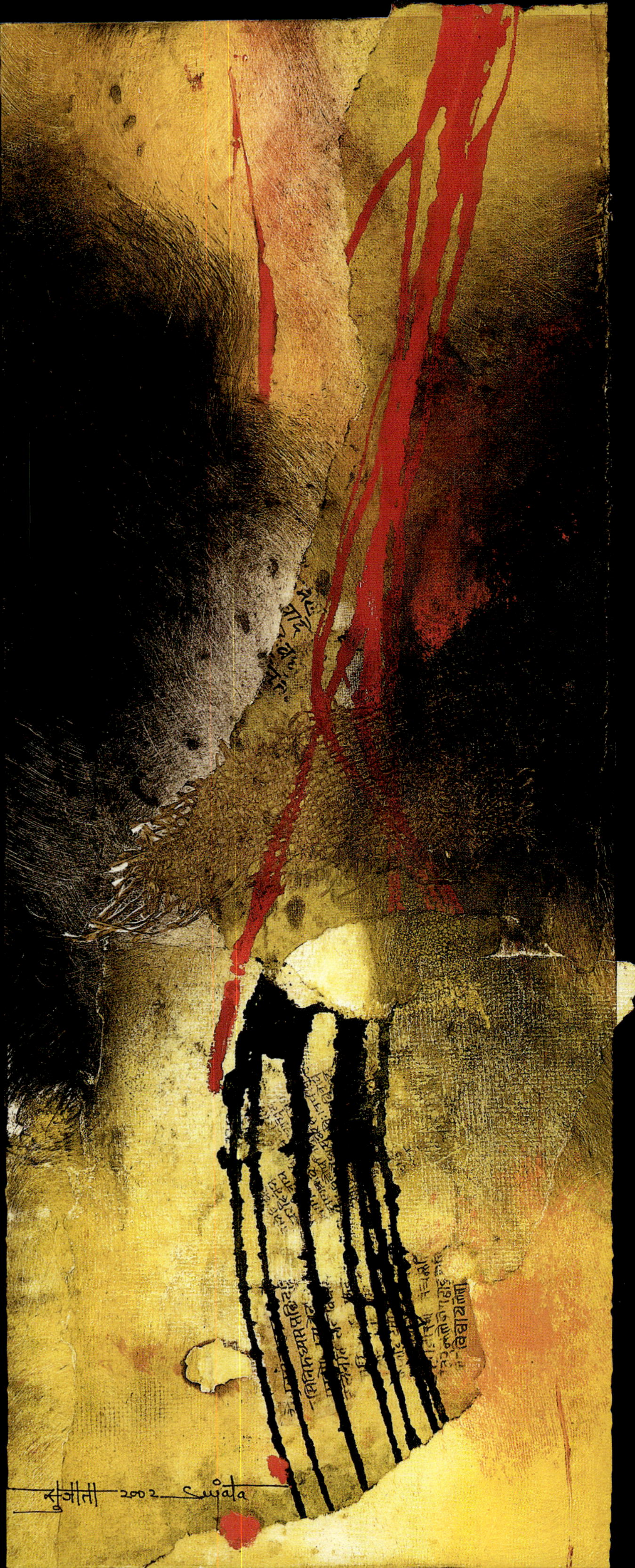
सुजाता 2002 Sujata

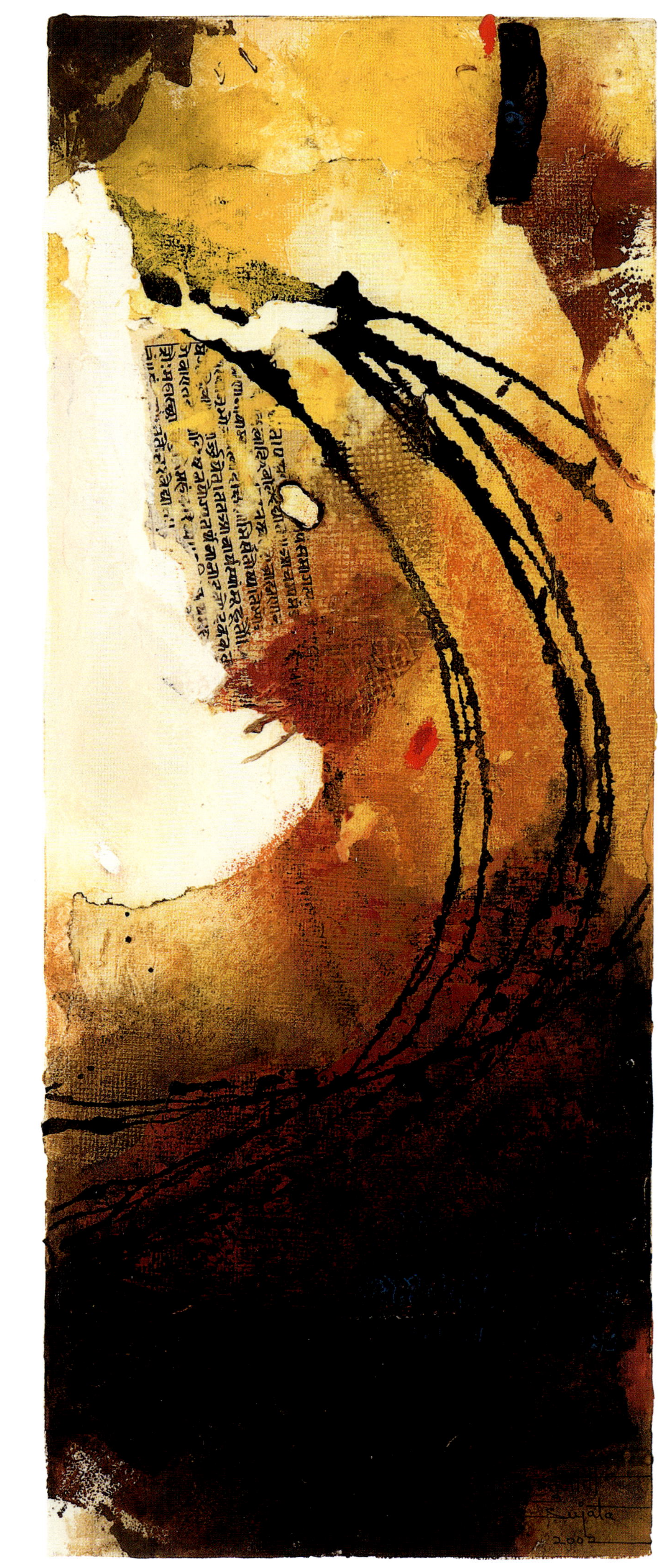
Sujata
2002

Is there something secretly written inside each of us?
Or is each of us a tiny fragment of the vast script which tells the story of the world?

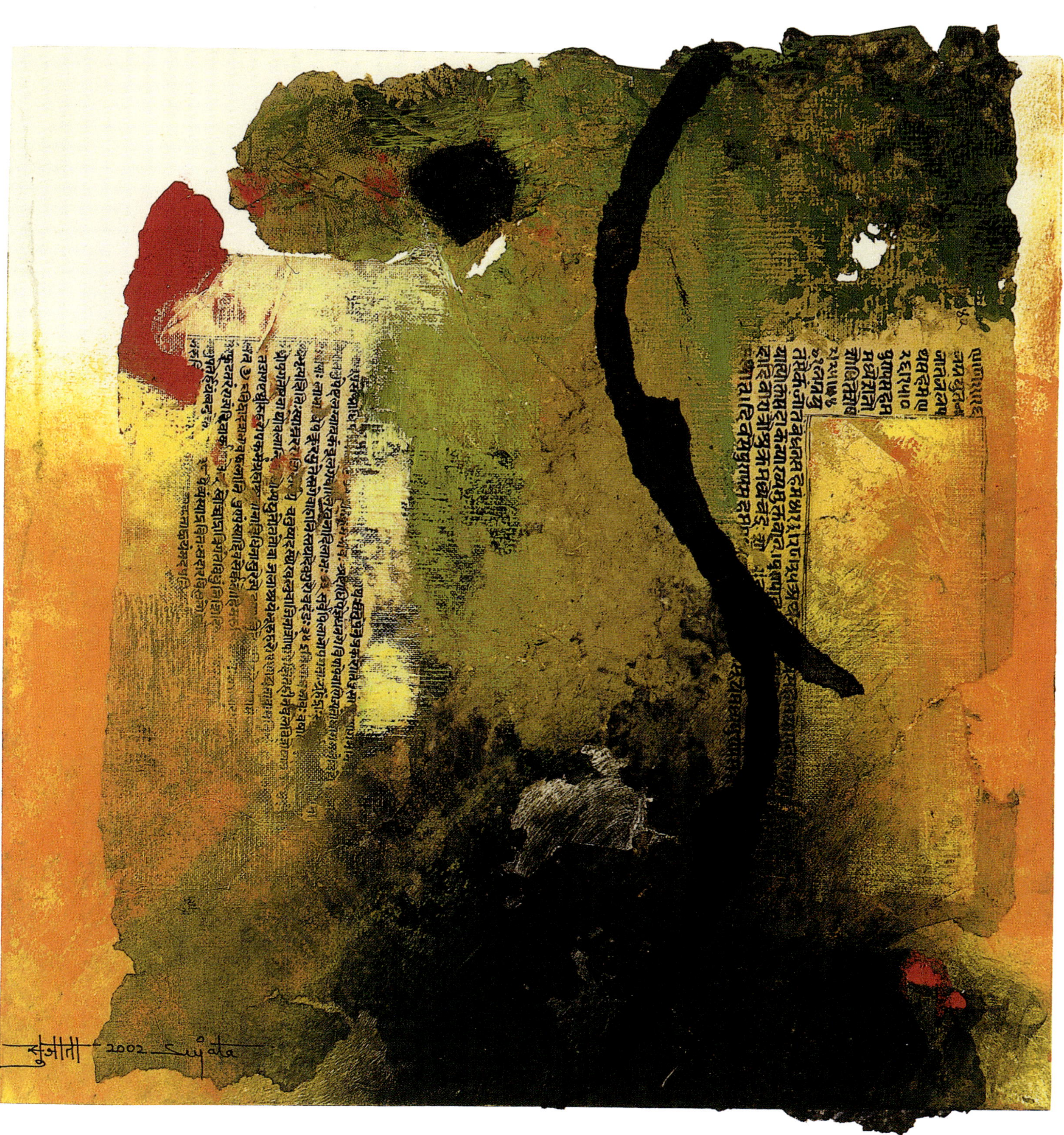
सुजाता 2002 Sujata

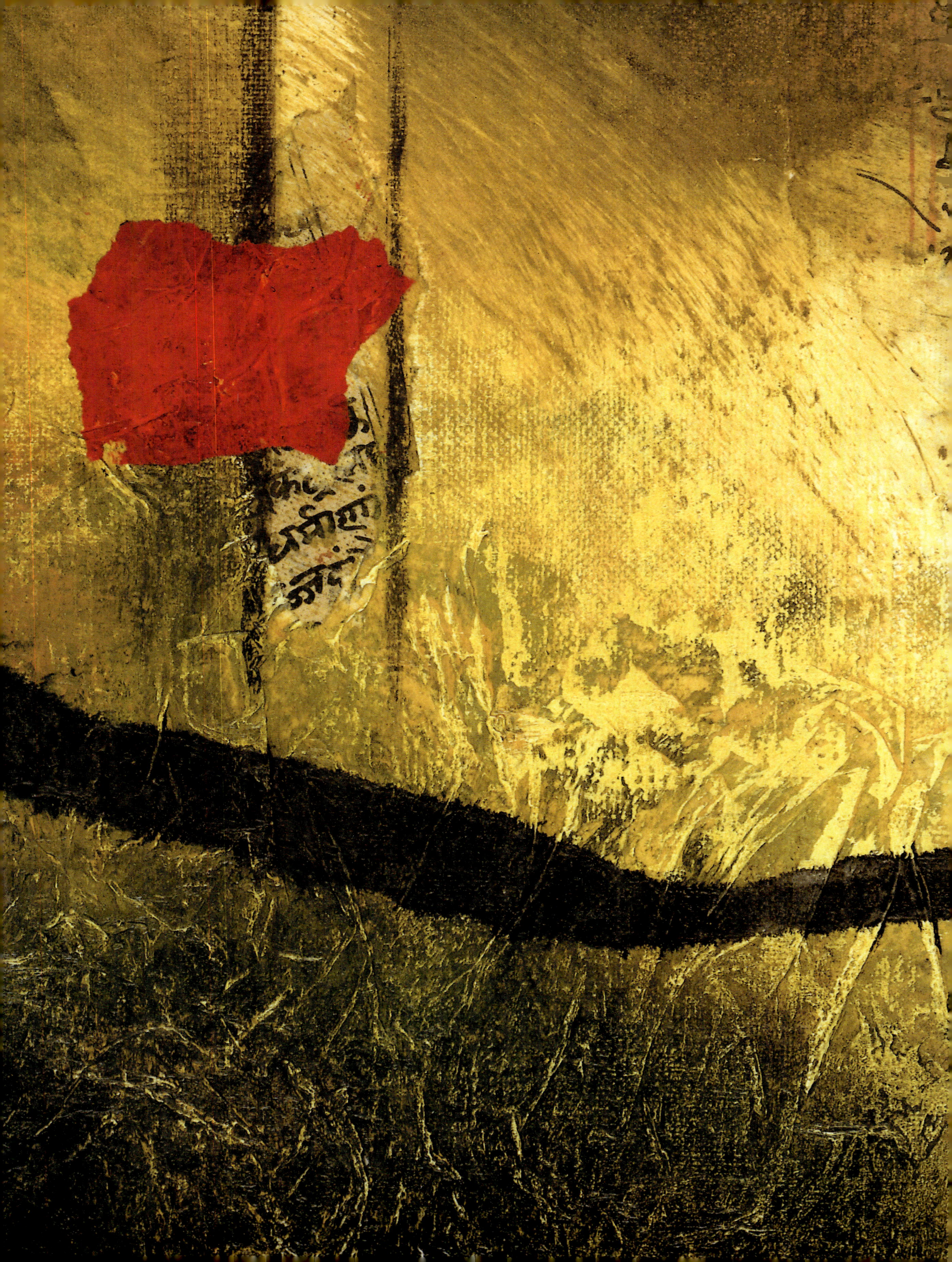

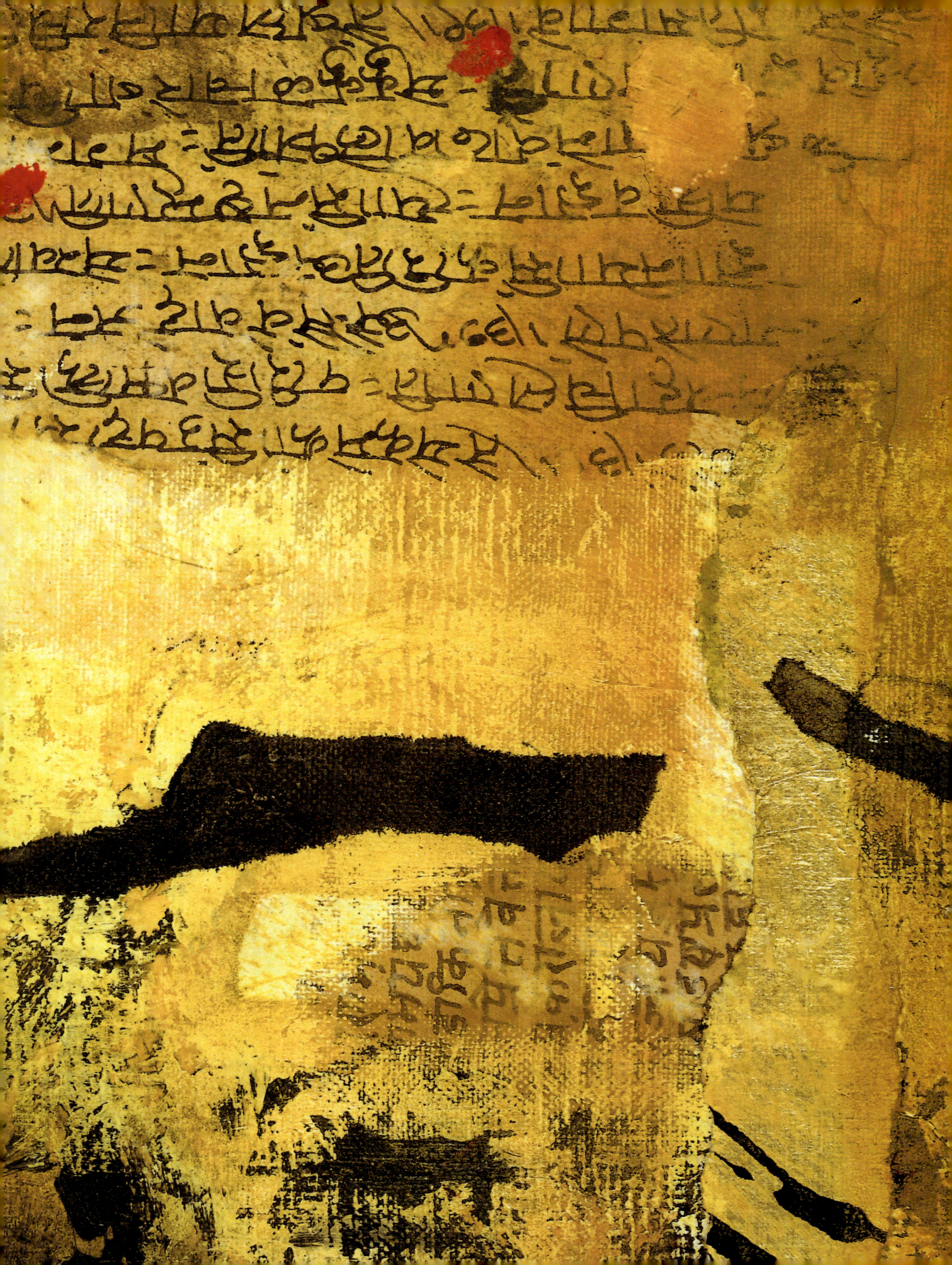

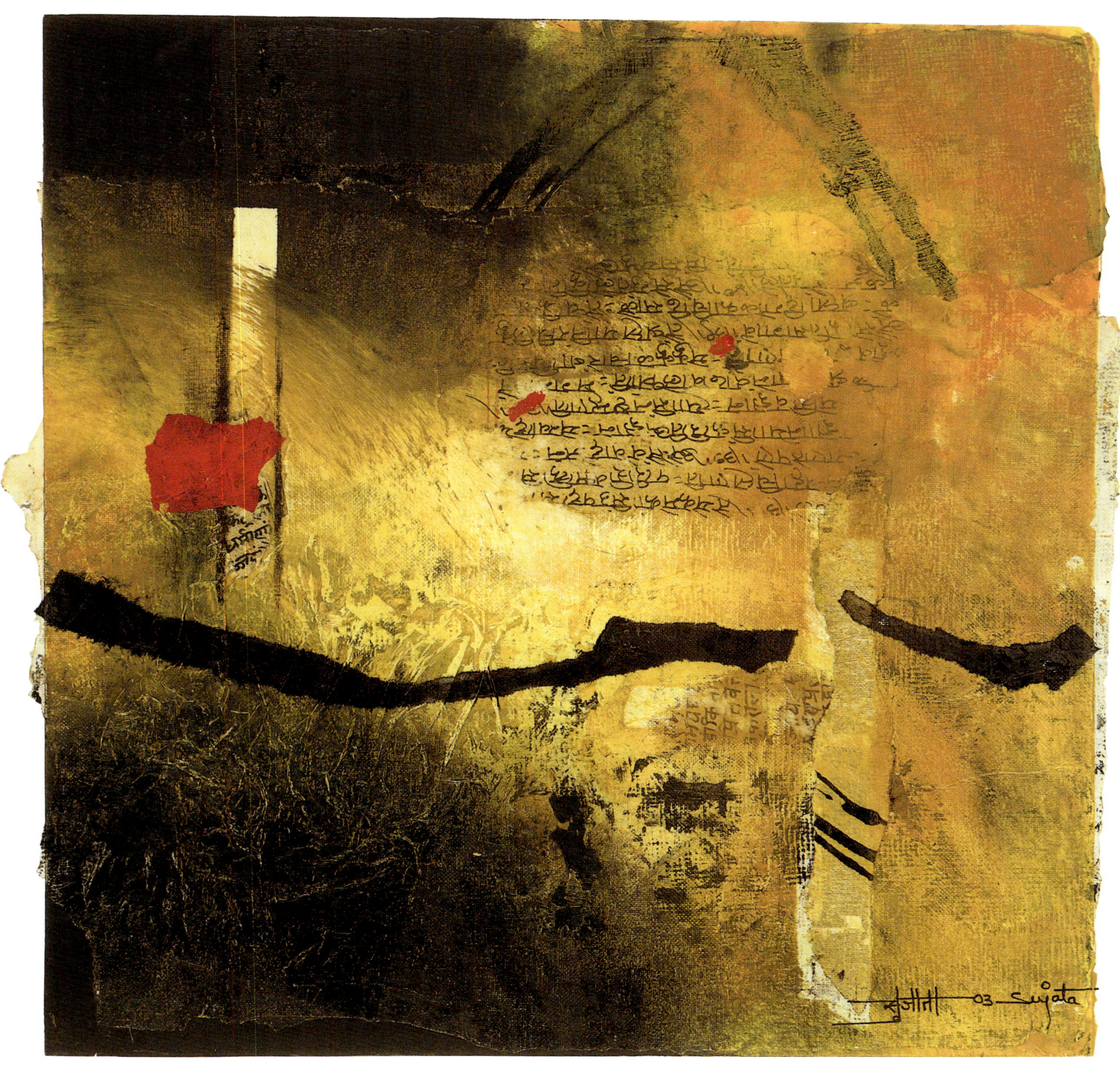
सुजाता 03 Sujata

The soft vibrations of the cosmos have been heard for billions and billions of years. Heard only vaguely, it was at first impossible to pinpoint their nature, especially since no one was there to notice them. Slowly, little by little, they grew stronger, more regular, and it transpired that they were musical.
These musical cosmic movements lasted for a very long time; they waxed and waned.

From this music, sounds emerged. The first sound to be heard was the syllable 'om', followed by more sounds which grew into syllables, then into words, then sentences.

And from these sentences were born the *Vedas.*
As the fruit of the whole cosmos, they are beyond discussion. They are the only texts without an author. They were born of the world. And from these sentences everything was born, even the Gods, even the stars, even our fellow beings.

It was not man that created these first texts but the texts that created man.

Destiny crept into my voice, as if by surprise.

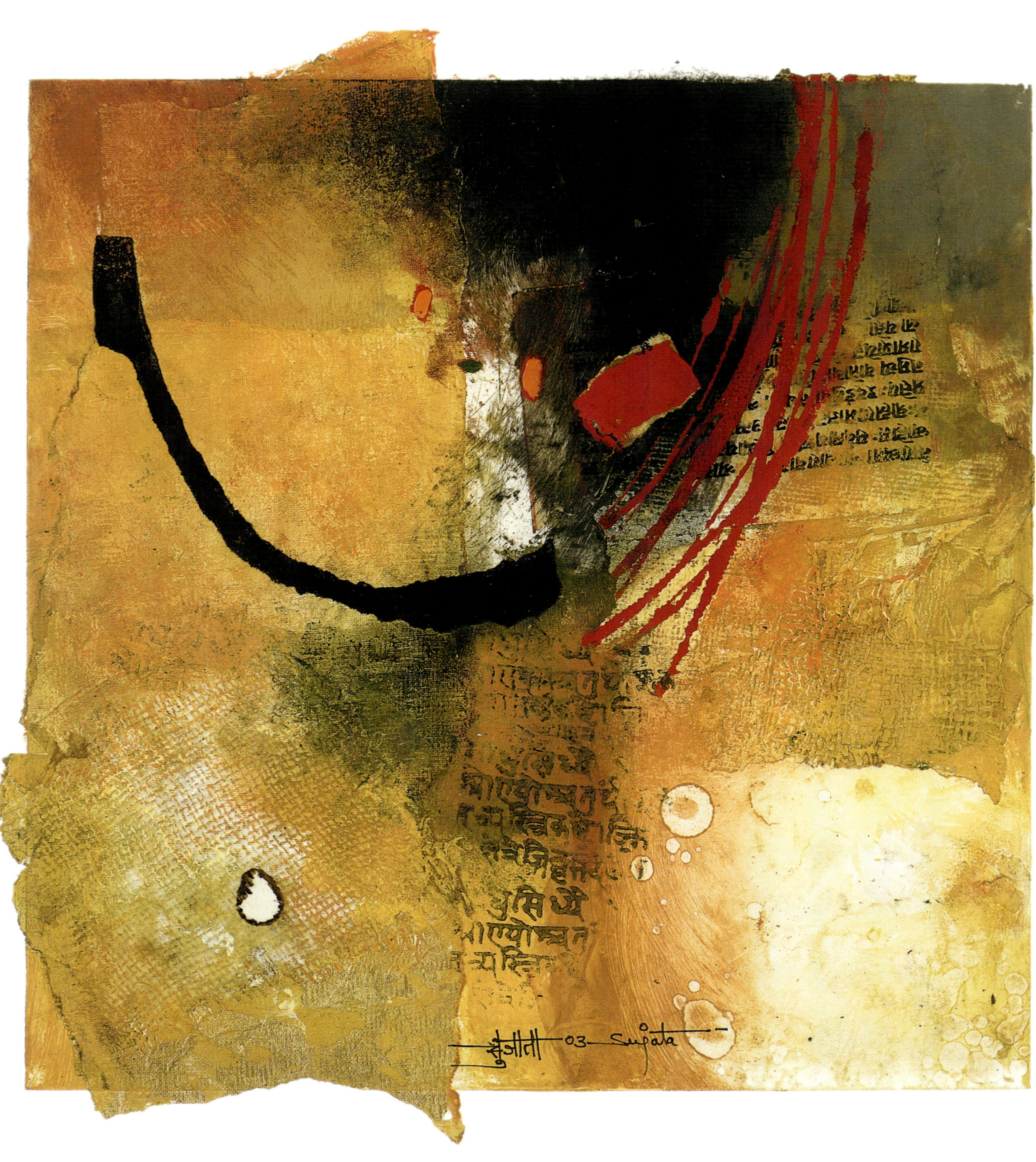
सुजाता 03 Sujata

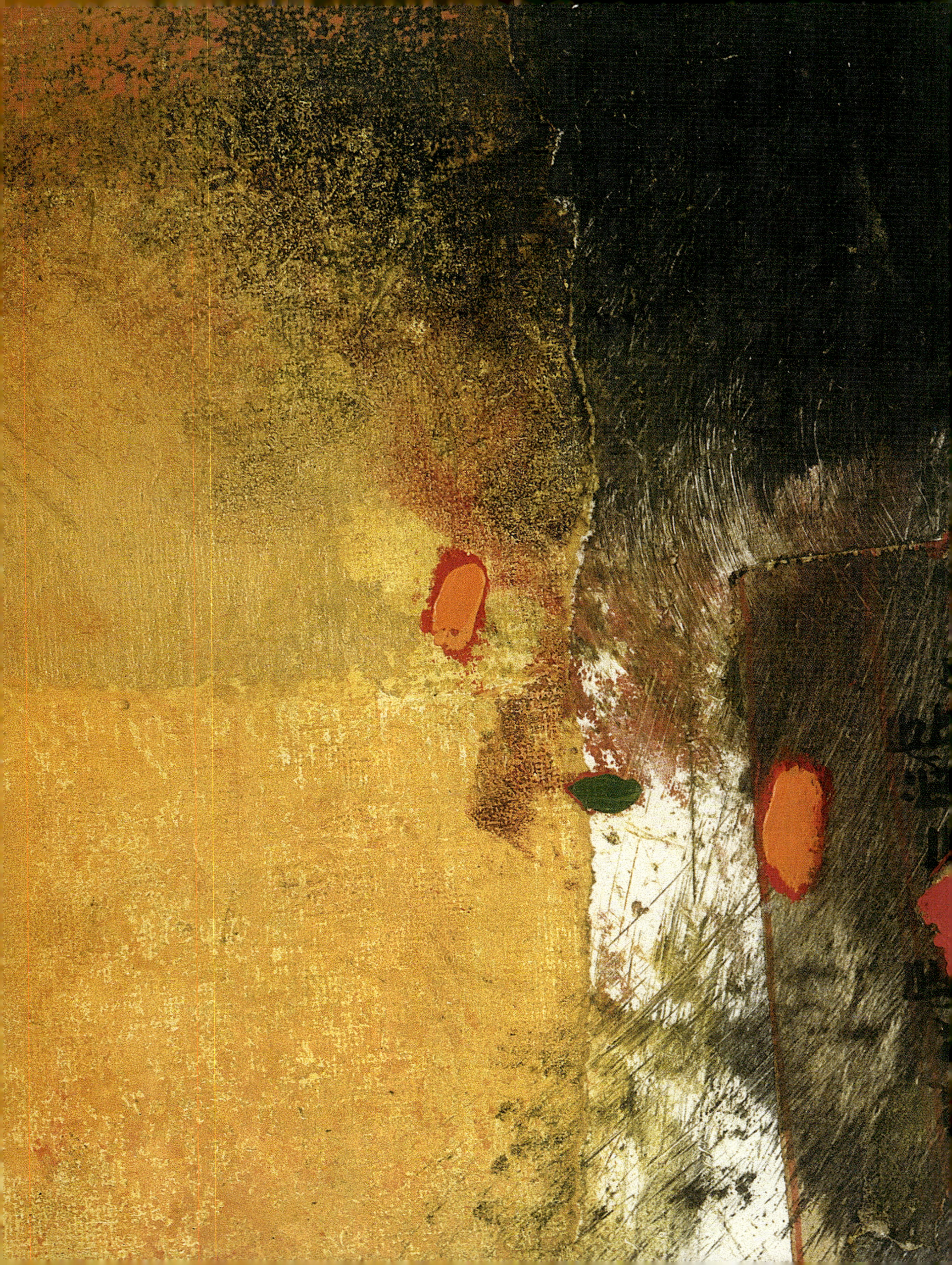

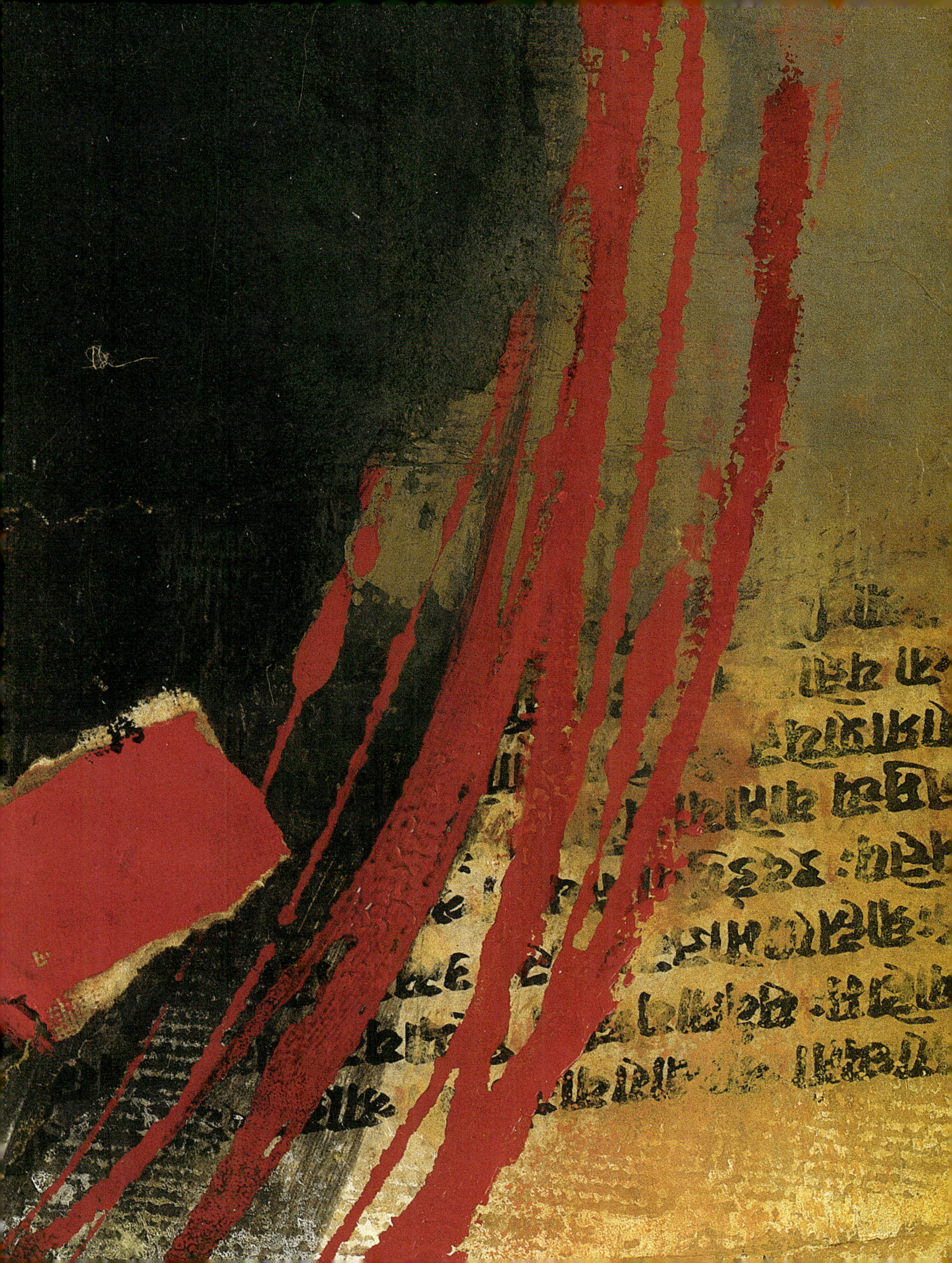

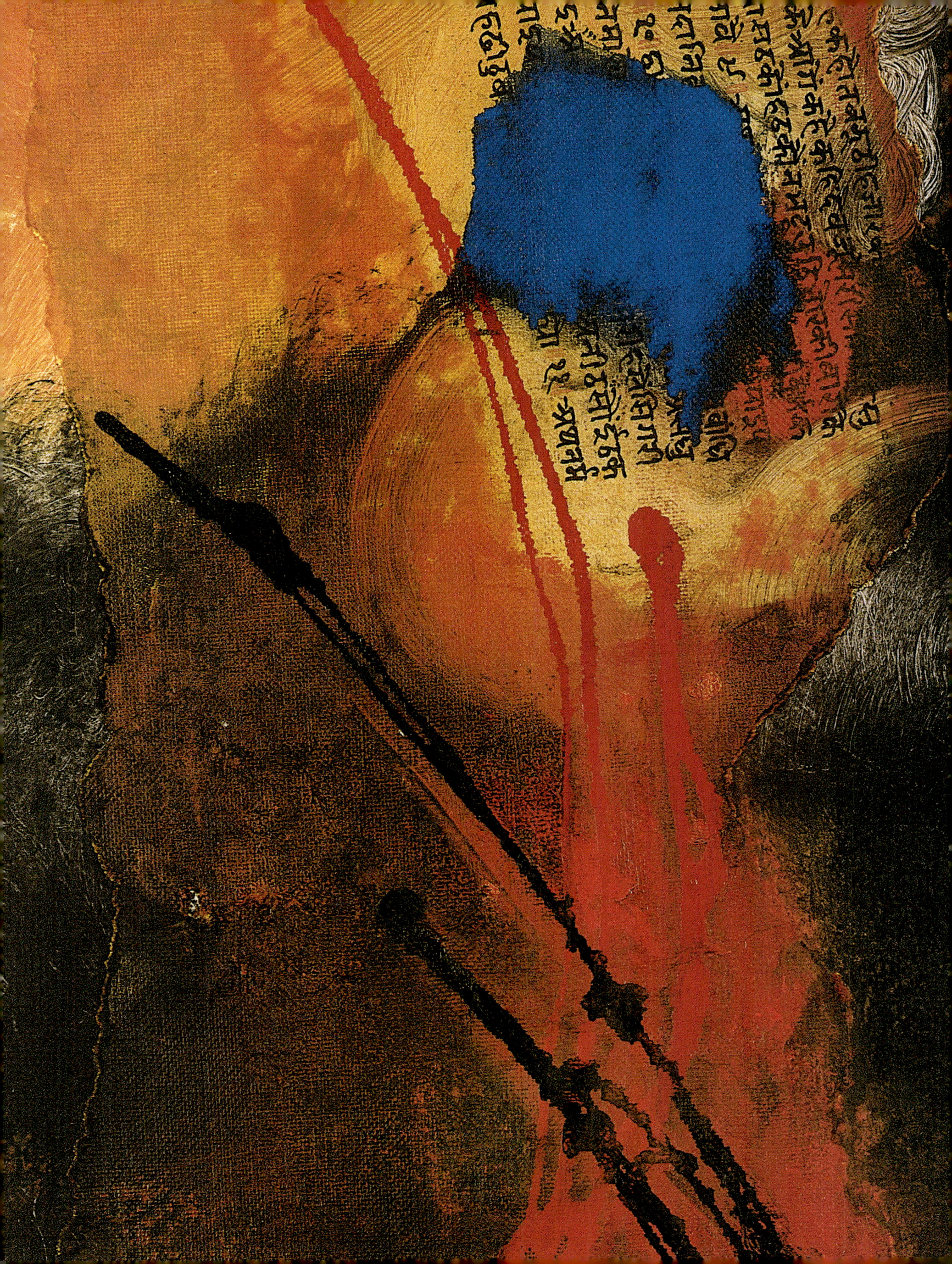

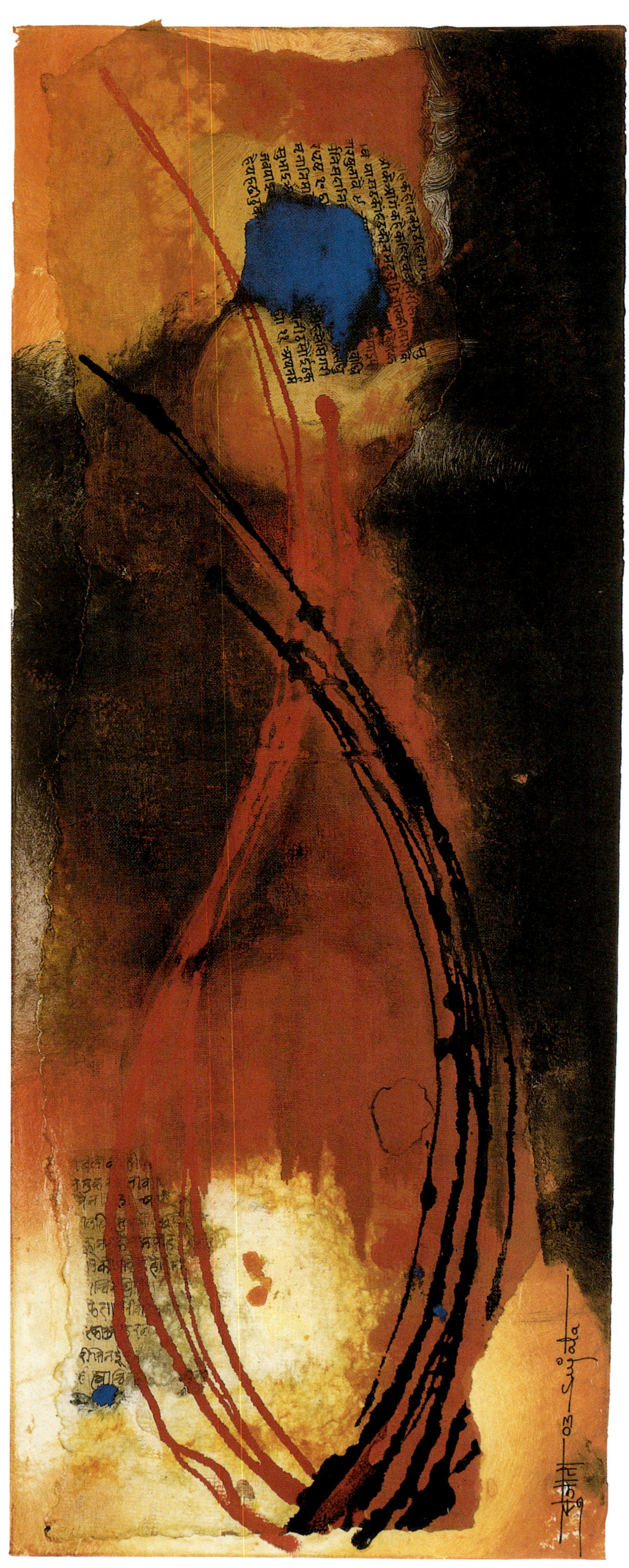

Remember at all times what I have told you:
if your heart breaks or closes, if it grows bitter,
sombre or hard, the light has been lost.

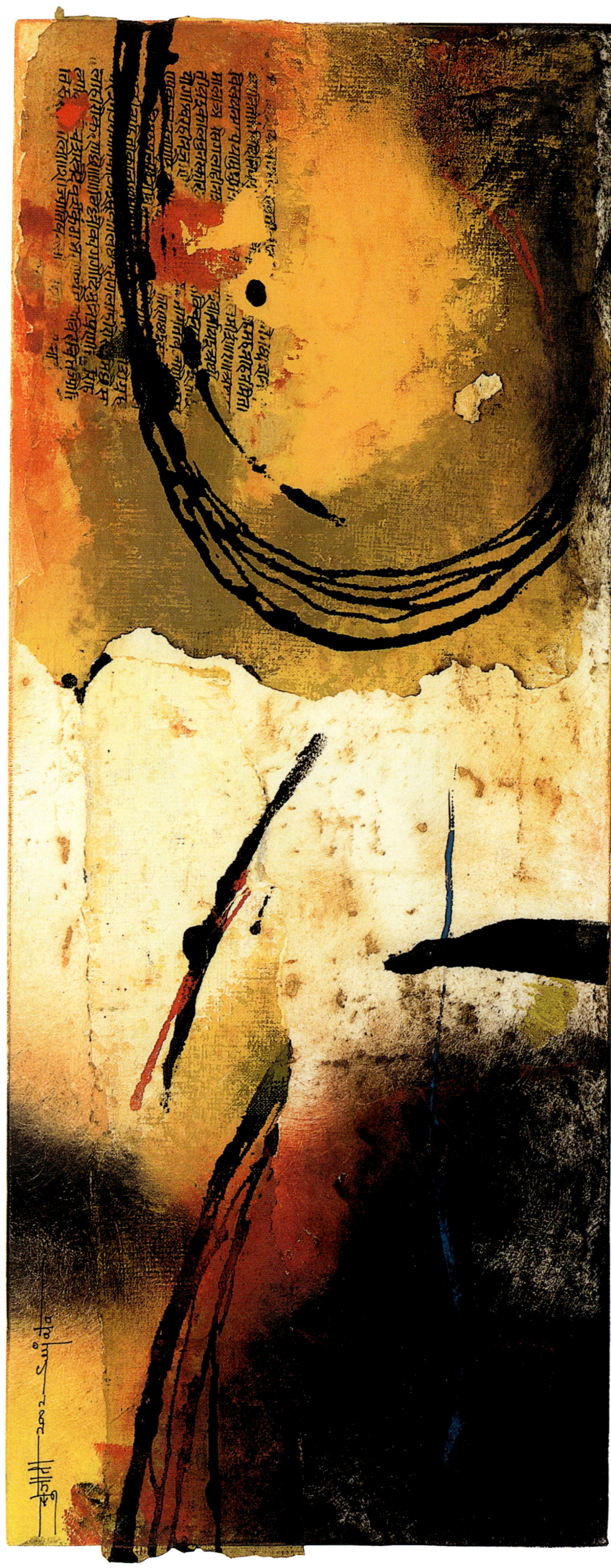

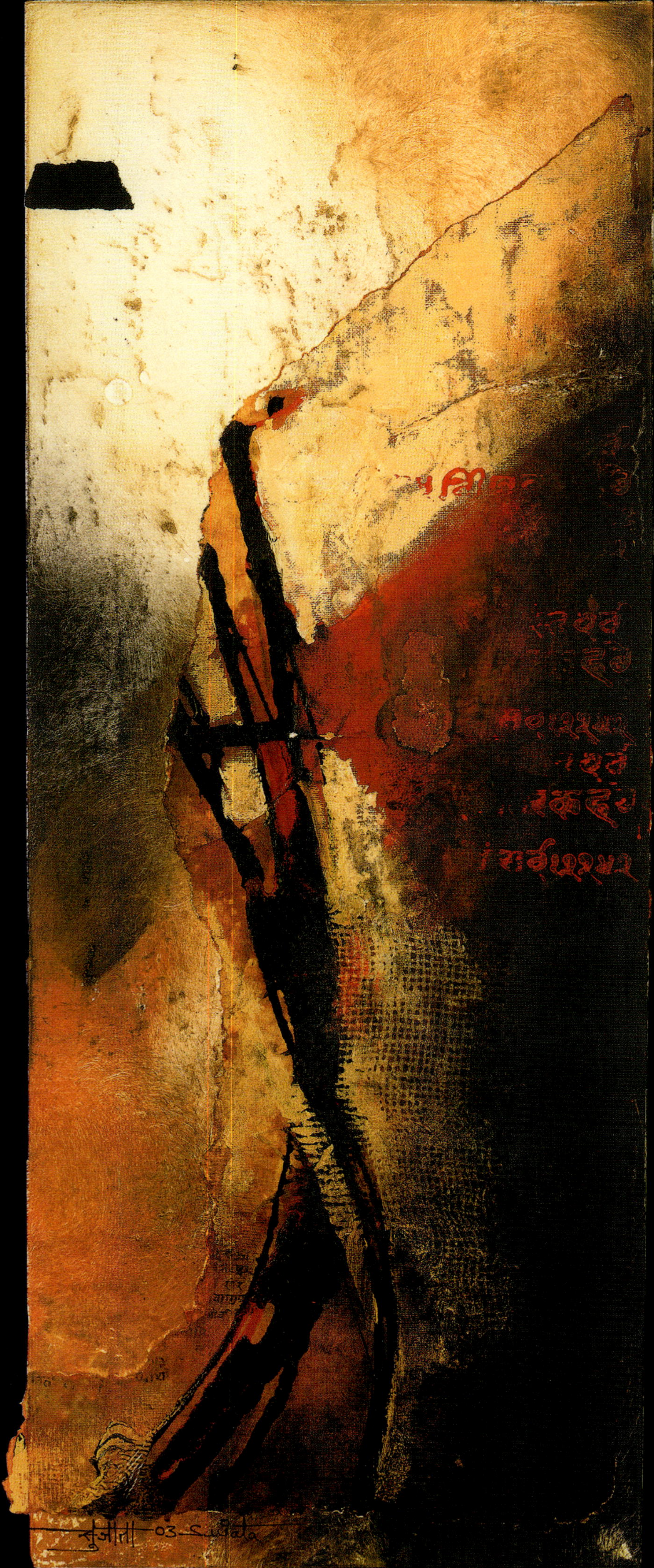
सुजाता 03 Sujata

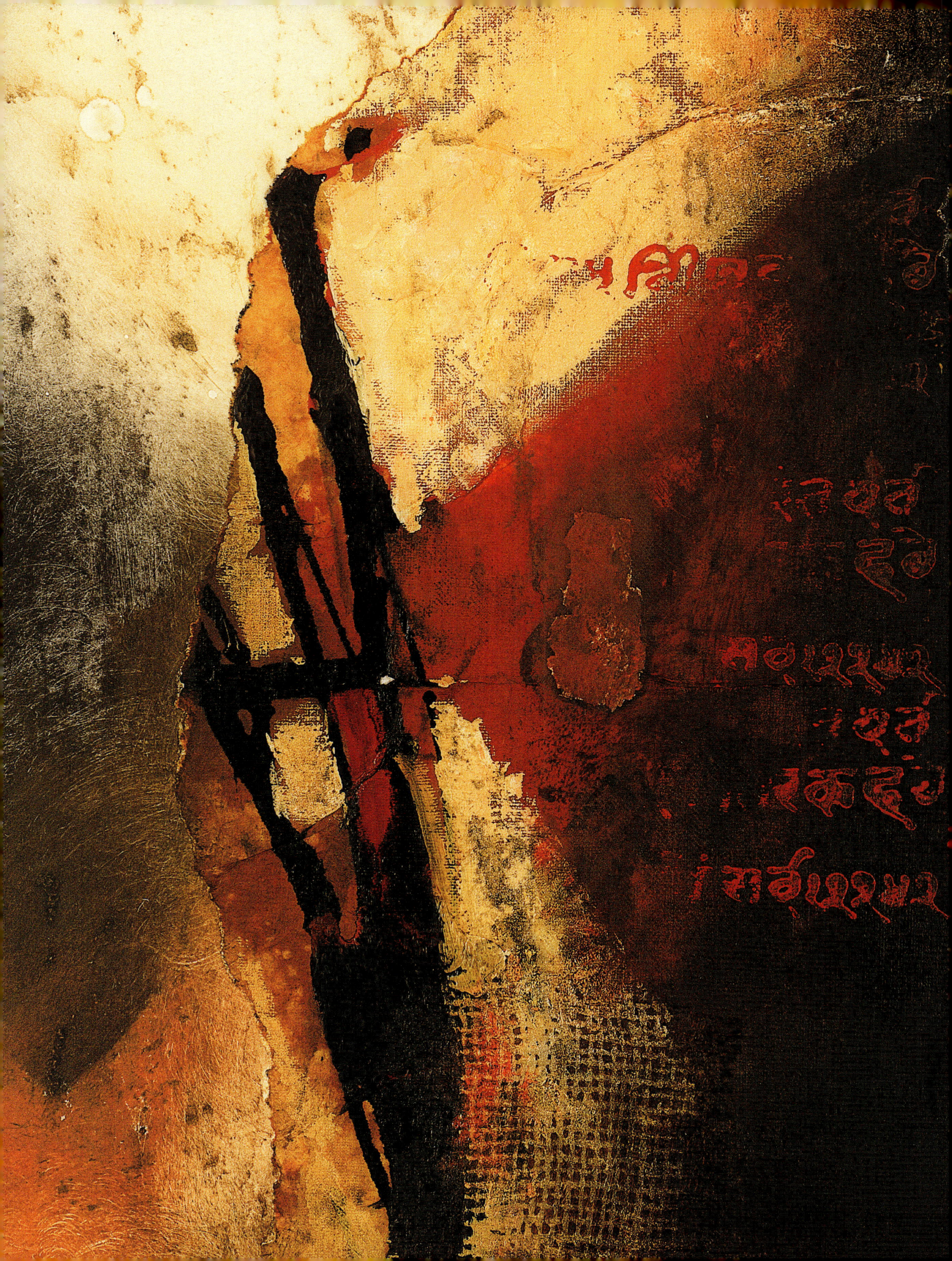

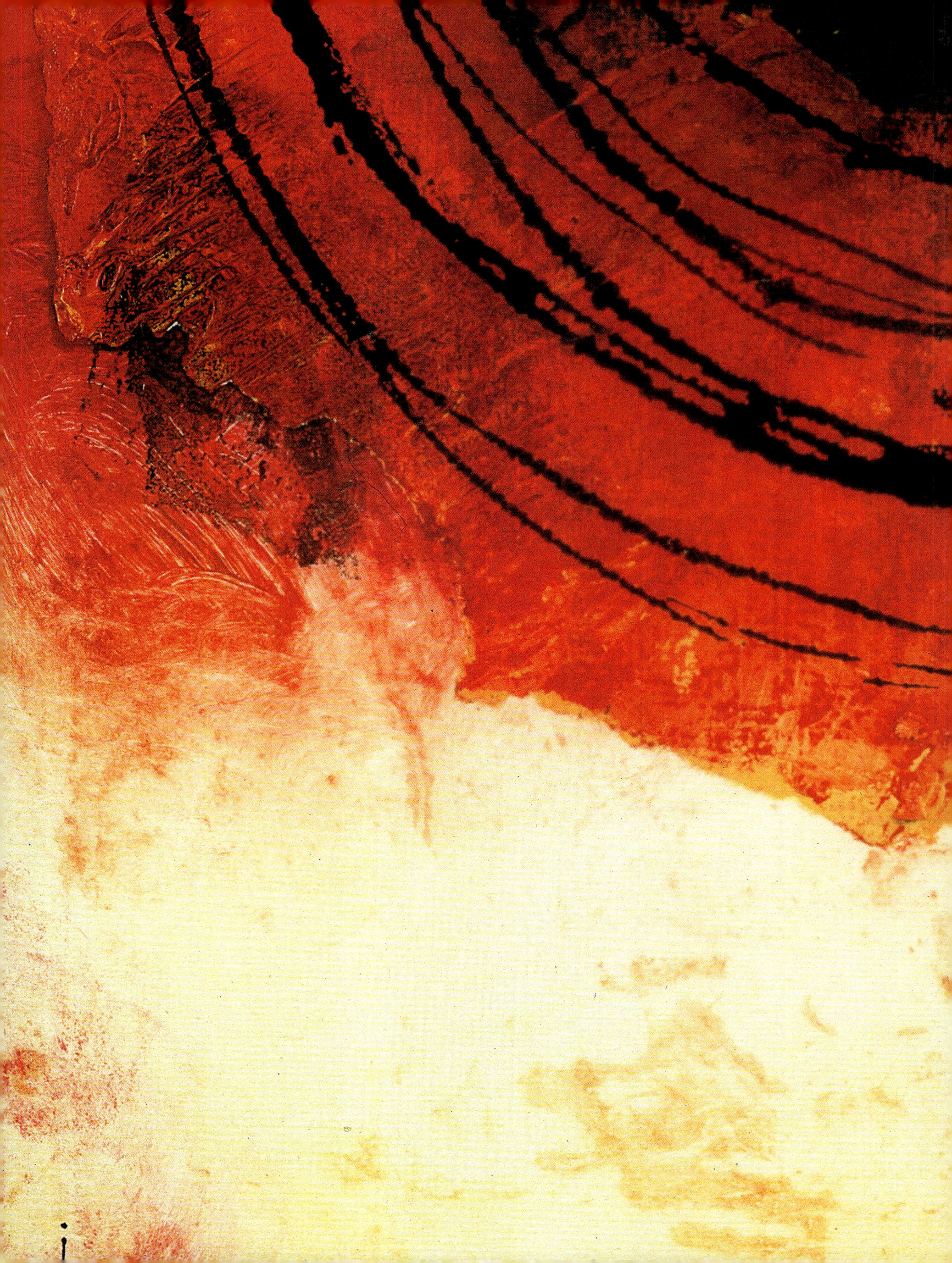

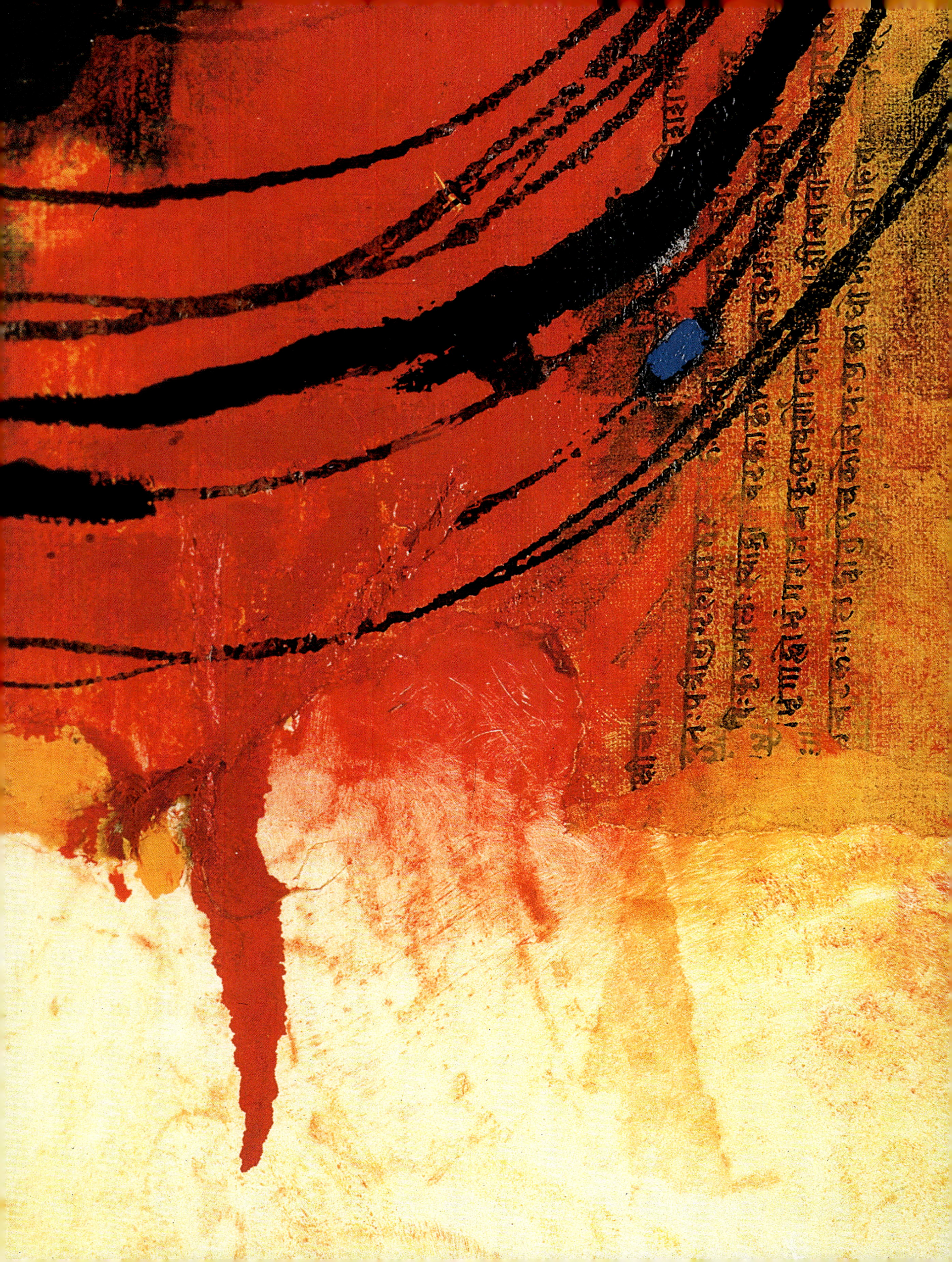

Everything depends on me, like the pearls on a string.
I am the perfume of the earth, the warmth of the fire; I am appearance and disappearance,
I am the game of tricksters and the brilliance of all that shines.
Arms cannot pierce this life that inhabits you, nor fire burn it; waters cannot wet it nor the wind dry it.

Be not afraid, rise, for I love you.

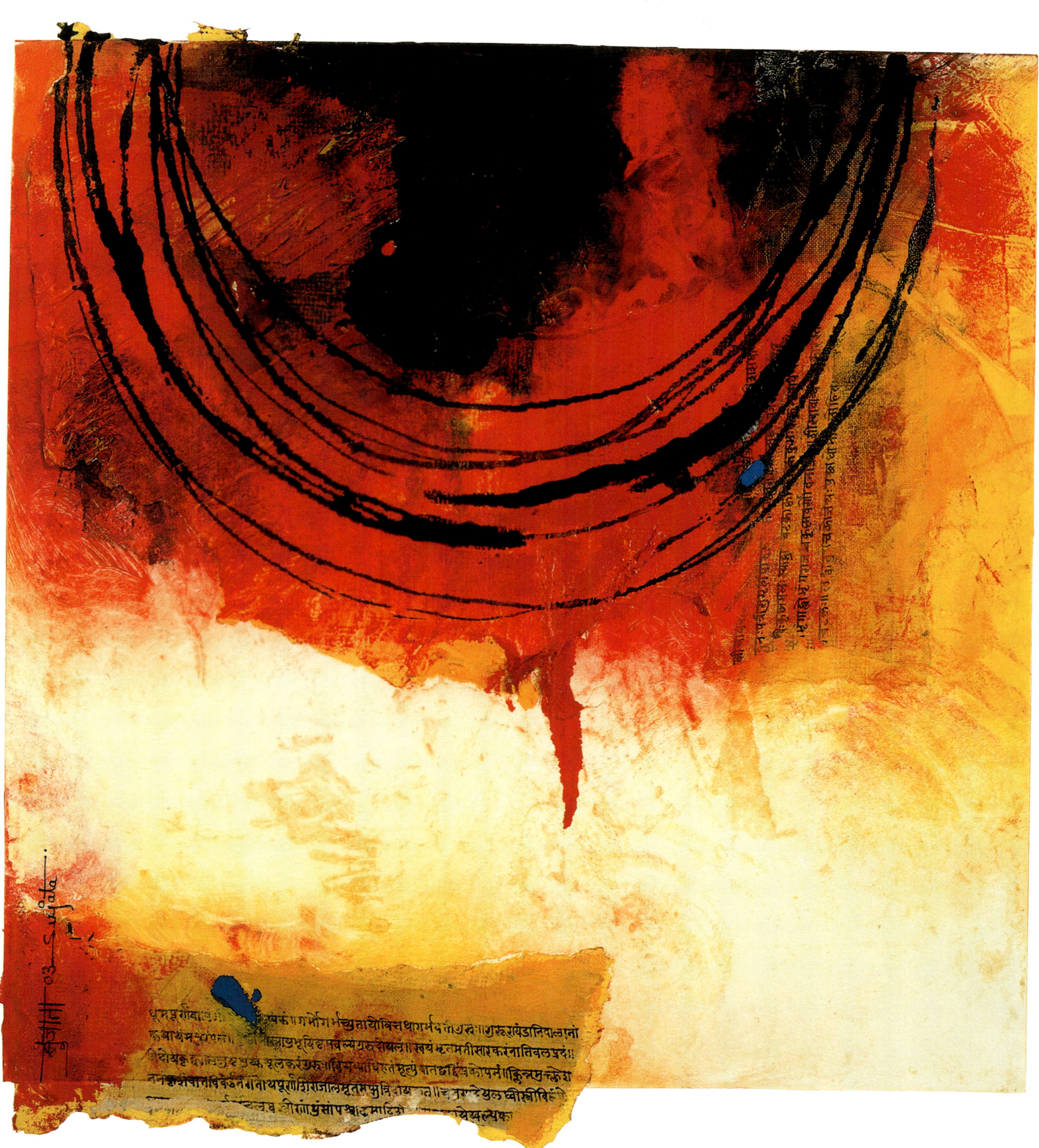

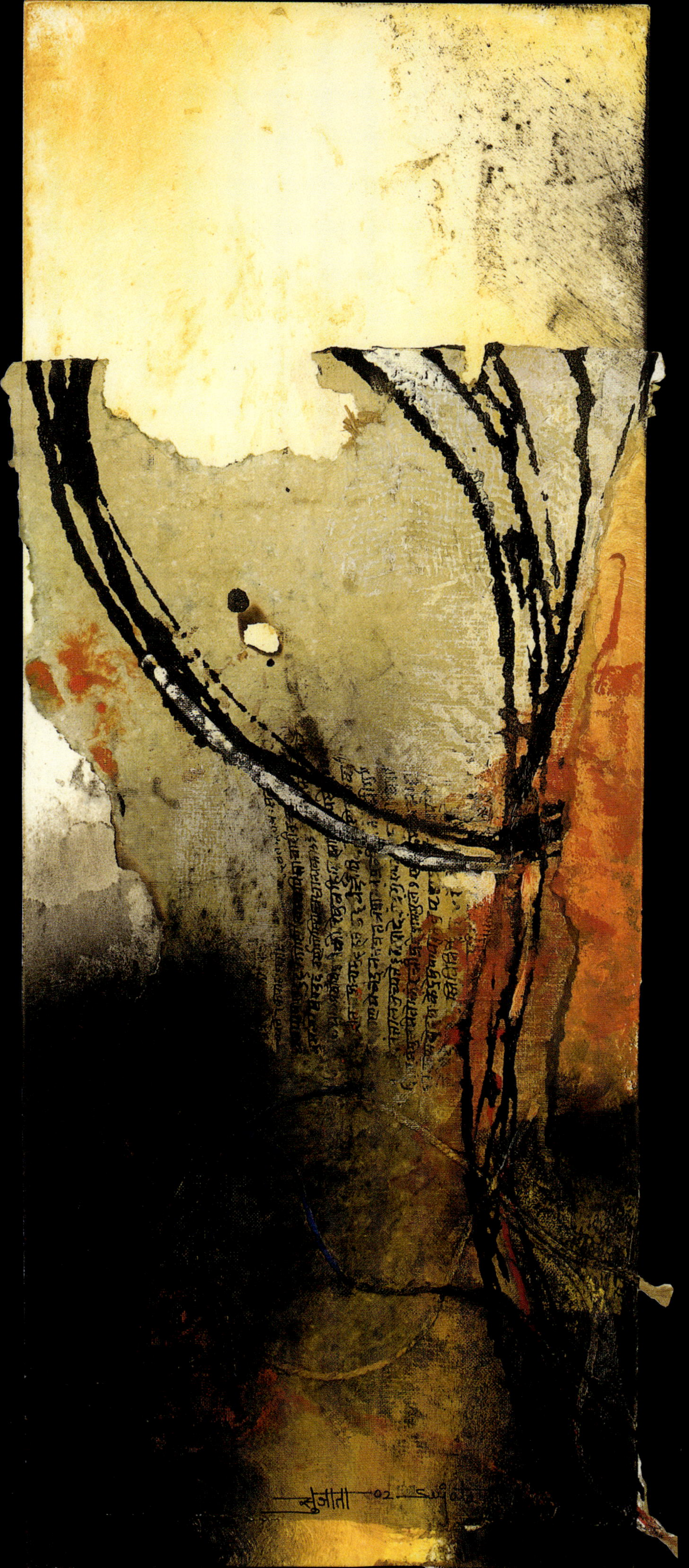

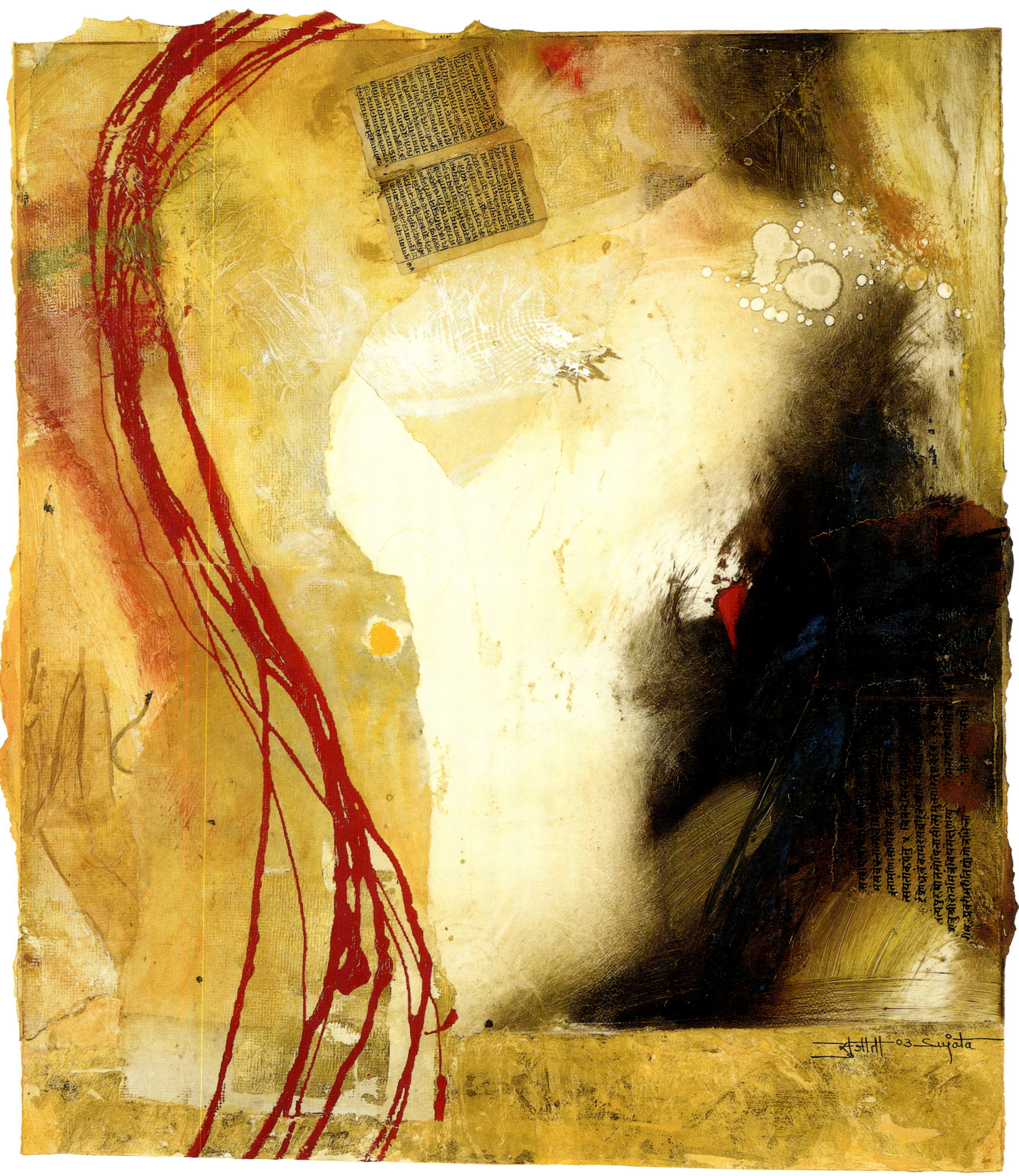

The original word is obscure.
No one yet knows how to speak, nor how to listen.
No one knows how to write and no one how to read.

All speech surrenders itself to the wind;
which is why it invites commentary.
And because these commentaries contradict one another
or lose themselves, they invite further commentaries,
which, in turn, are lost in the sands of our intentions.
In the end, therefore, all is but commentary.
The only question to be asked is: what is its purpose?
Who remembers?

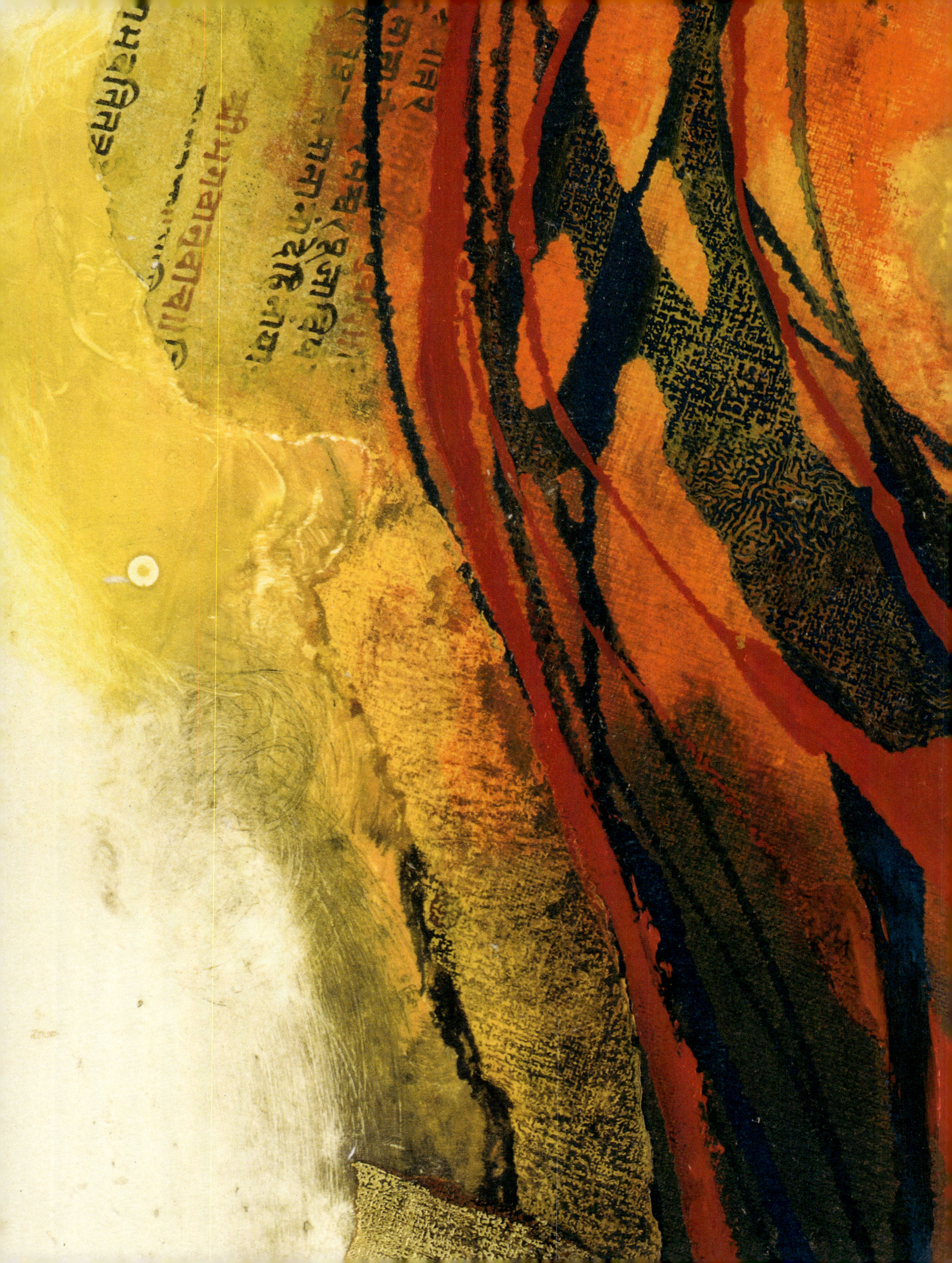

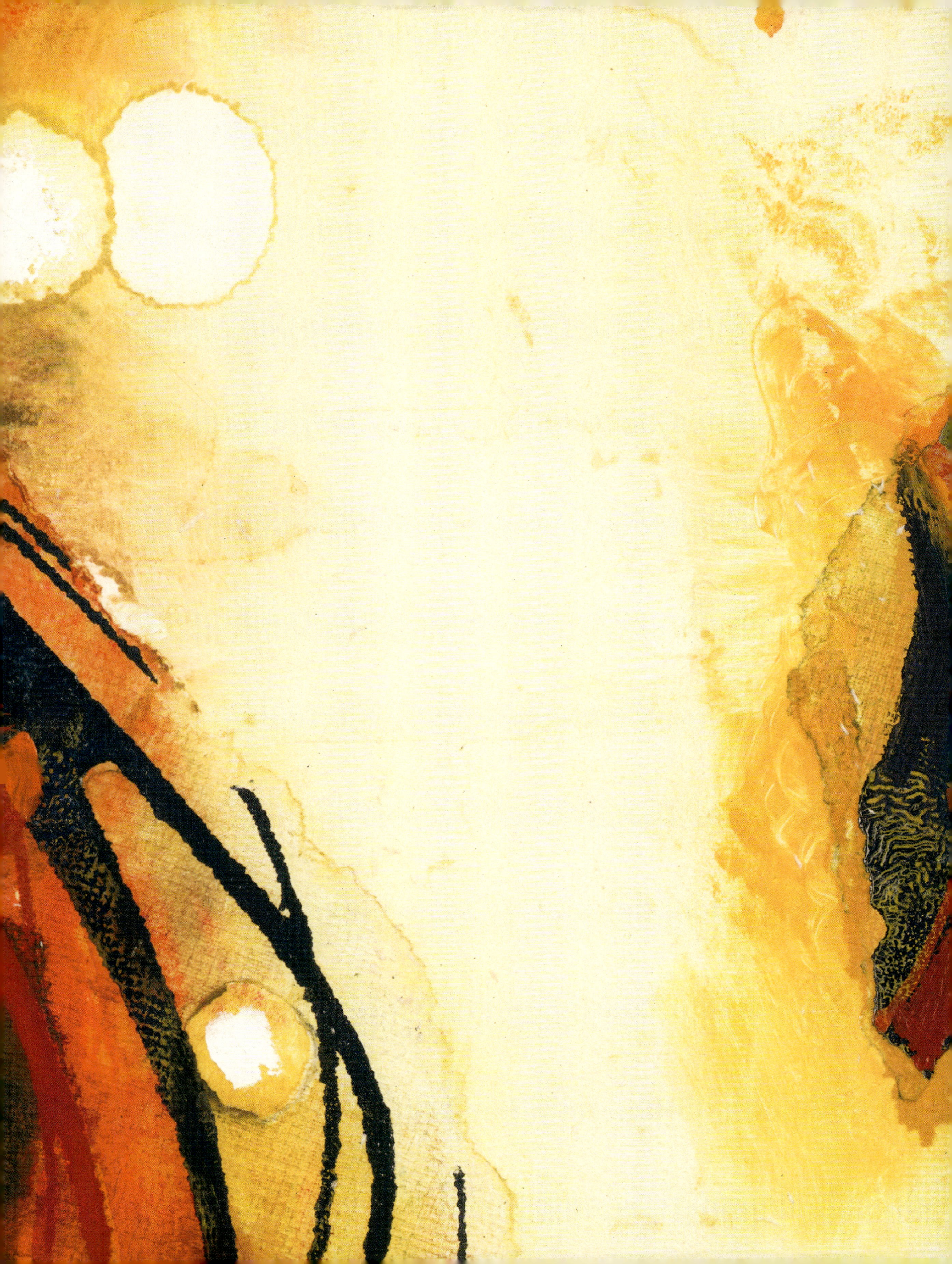

I heard the plaint of the earth. It said: men have become arrogant,
they inflict wounds upon me. They are countless in number and violent,
driven by the spirit of conquest. I tremble under the foot of man
devoid of wisdom and I wonder: what will he do to me next?

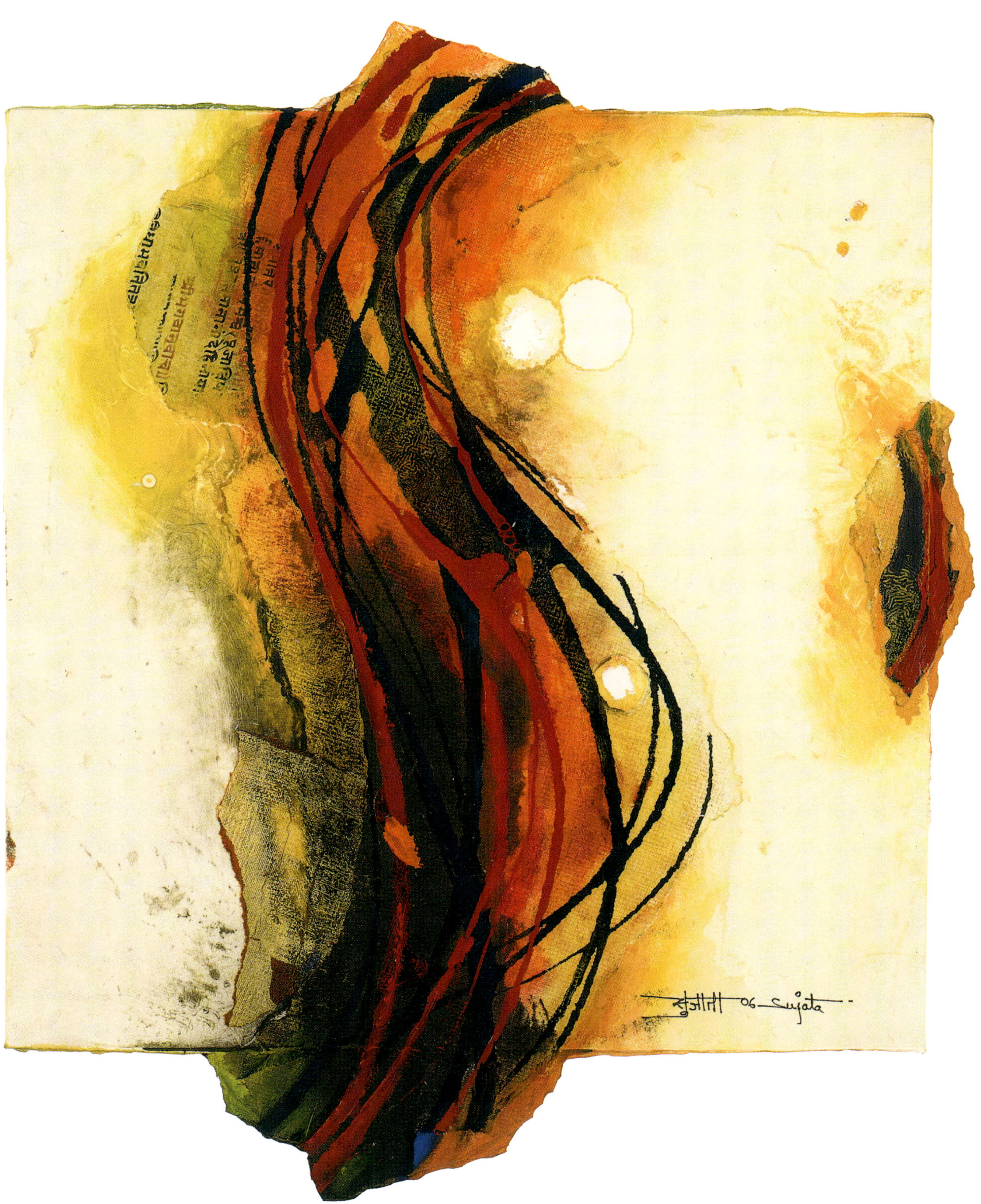
सुजाता 06 Sujata

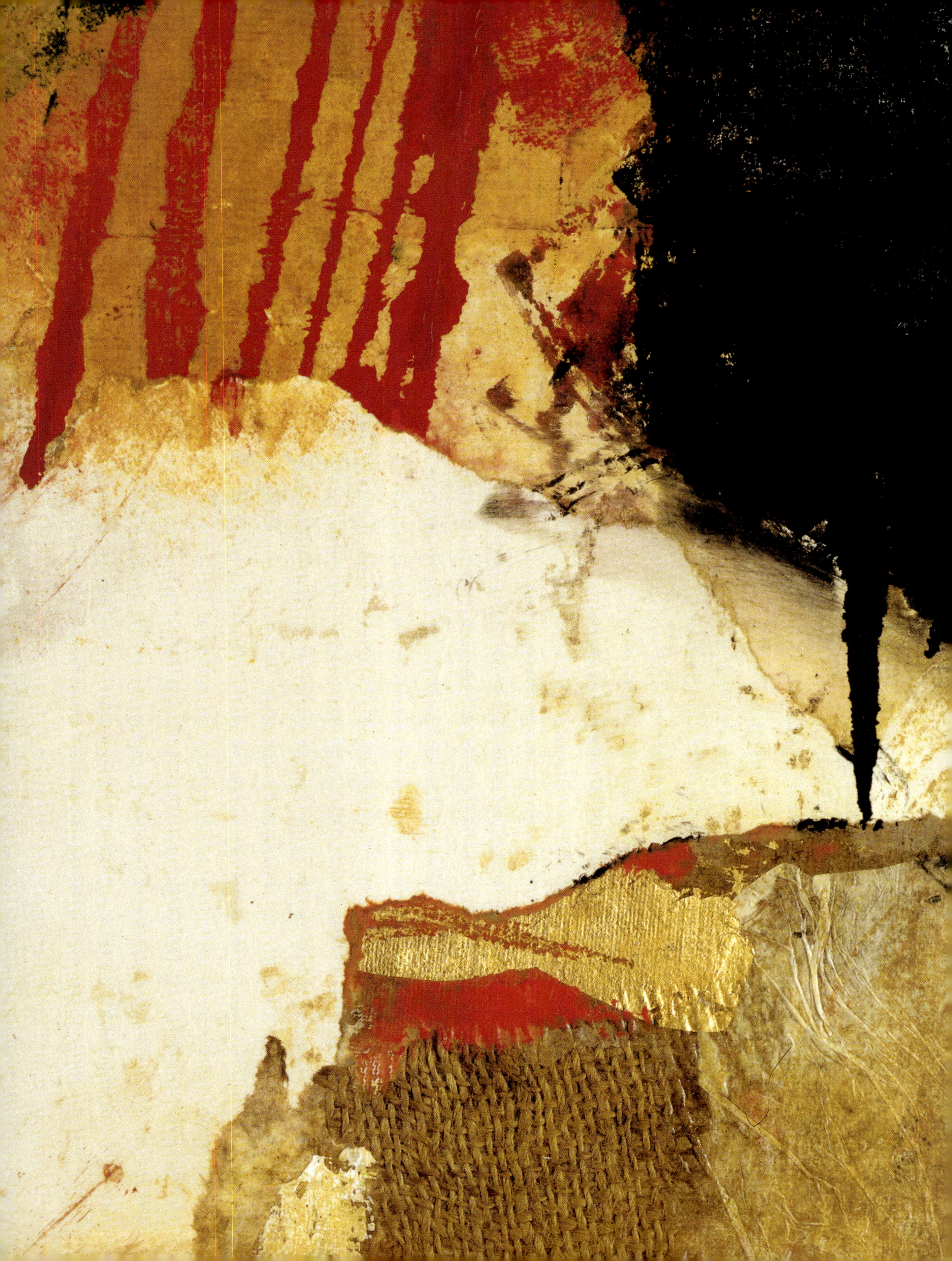

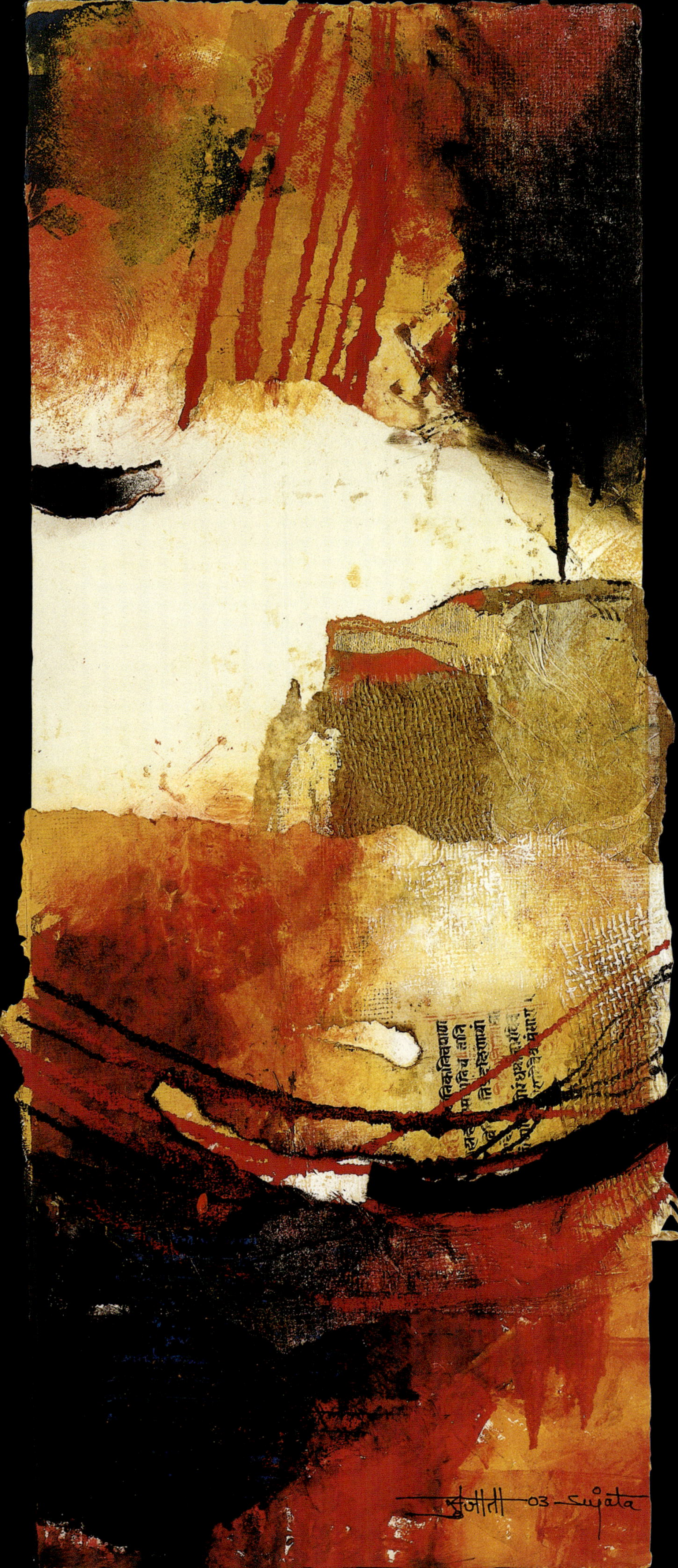
03 Sujata

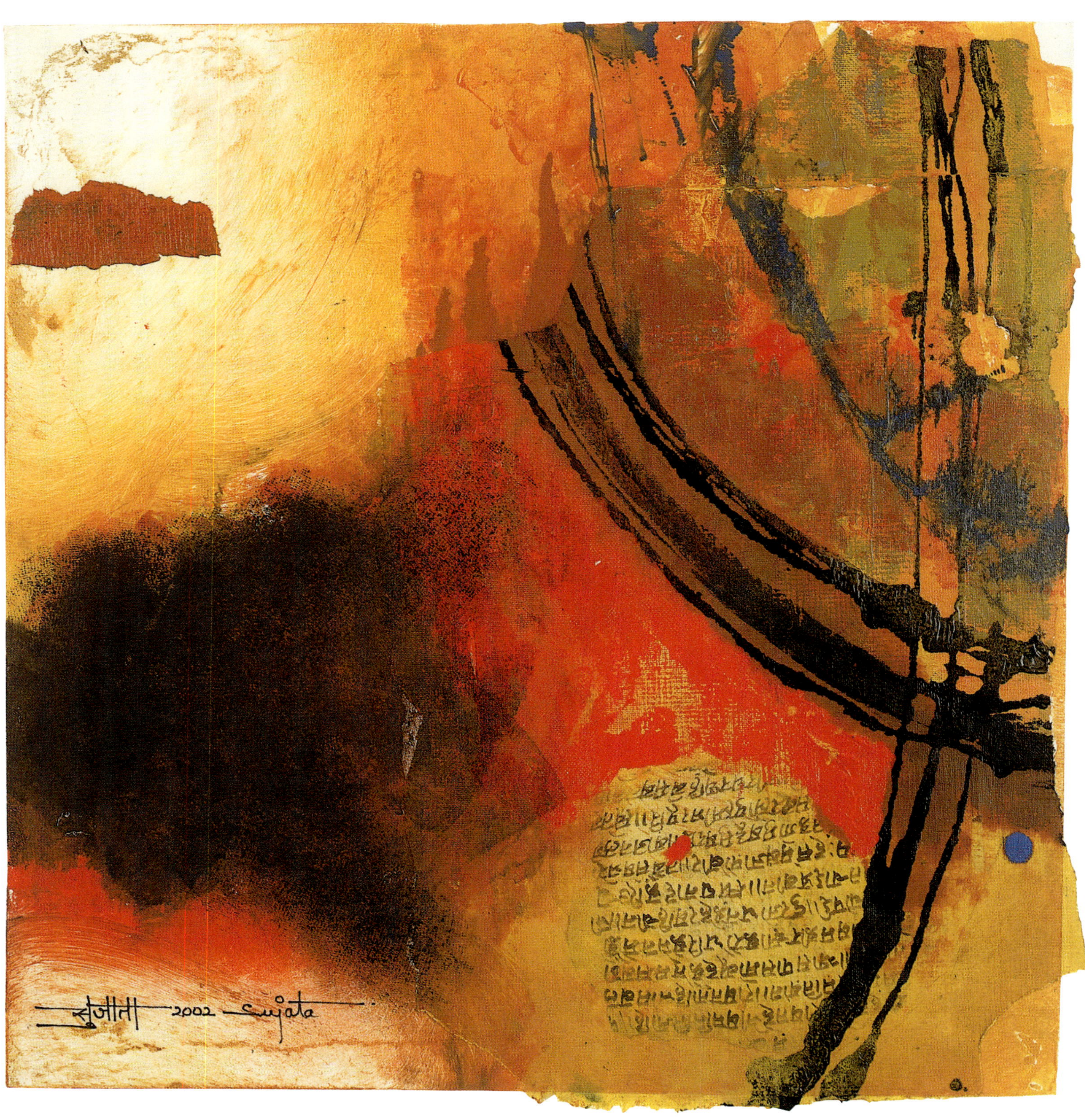
सुजाता 2002 Sujata

Reward or no reward, I do what I must do, with all my strength. It is my *dharma,* my only vessel.
If I did not do my duty, all that is solid and substantial would vanish and the world would be plunged into a demeaning darkness.

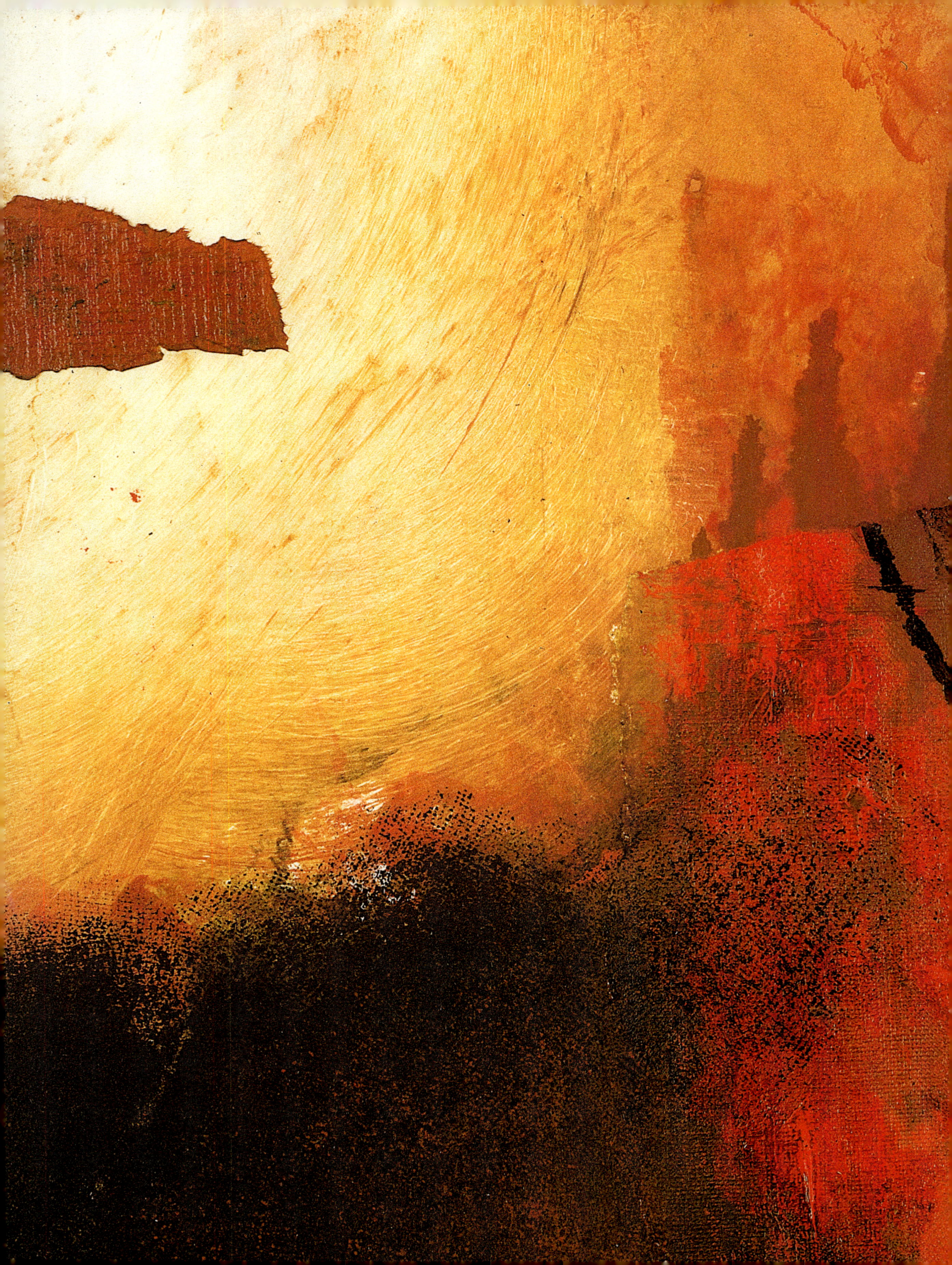

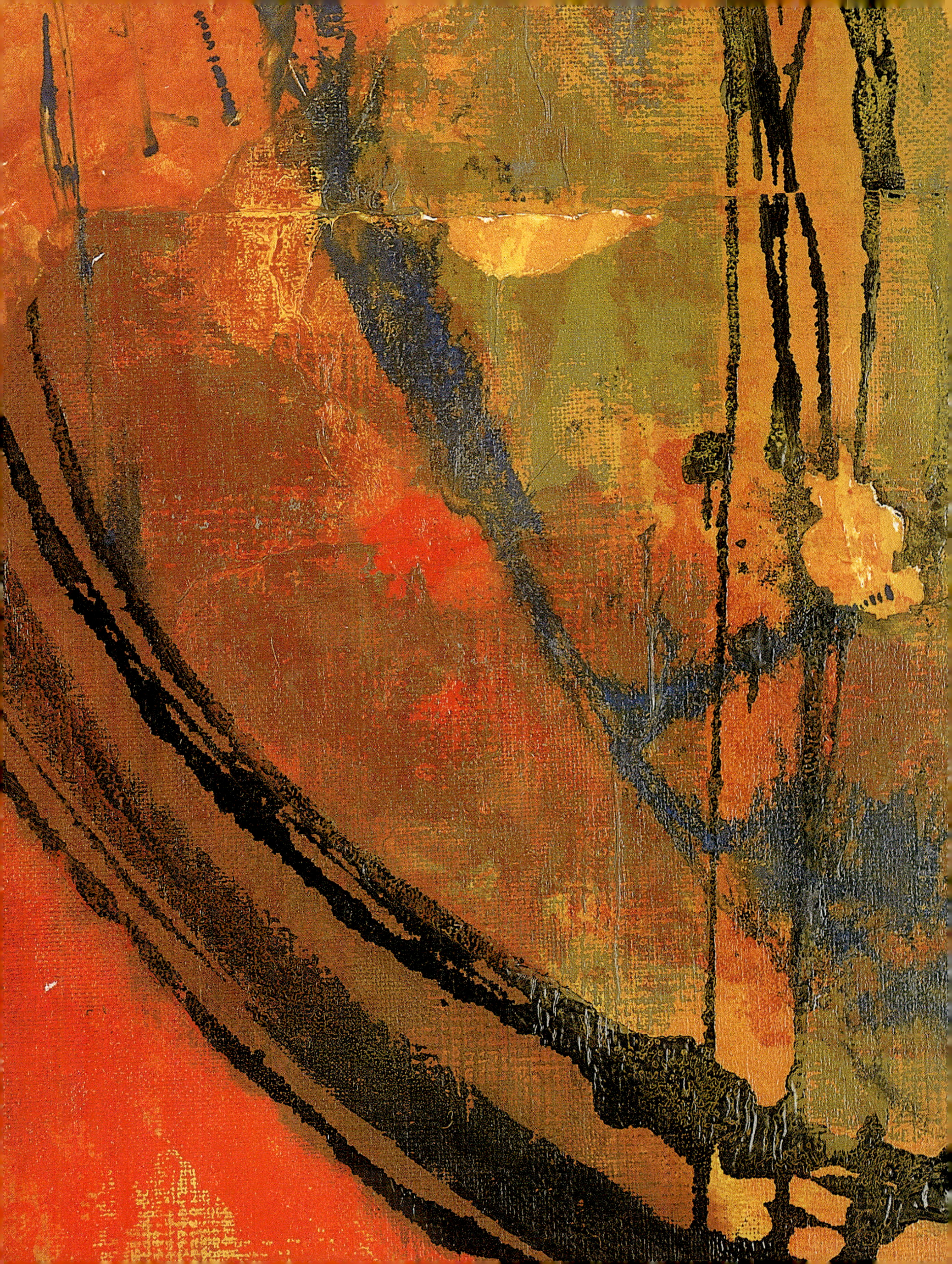

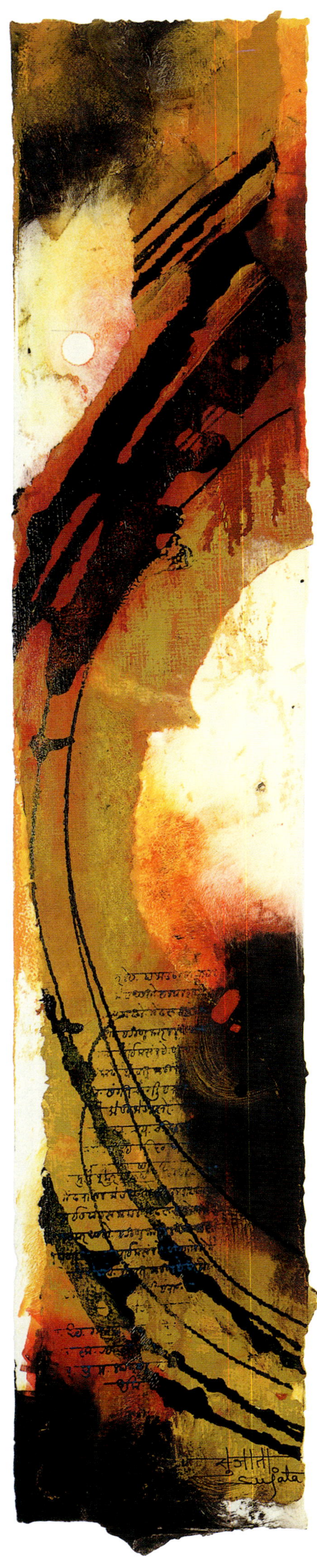

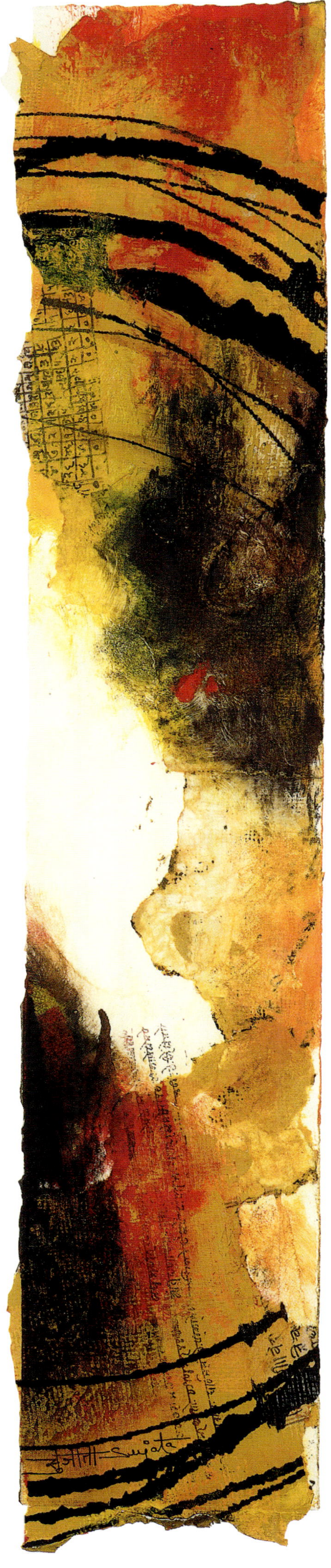

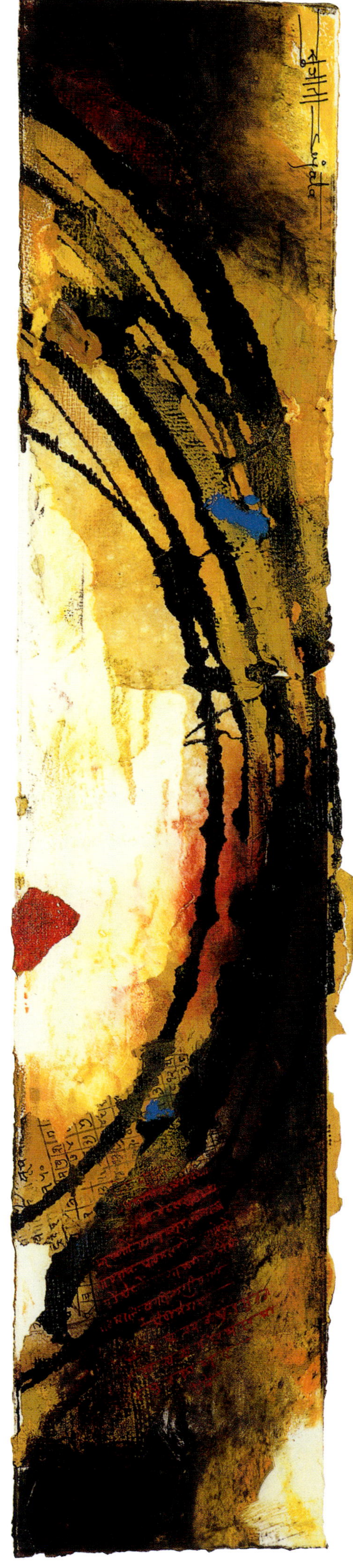

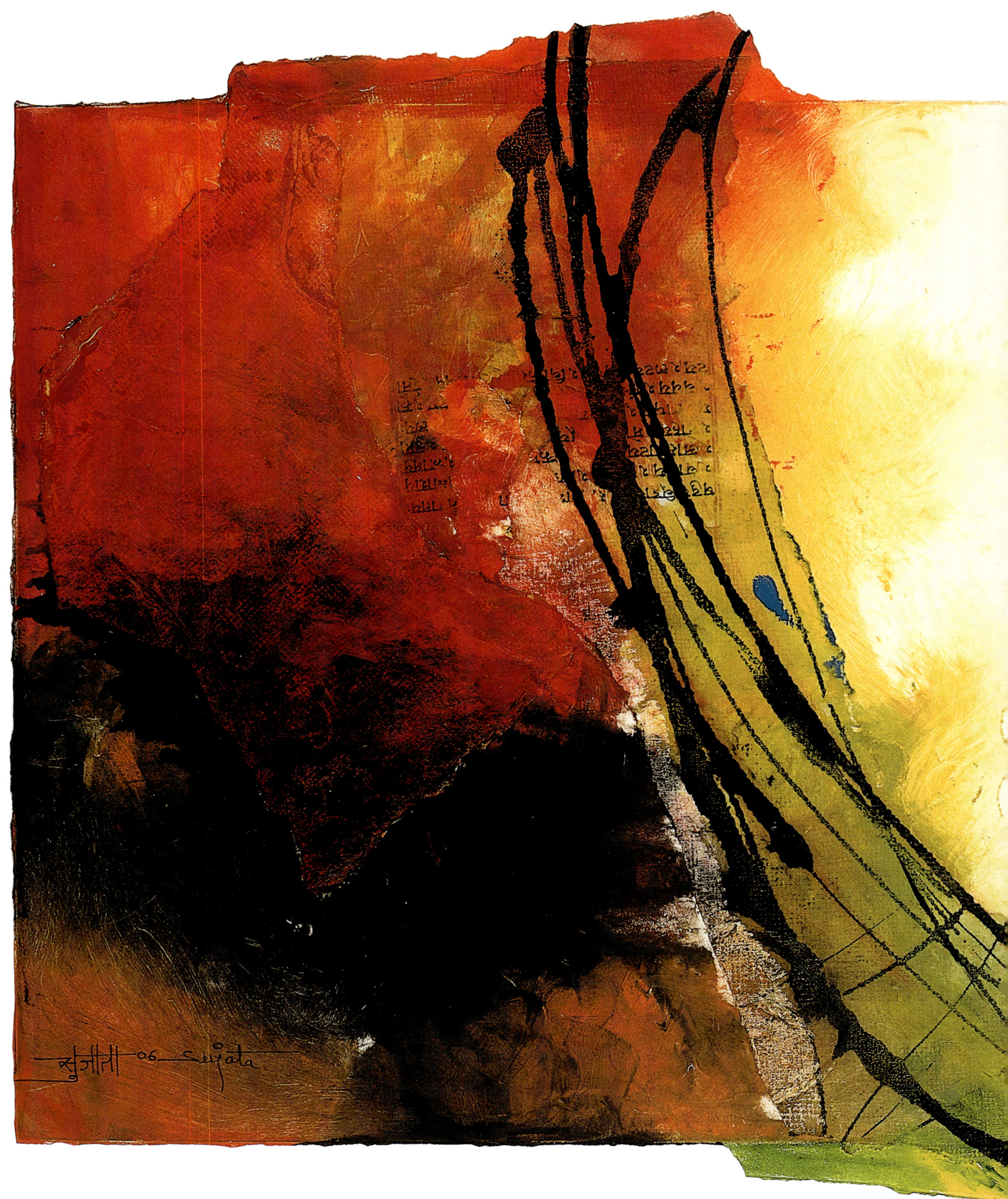

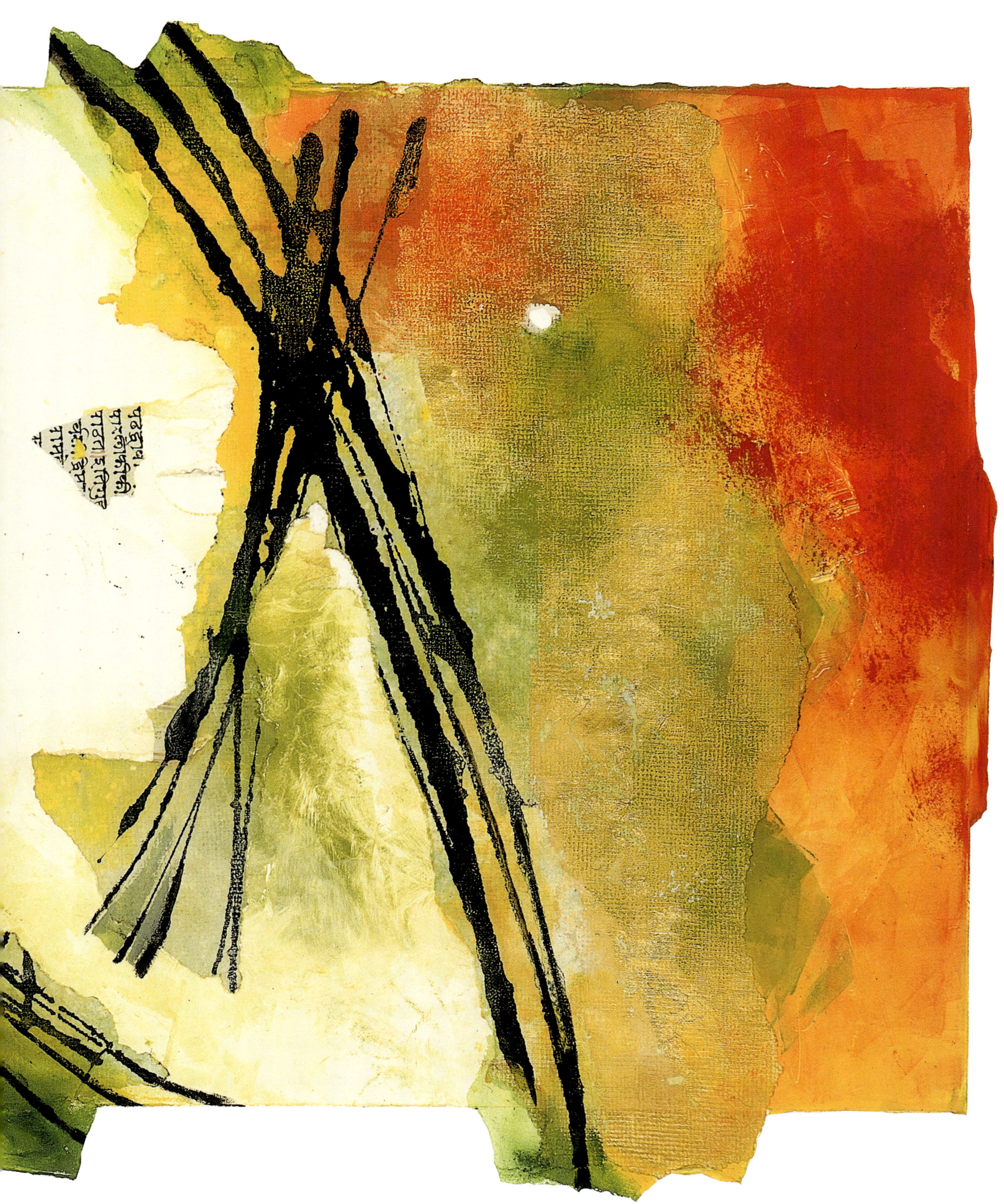

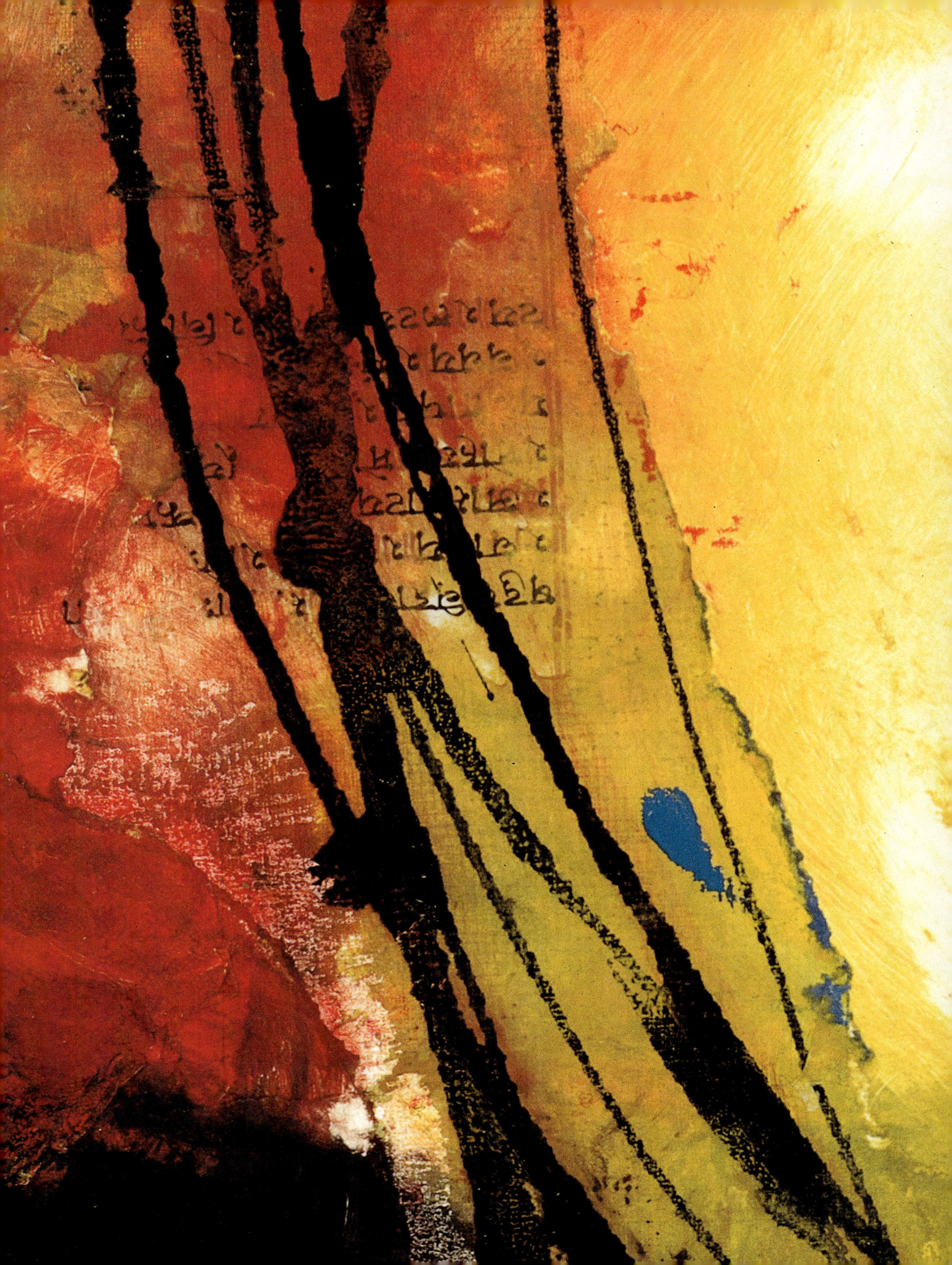

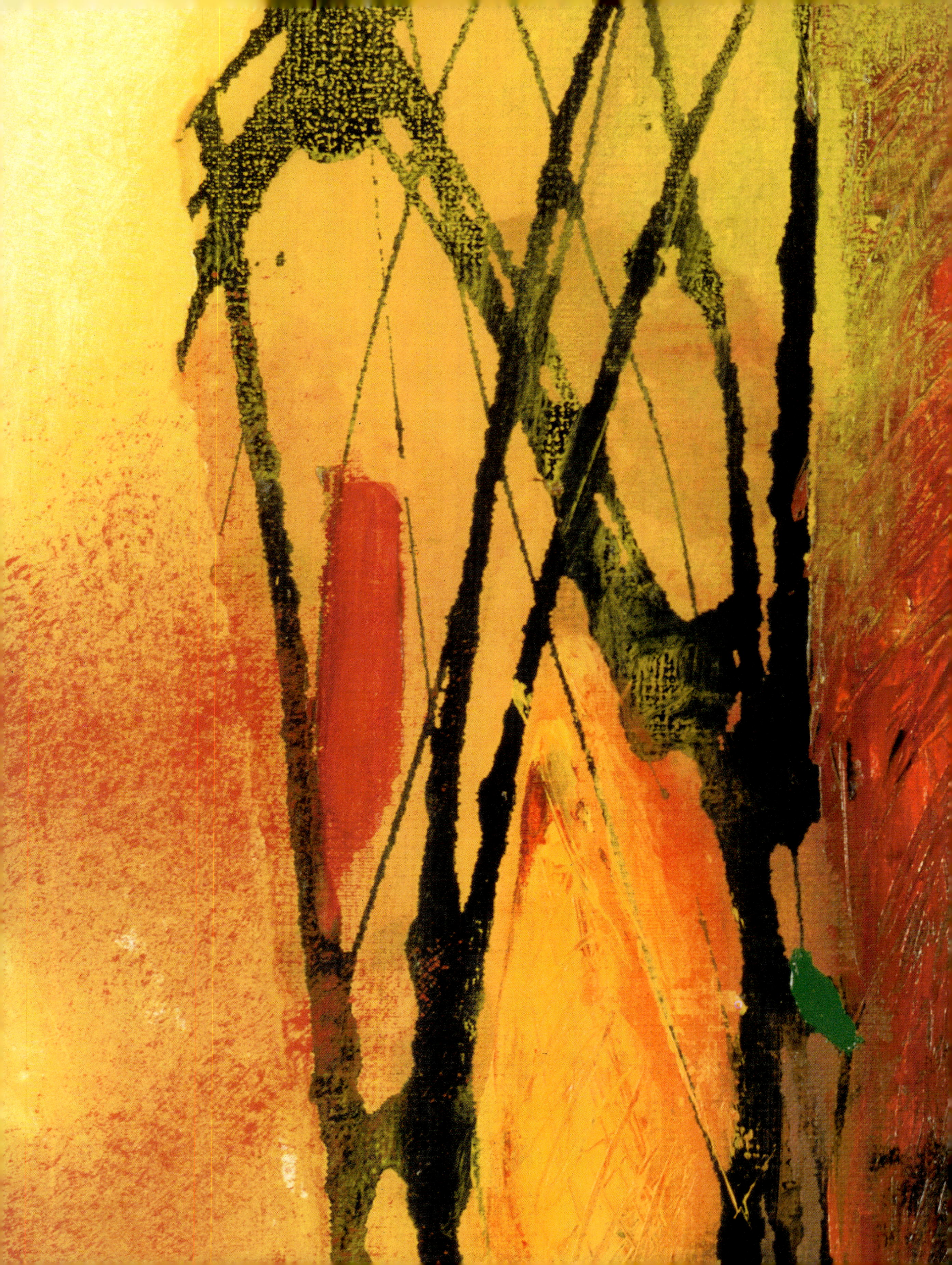

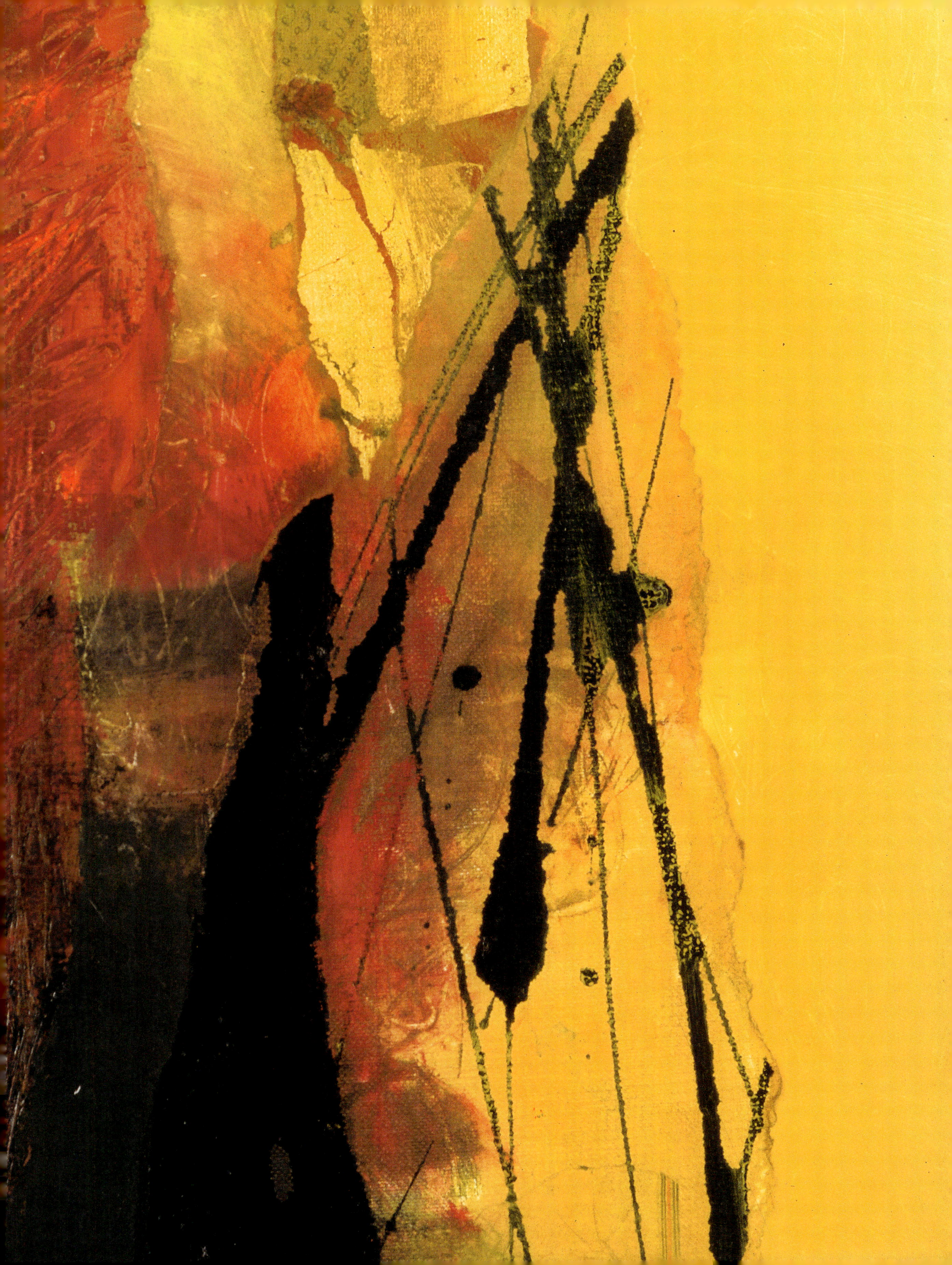

Through your body
I see the stars;
I see death and life;
I see silence.

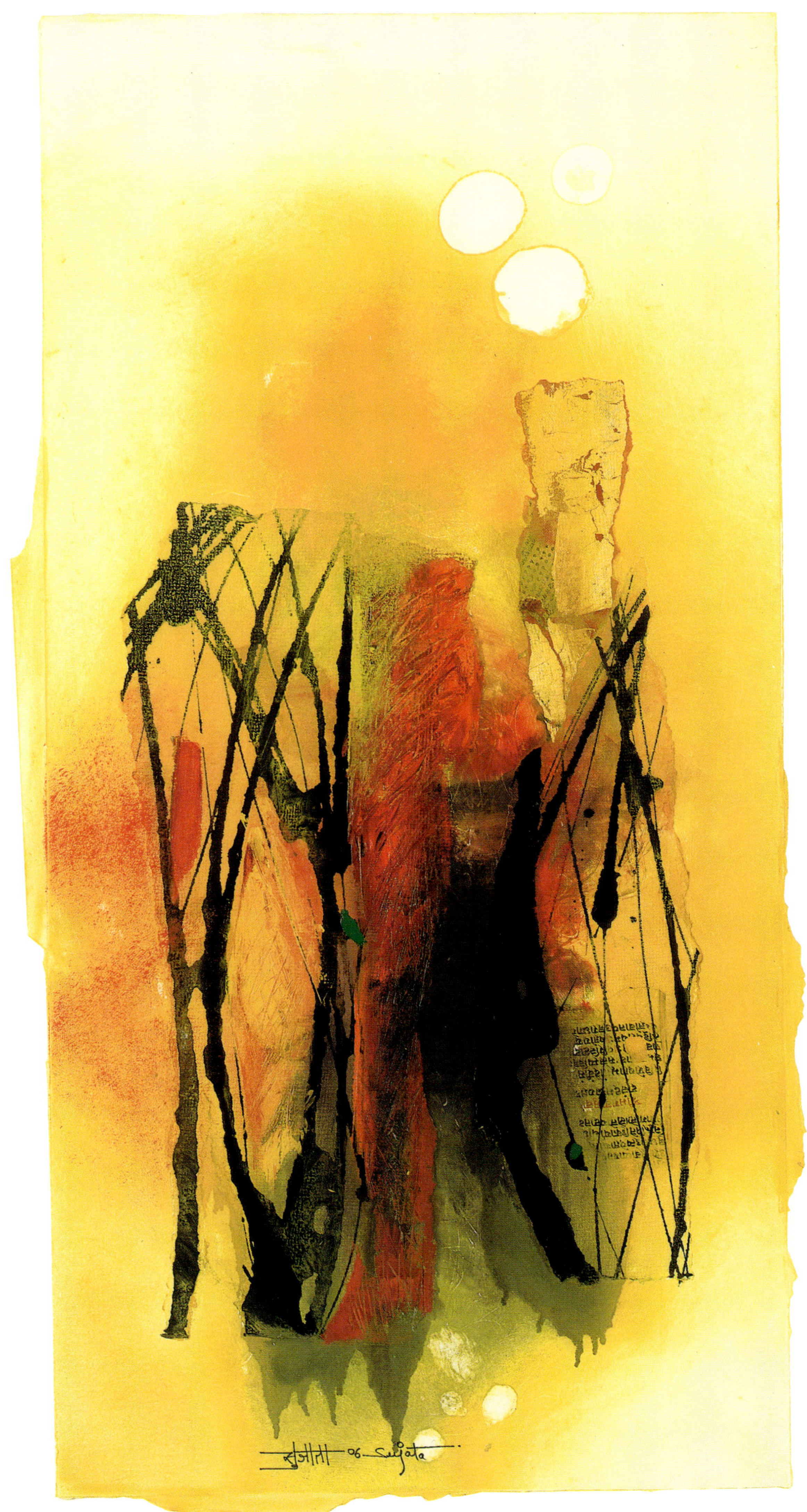
सुजाता 06 Sujata

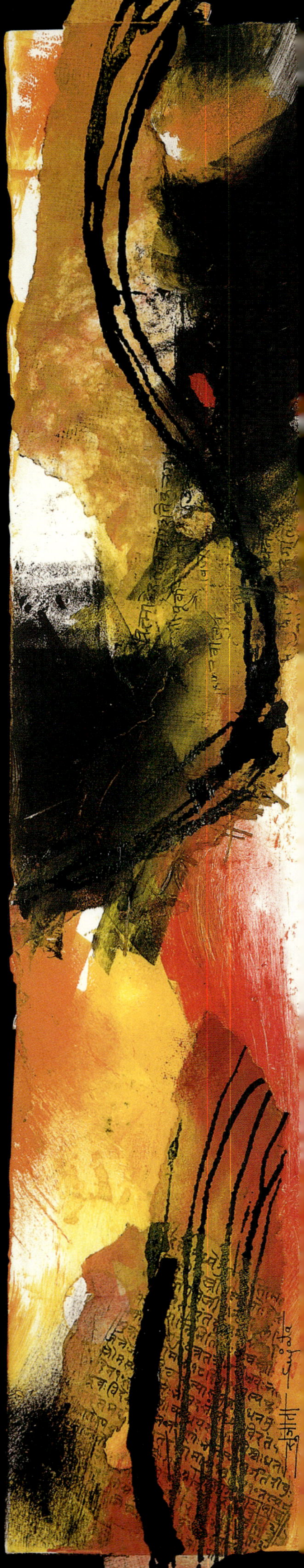

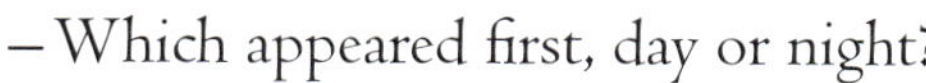

– Which appeared first, day or night?
– Day, but it preceded night by just one day.

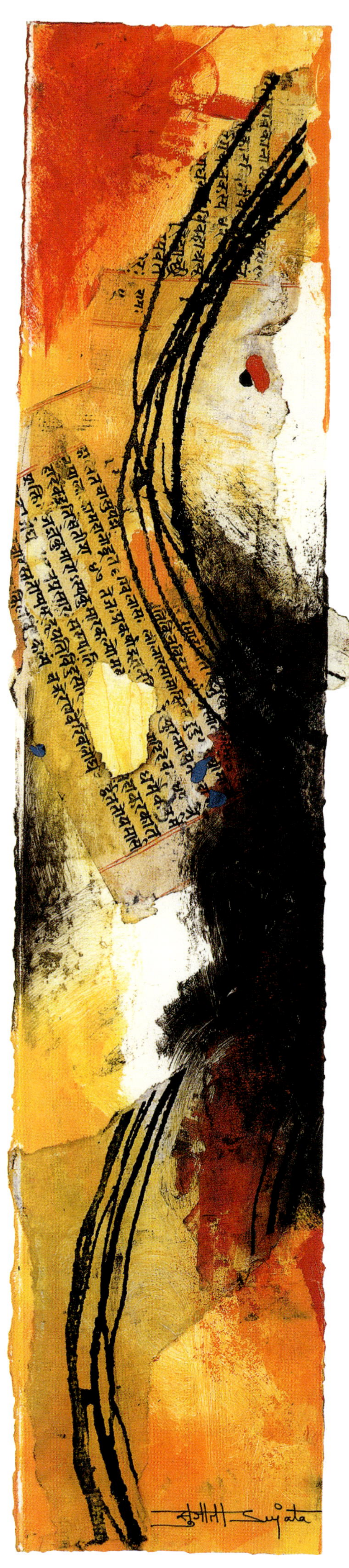

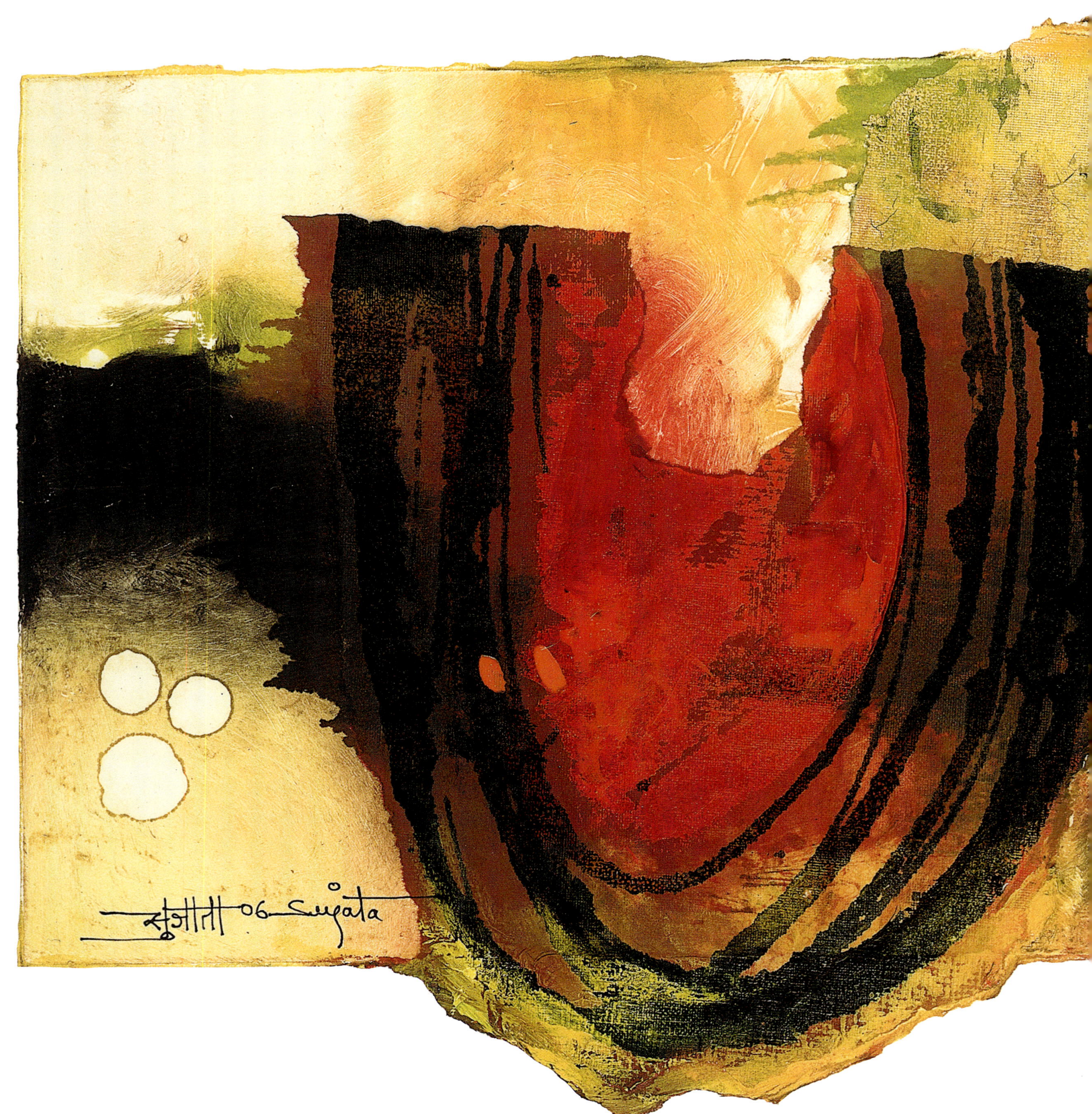
सुजाता 06 Sujata

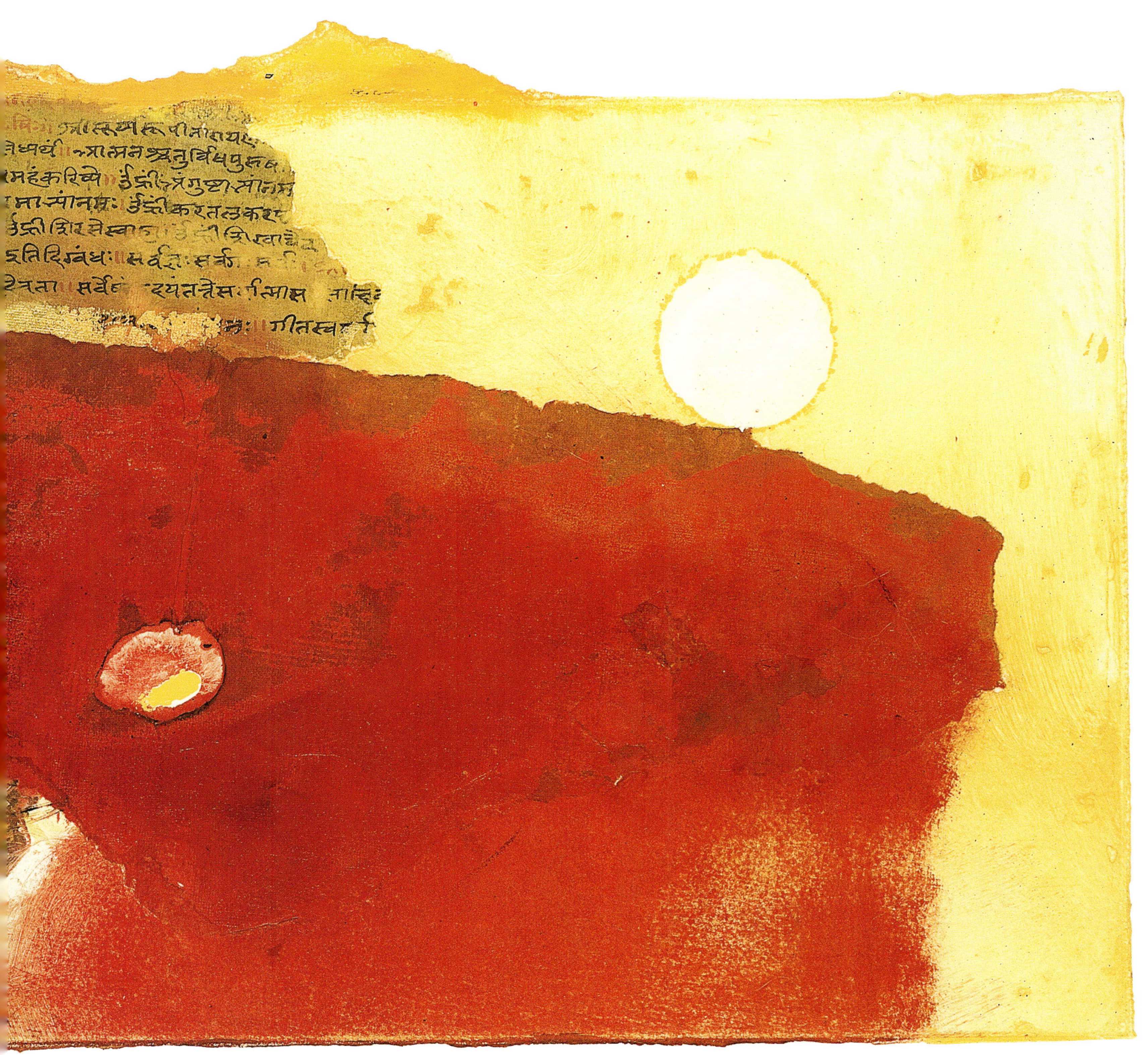

If I don't touch your heart, the ruin of the world is nigh.

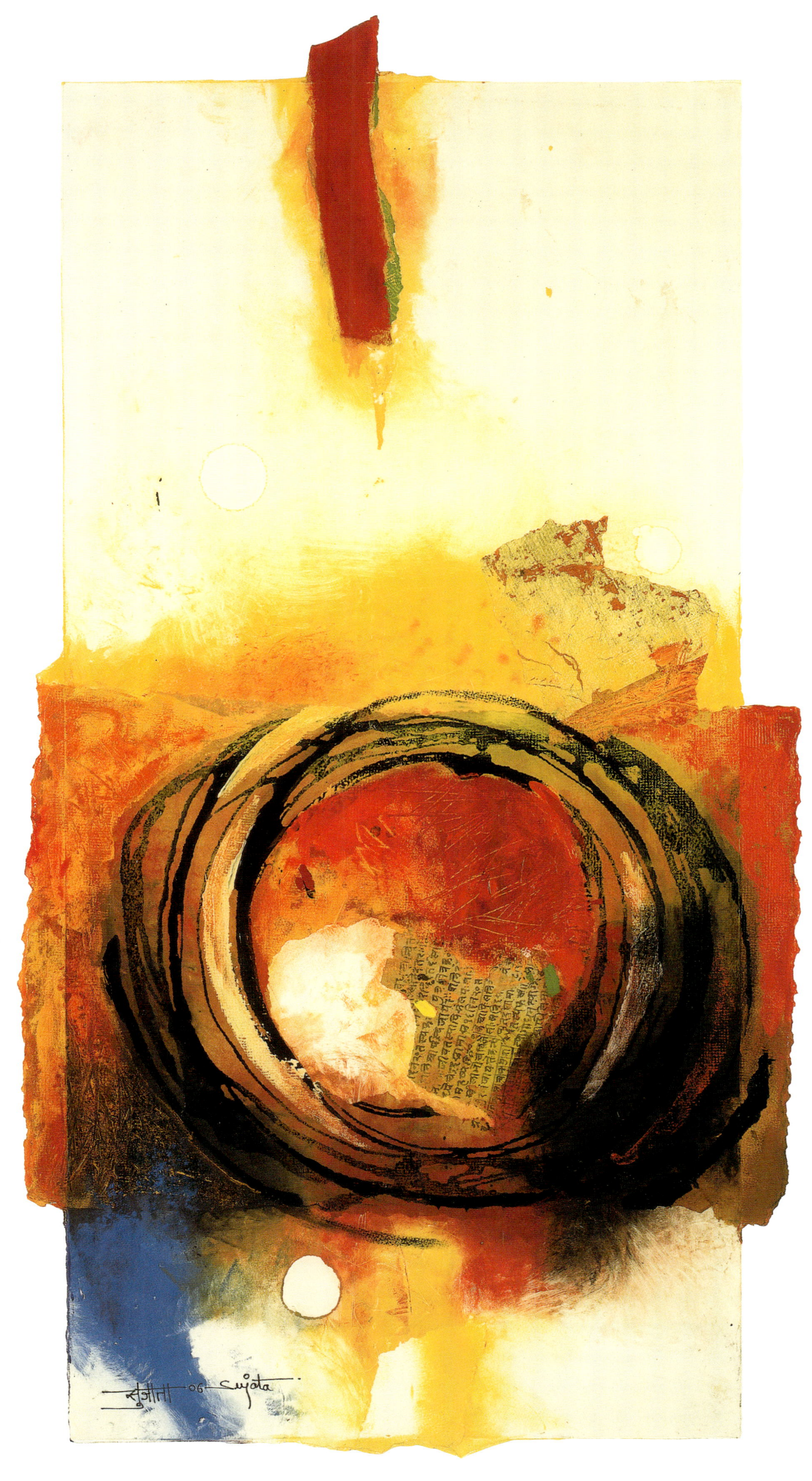
सुजाता 06 Sujata

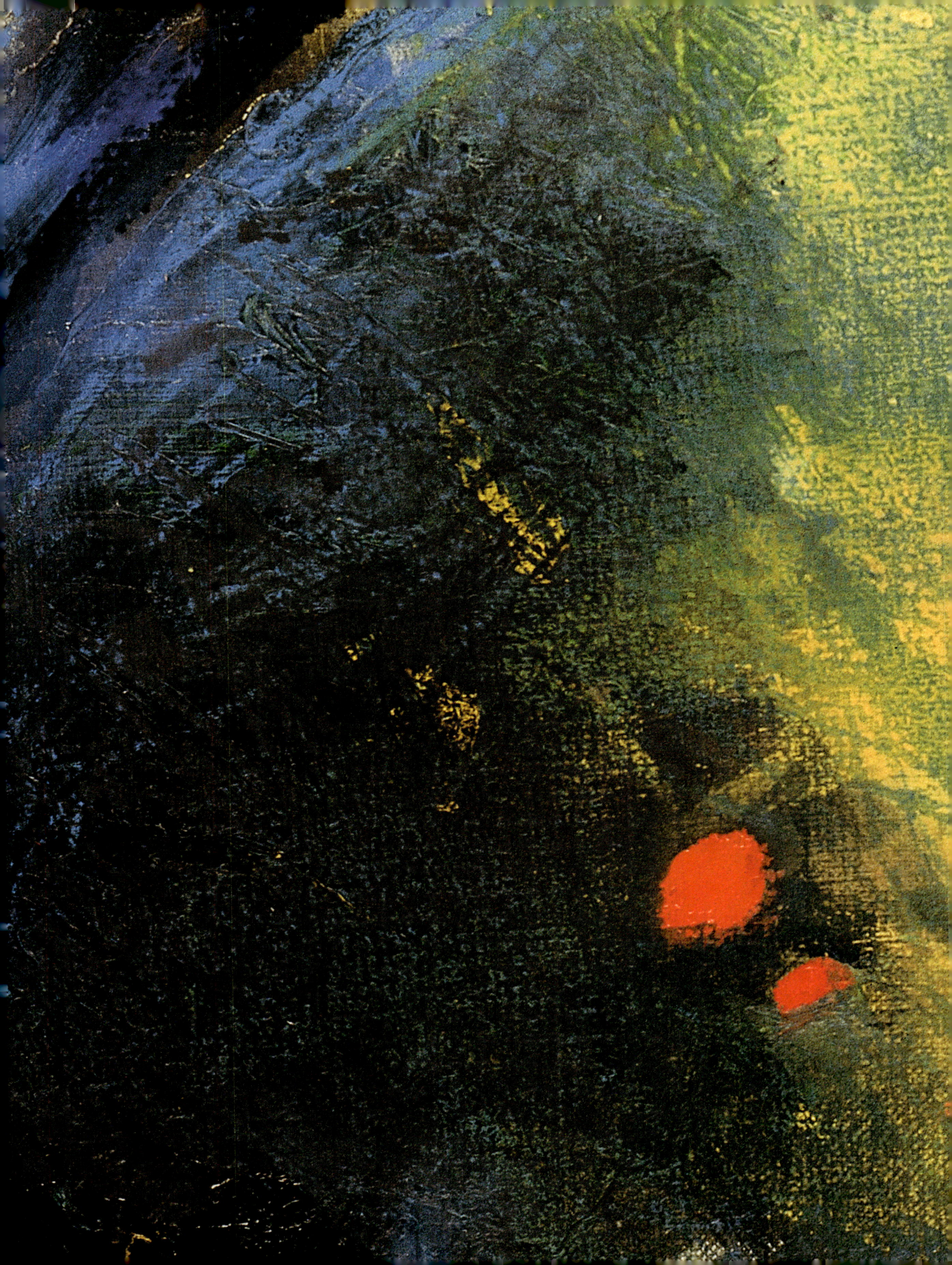

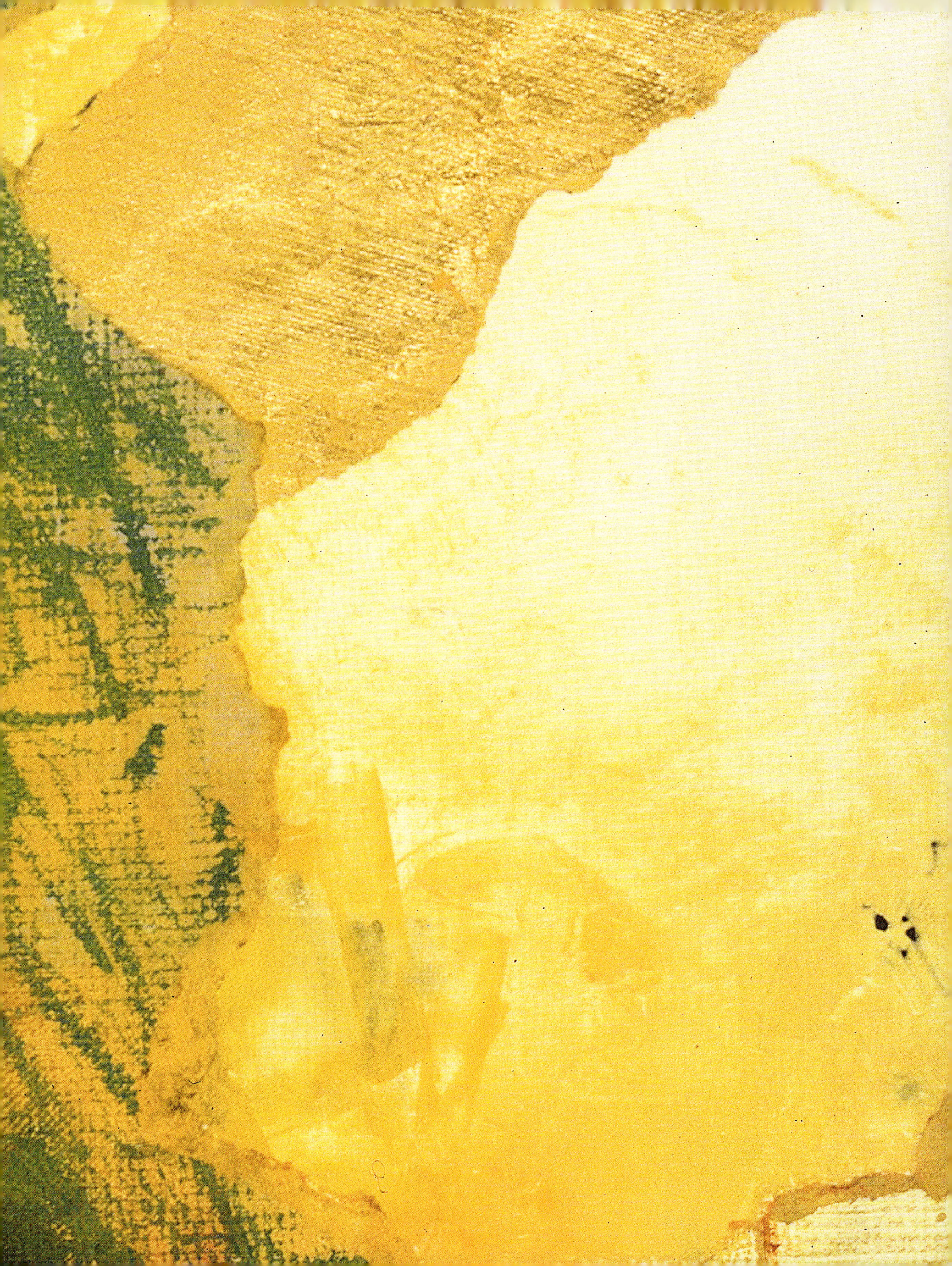

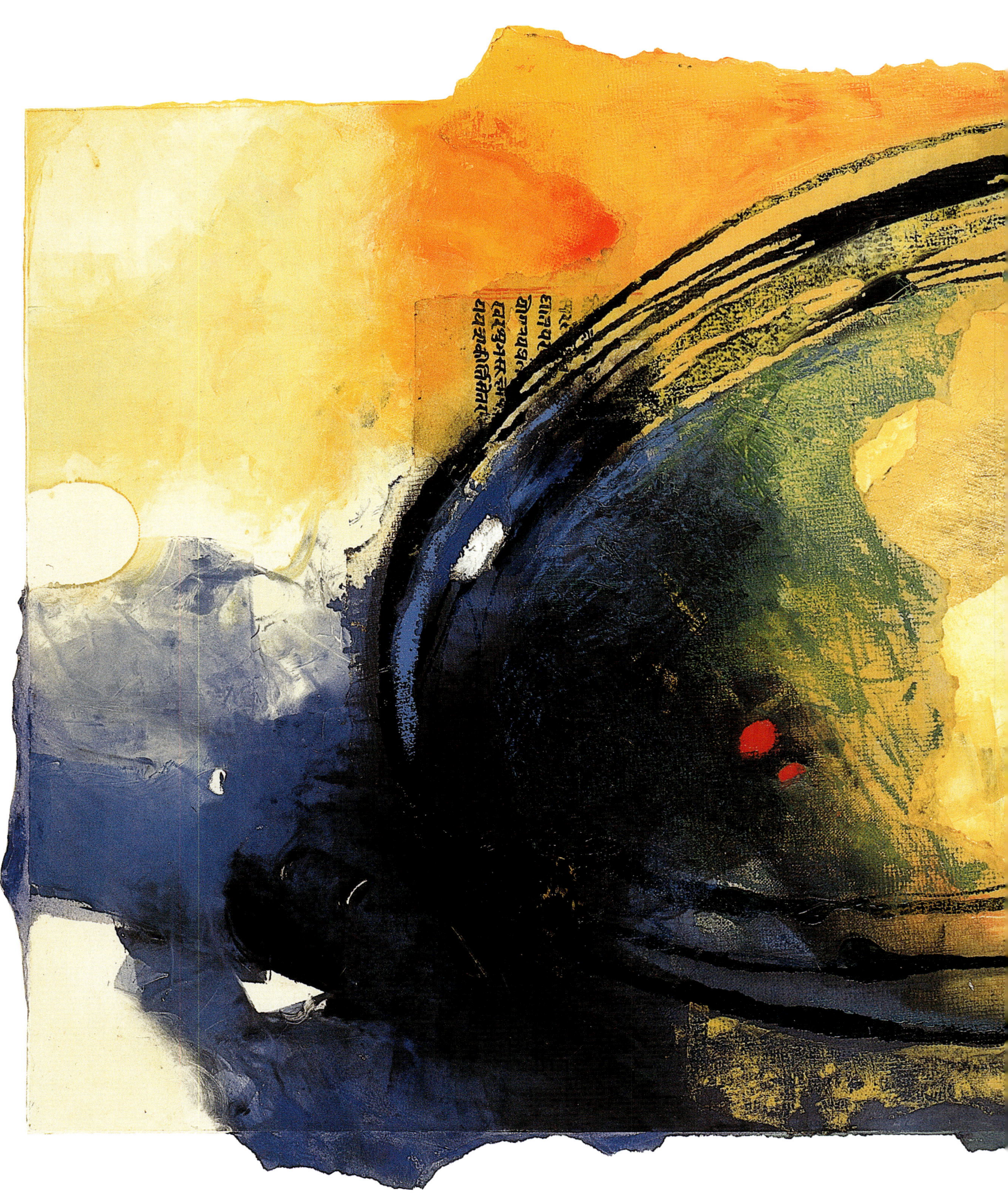

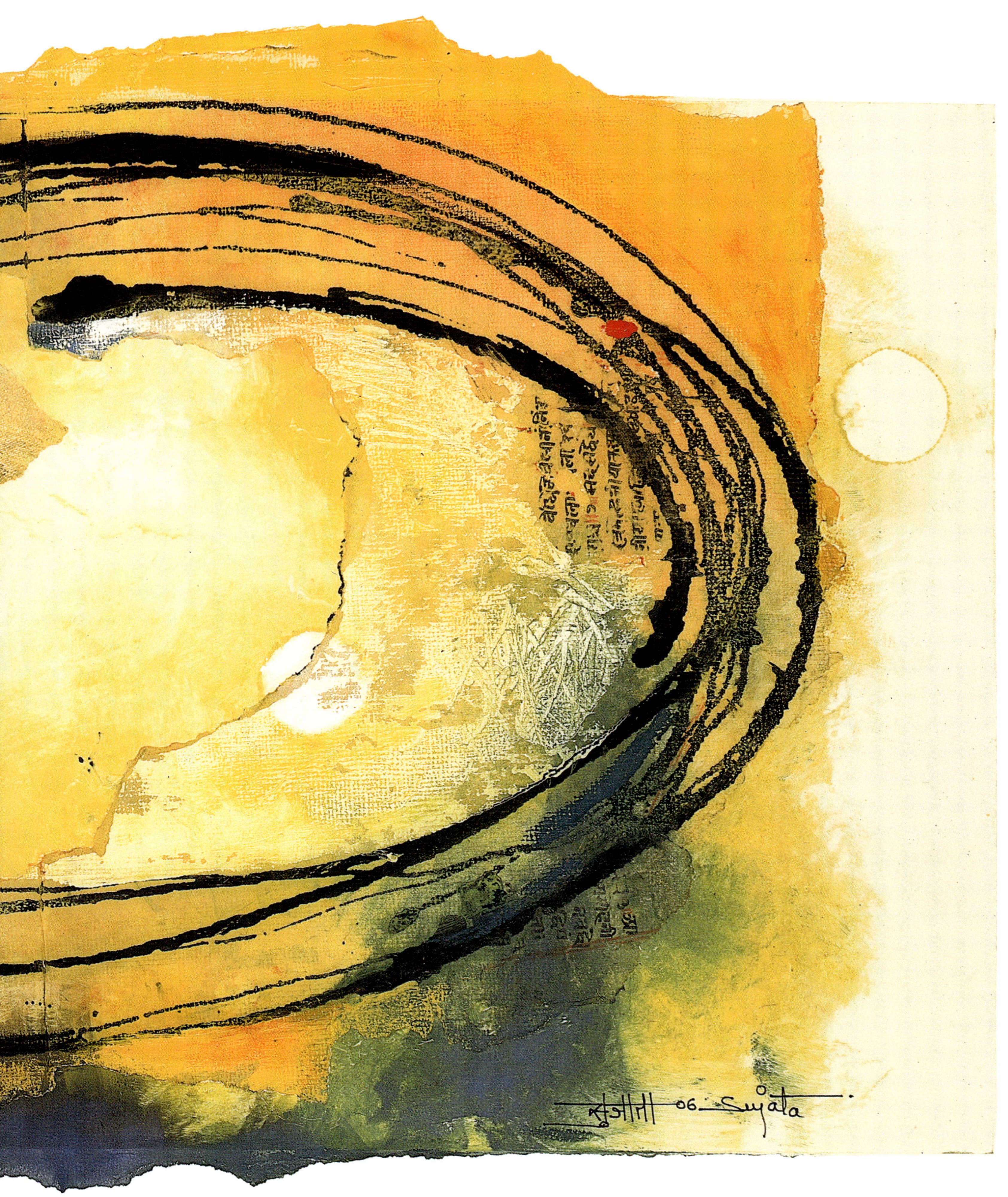

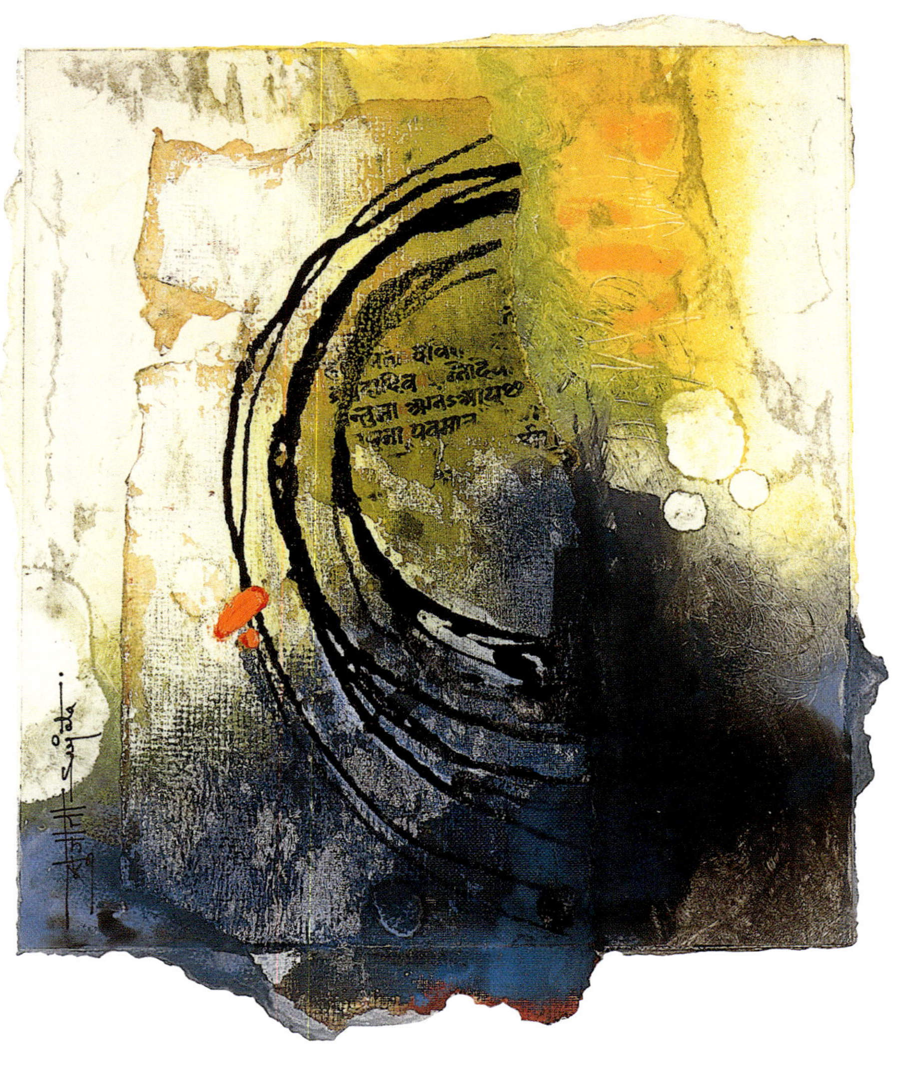

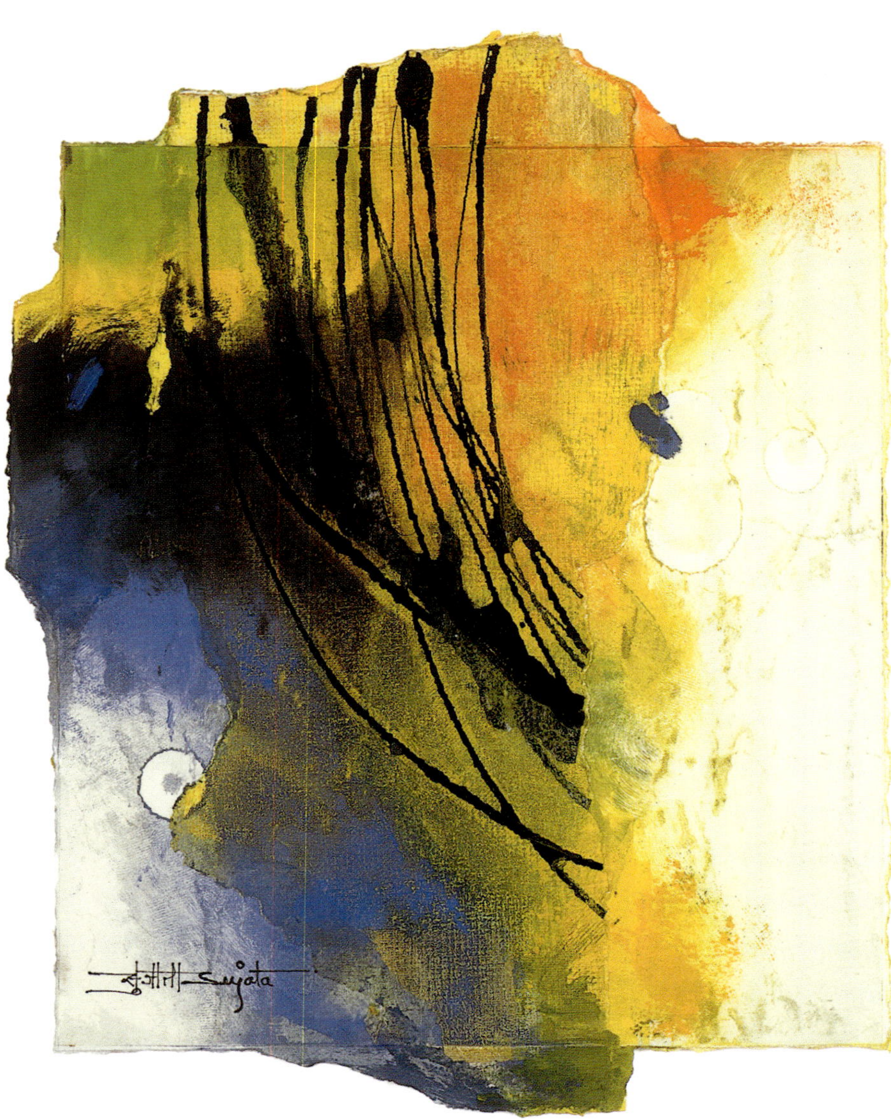

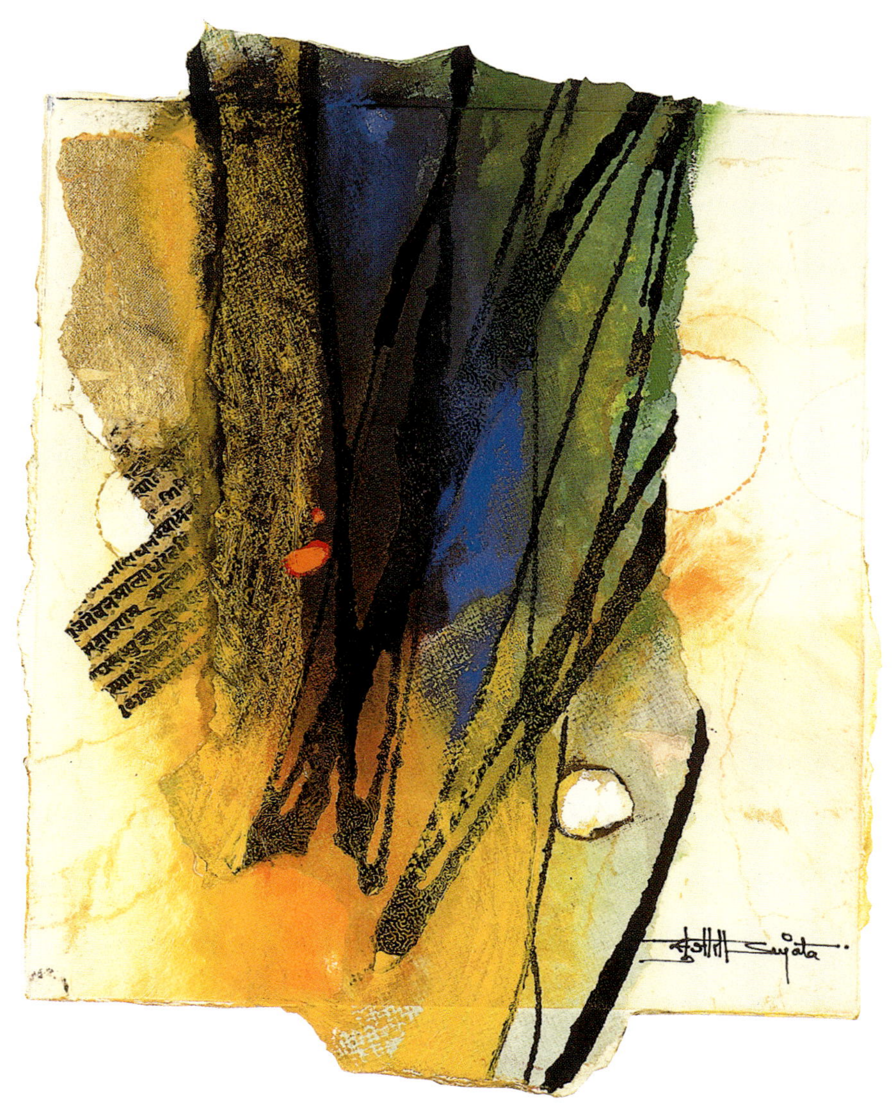

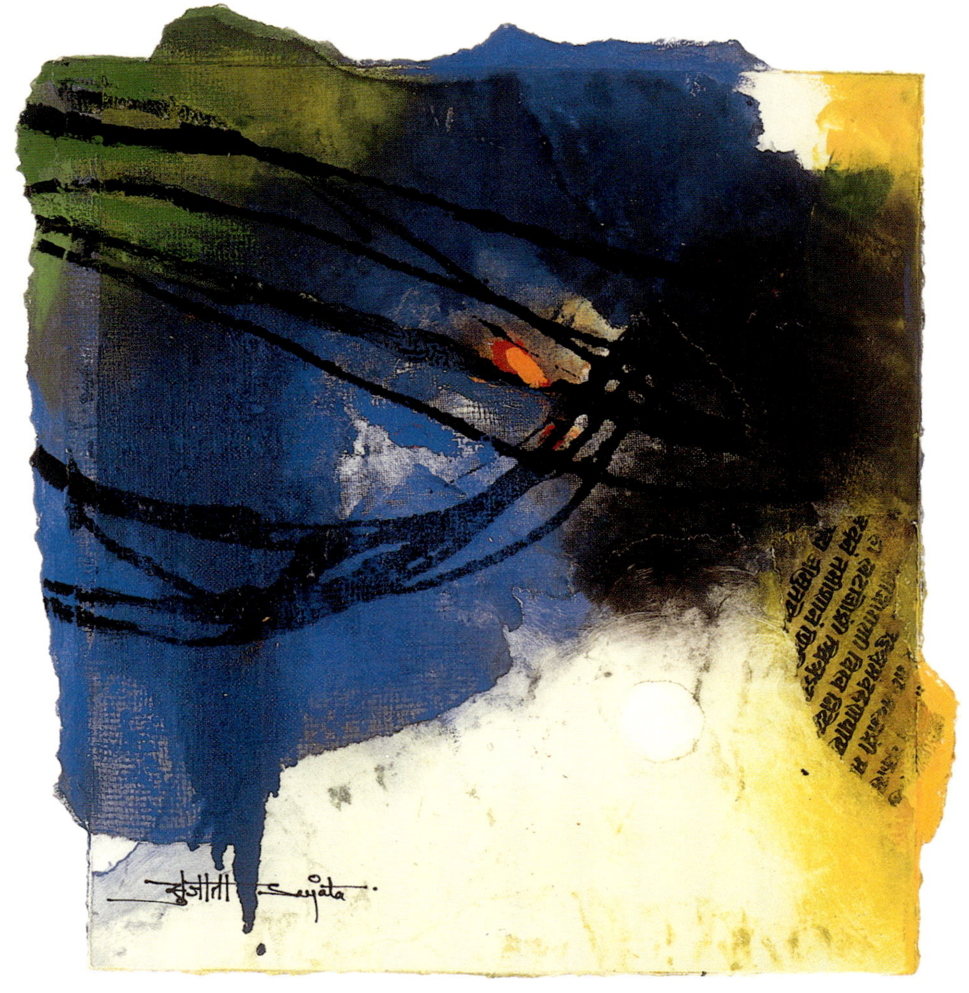

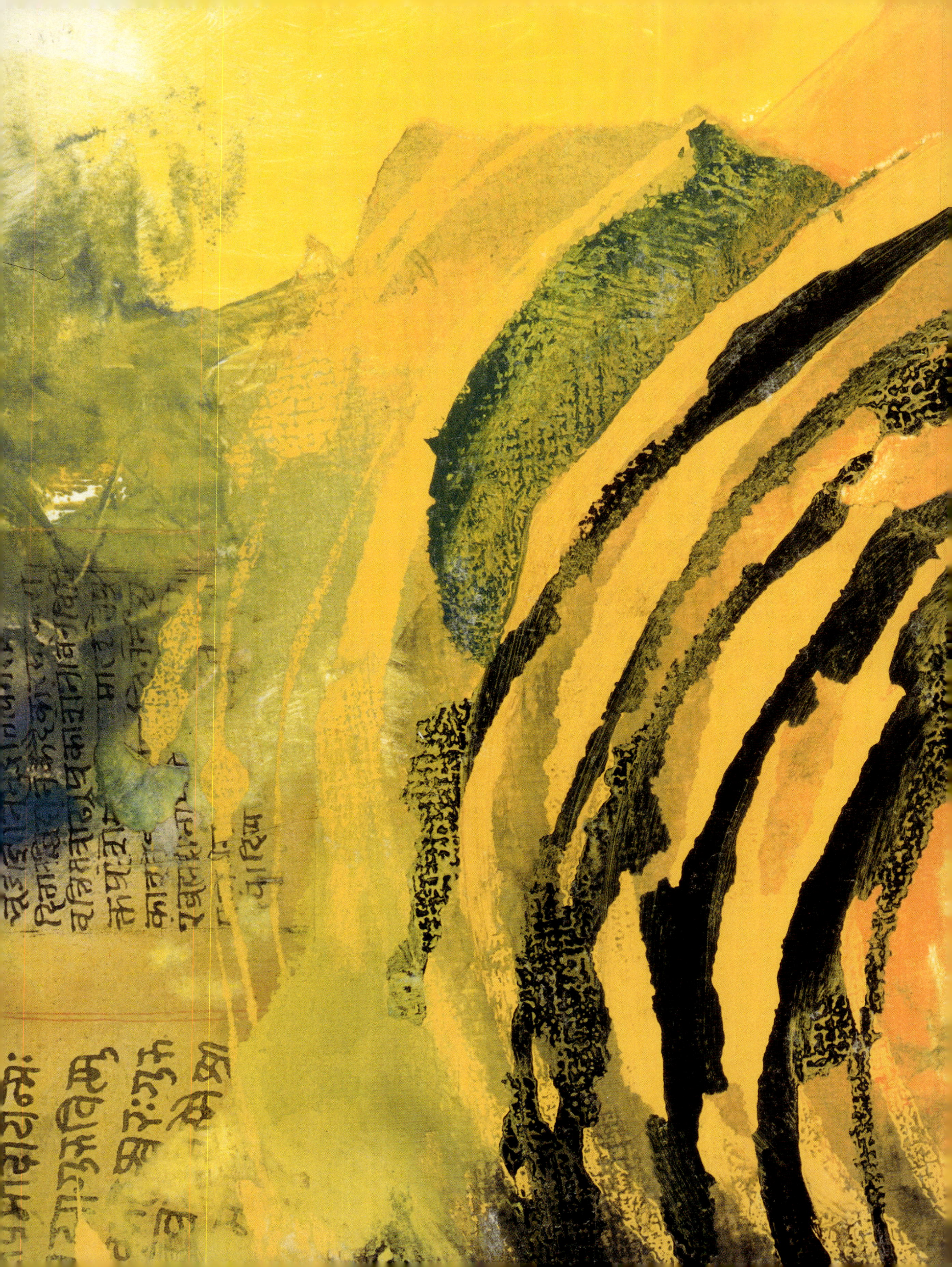

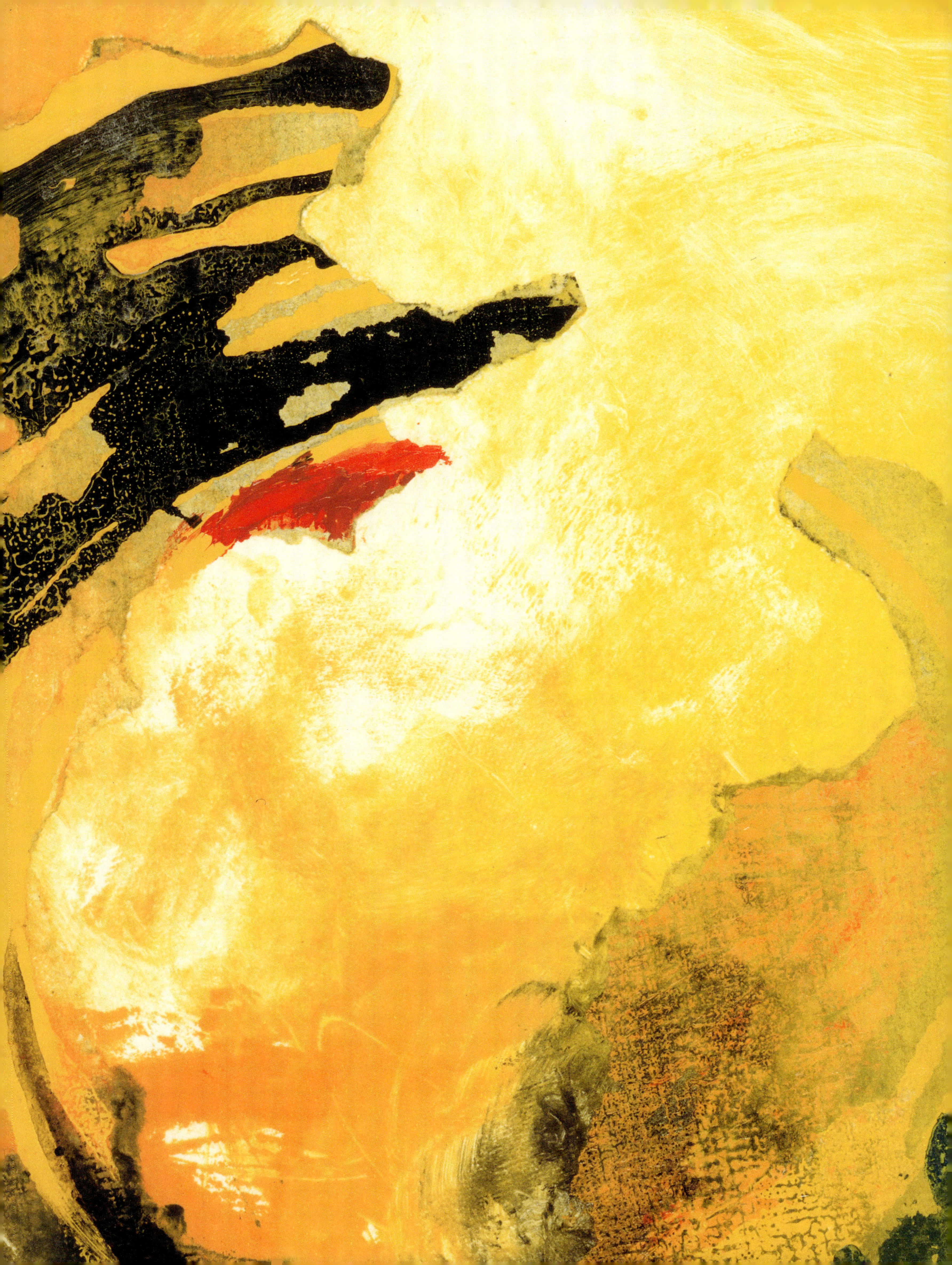

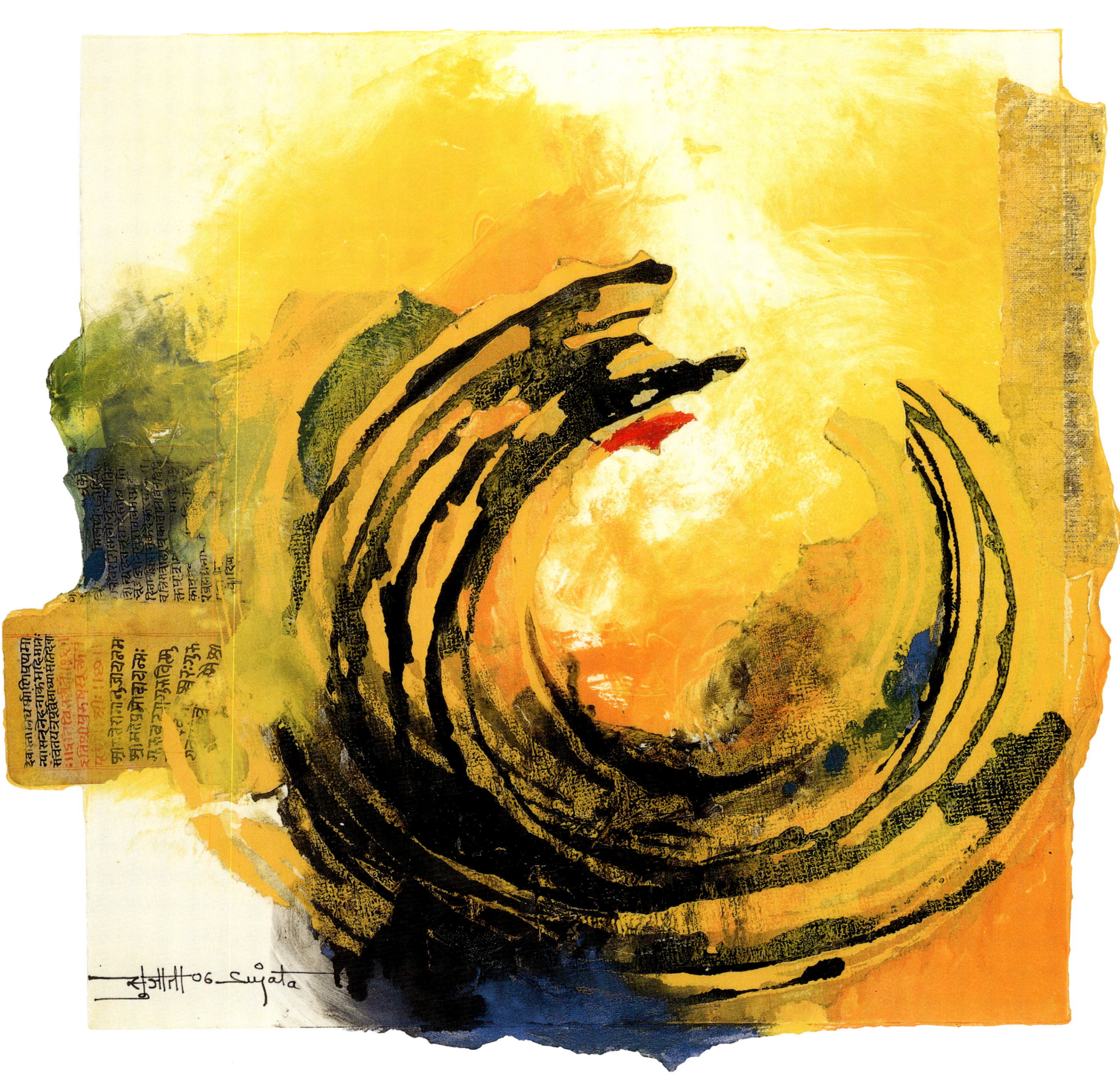
सुजाता 06 Sujata

Dharma, when it is protected, protects.
When it is destroyed, it destroys.
But to observe *dharma,* perhaps you need to forget it sometimes.

Night, on a terrace, calm, under a starry sky.
A young man says to an old man:
– What silence…
– Don't say: 'What silence.' Say: 'I hear nothing.'

सुजाता Sujata

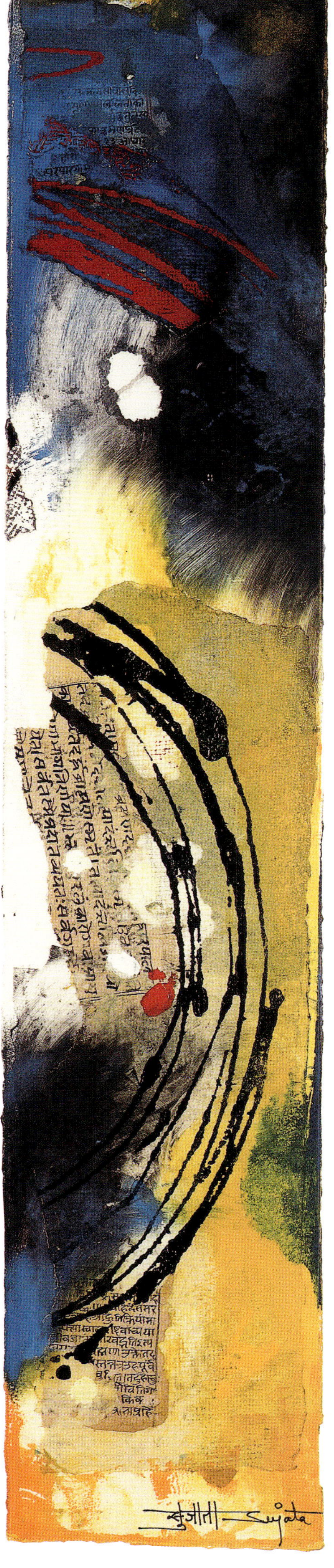
सुजाता Sujata

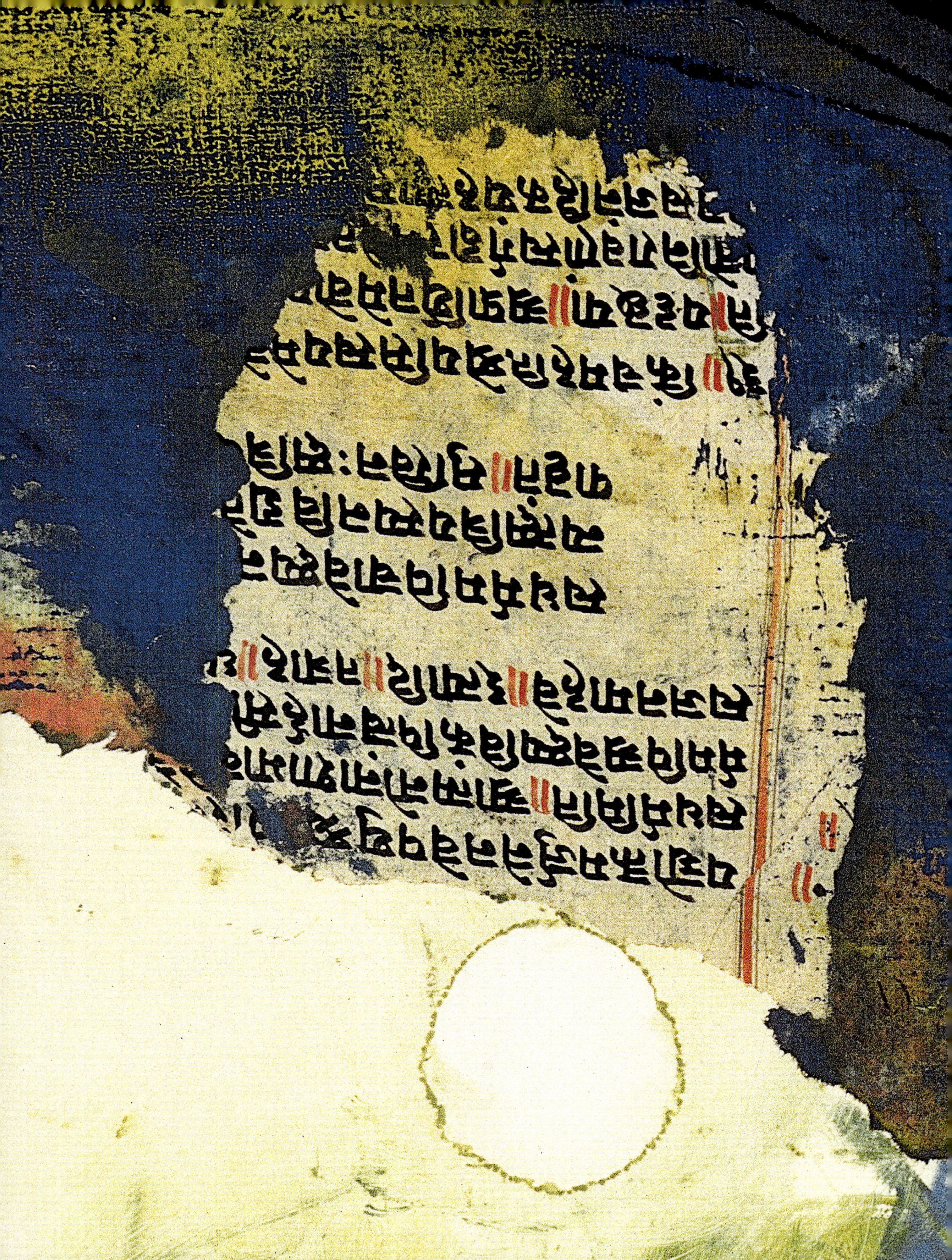

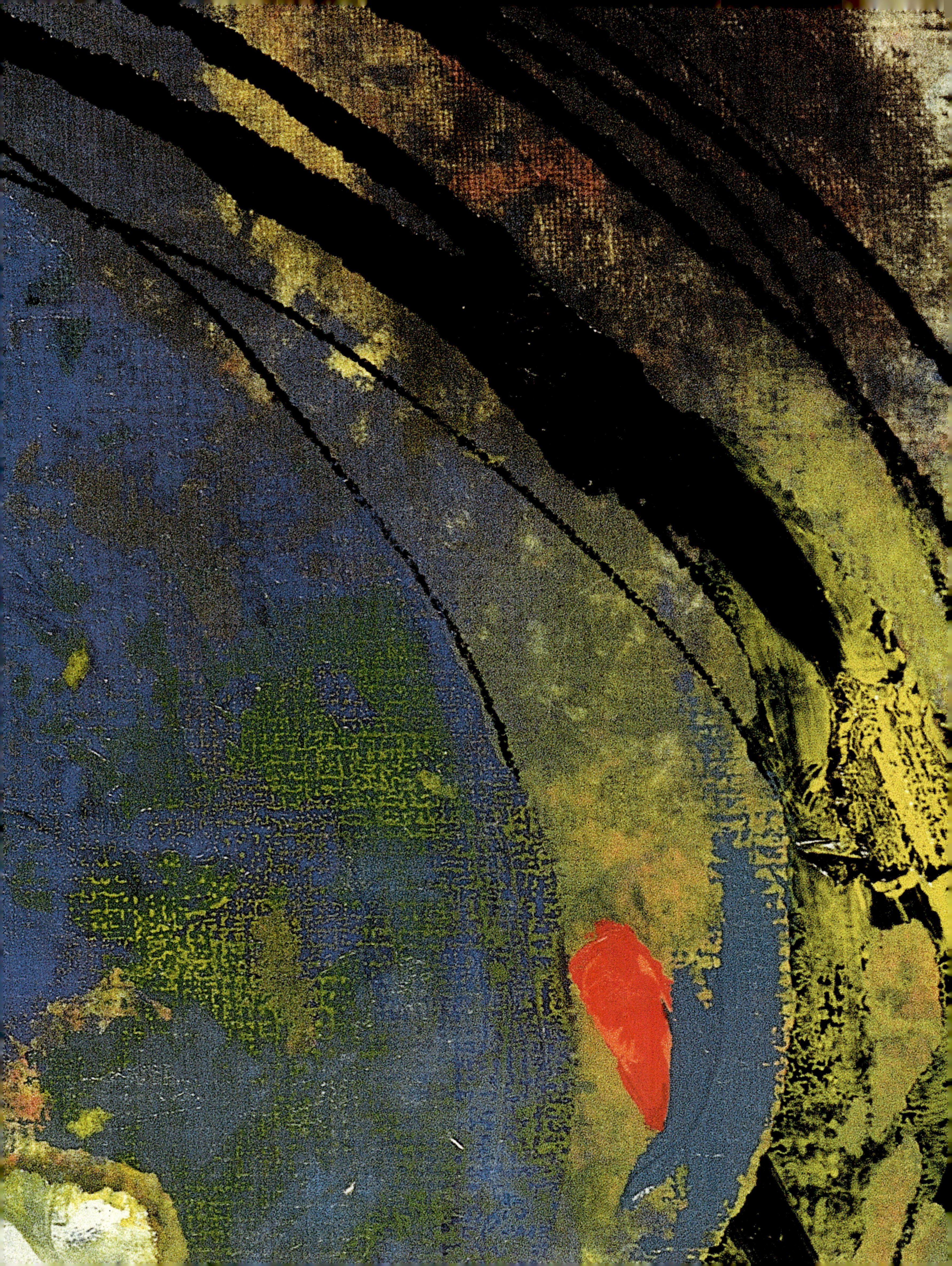

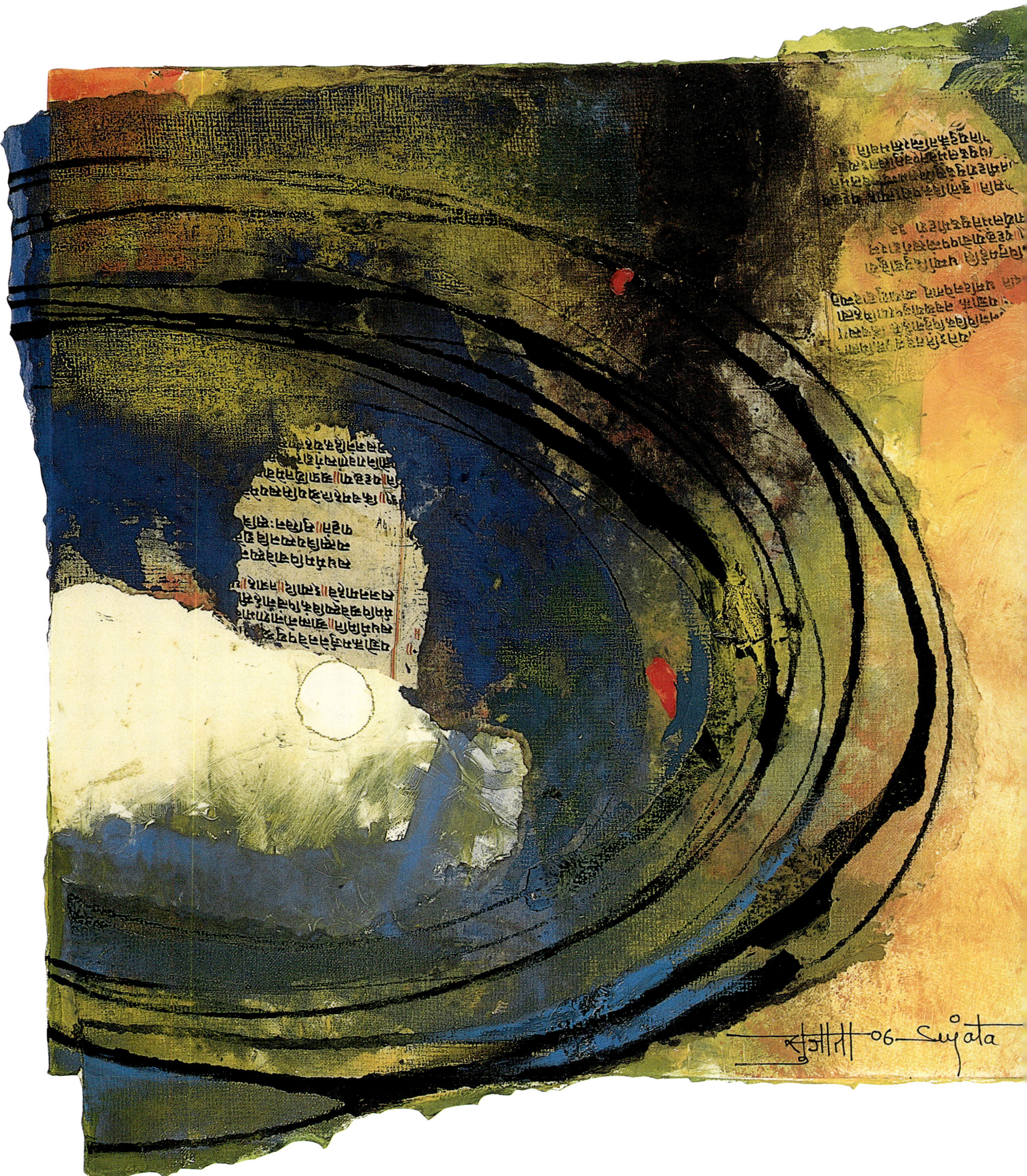
सुजाता 06 Sujata

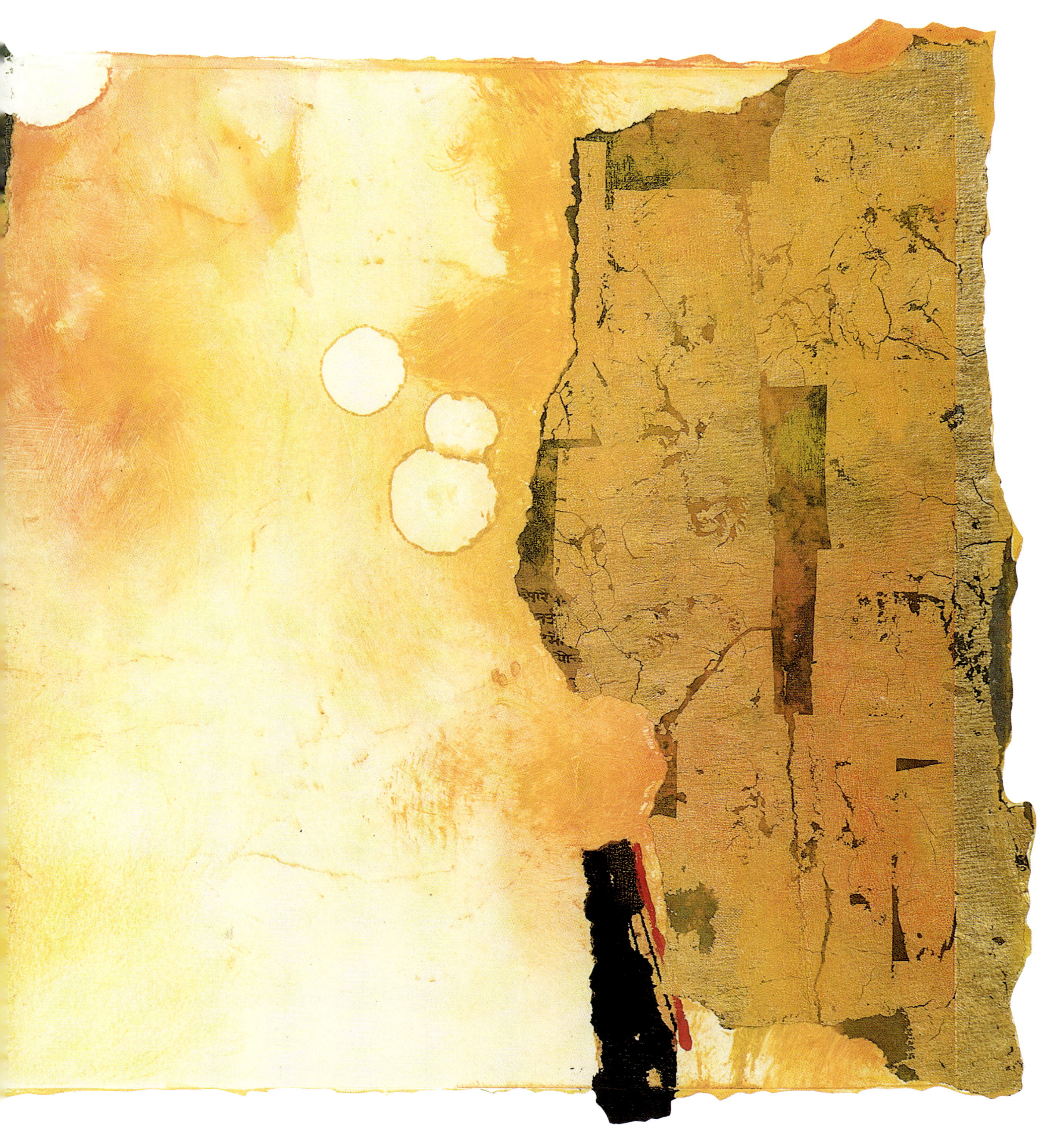

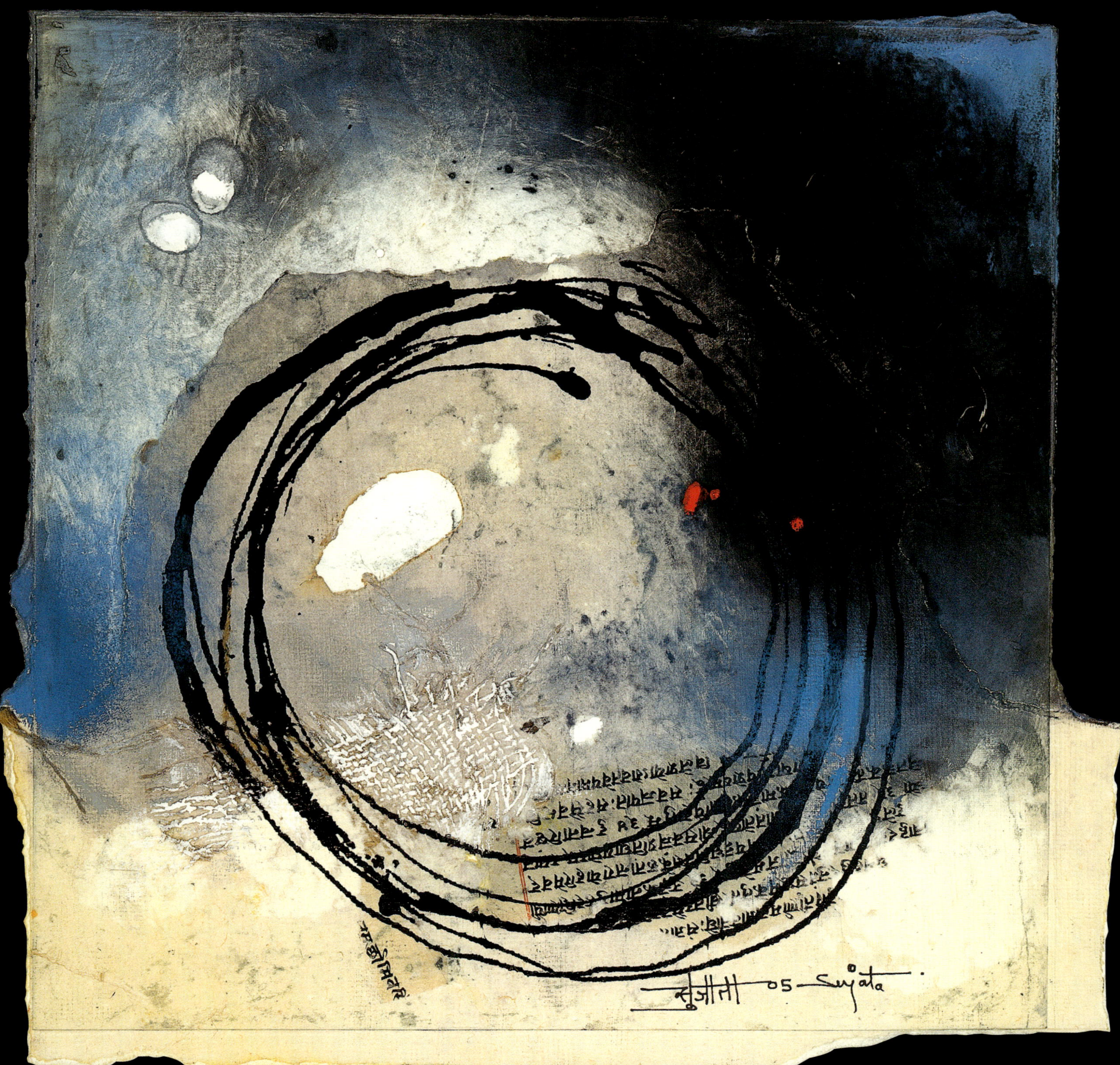
सुजाता 05 Sujata

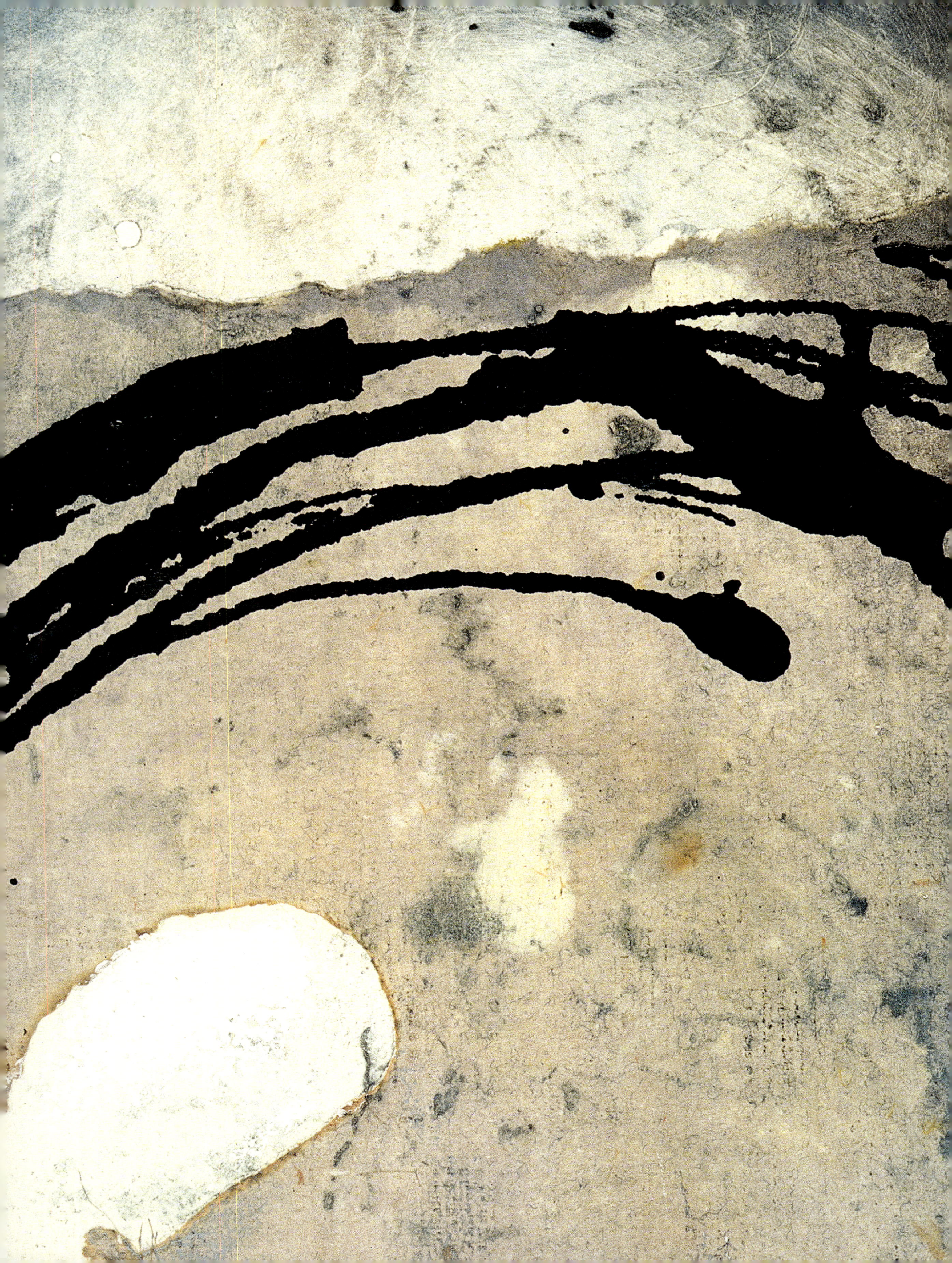

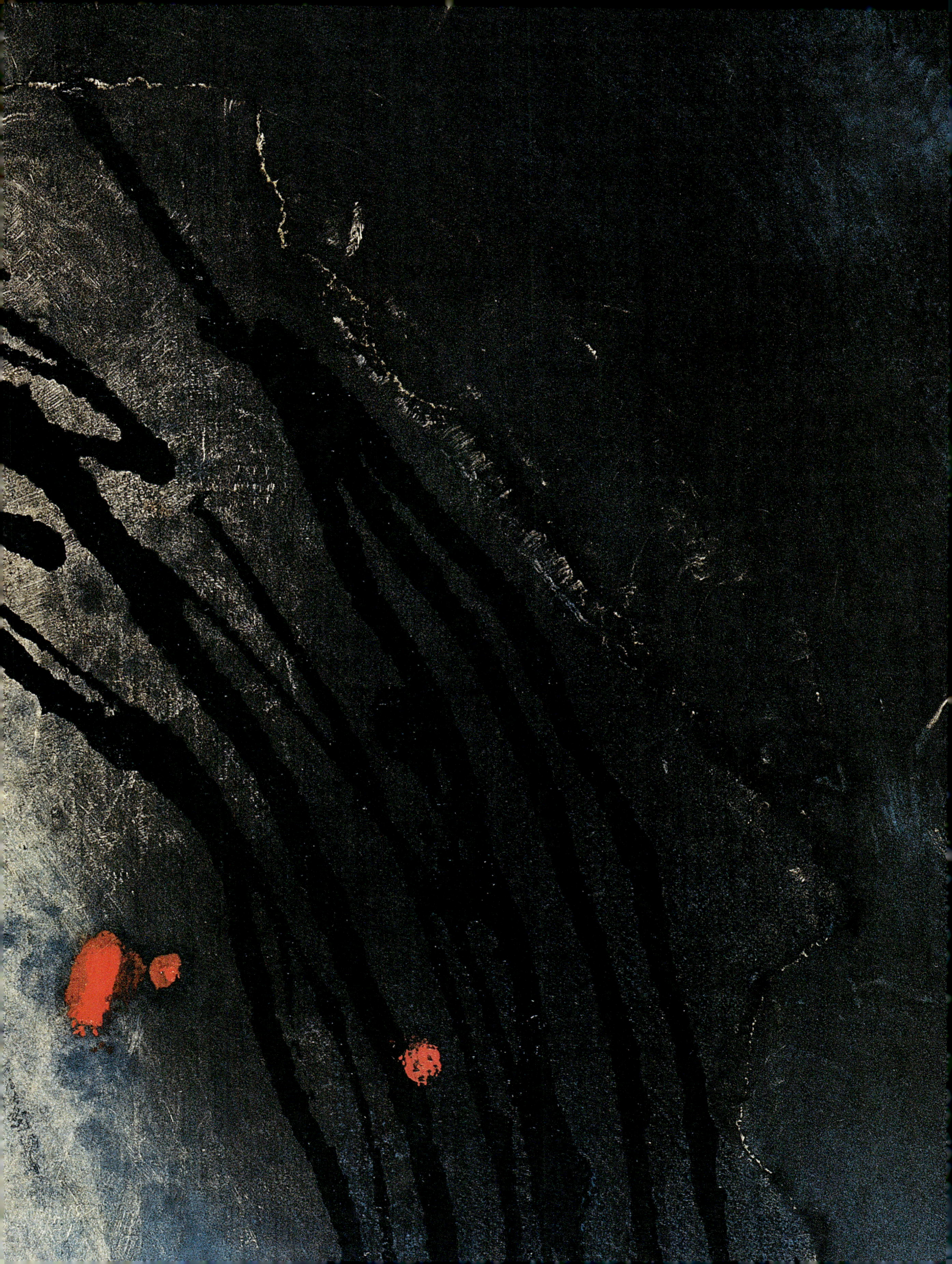

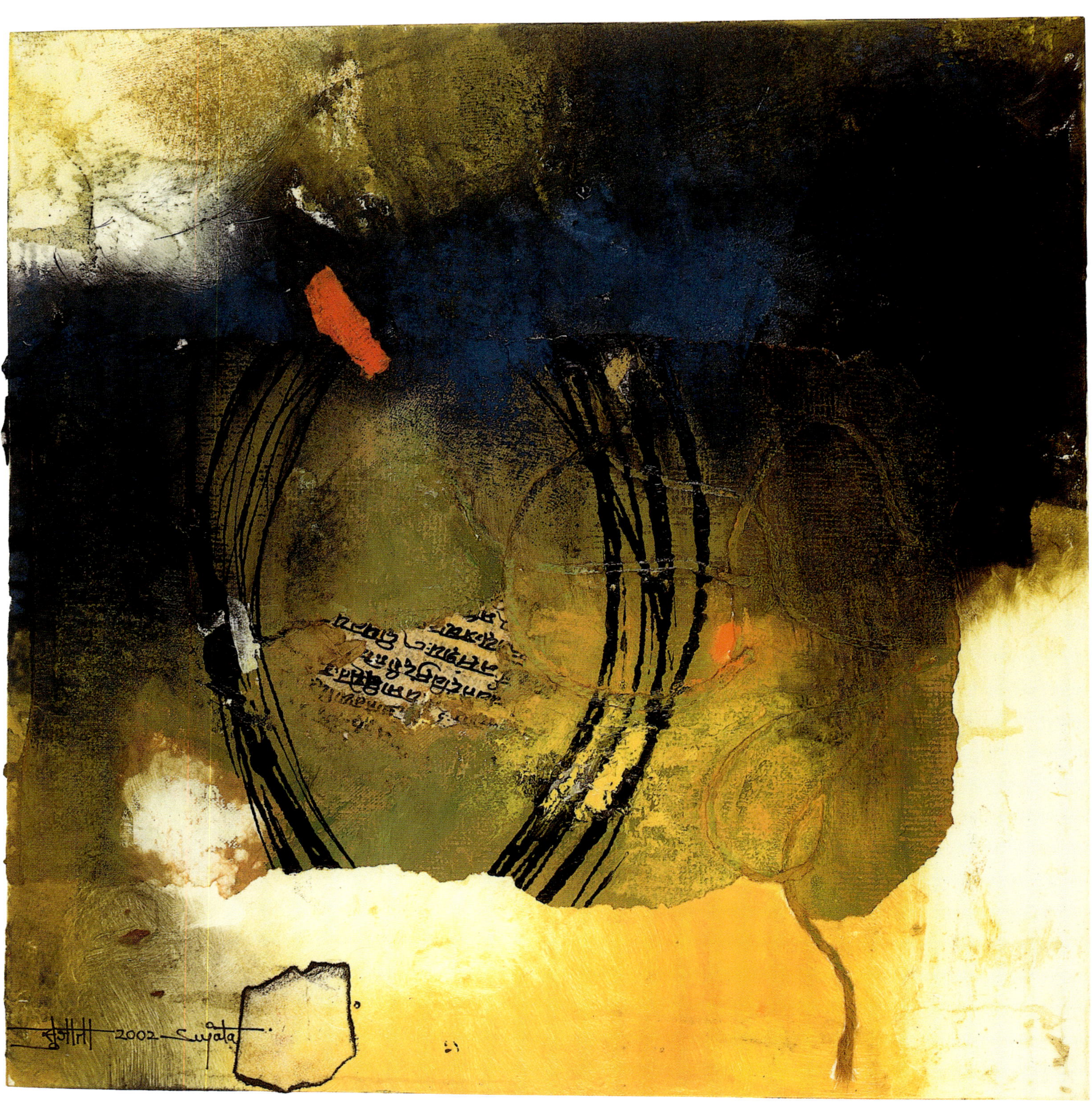

And what if silence was necessary for the harmony of our earth?
Silence, solitude, thought...

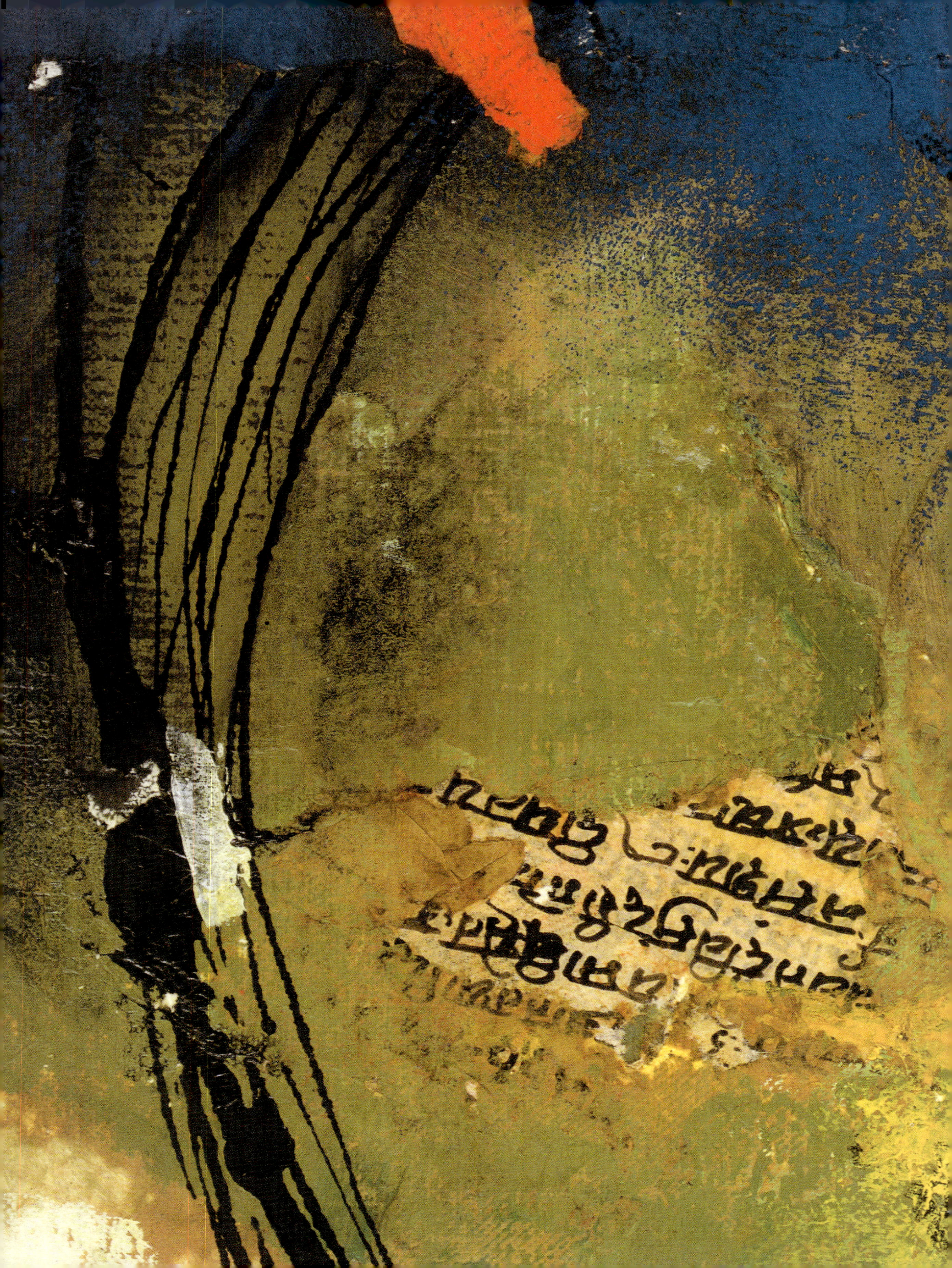

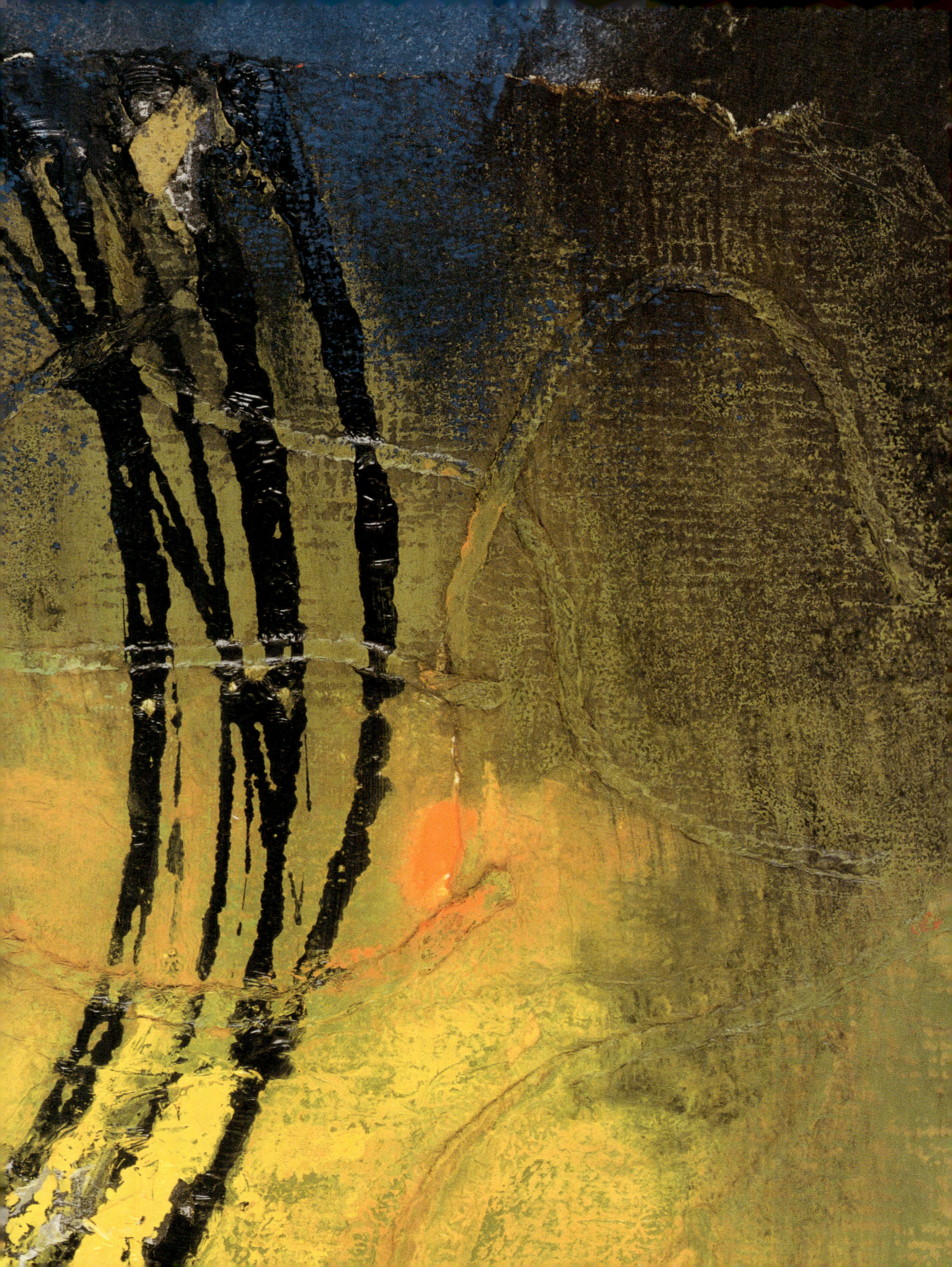

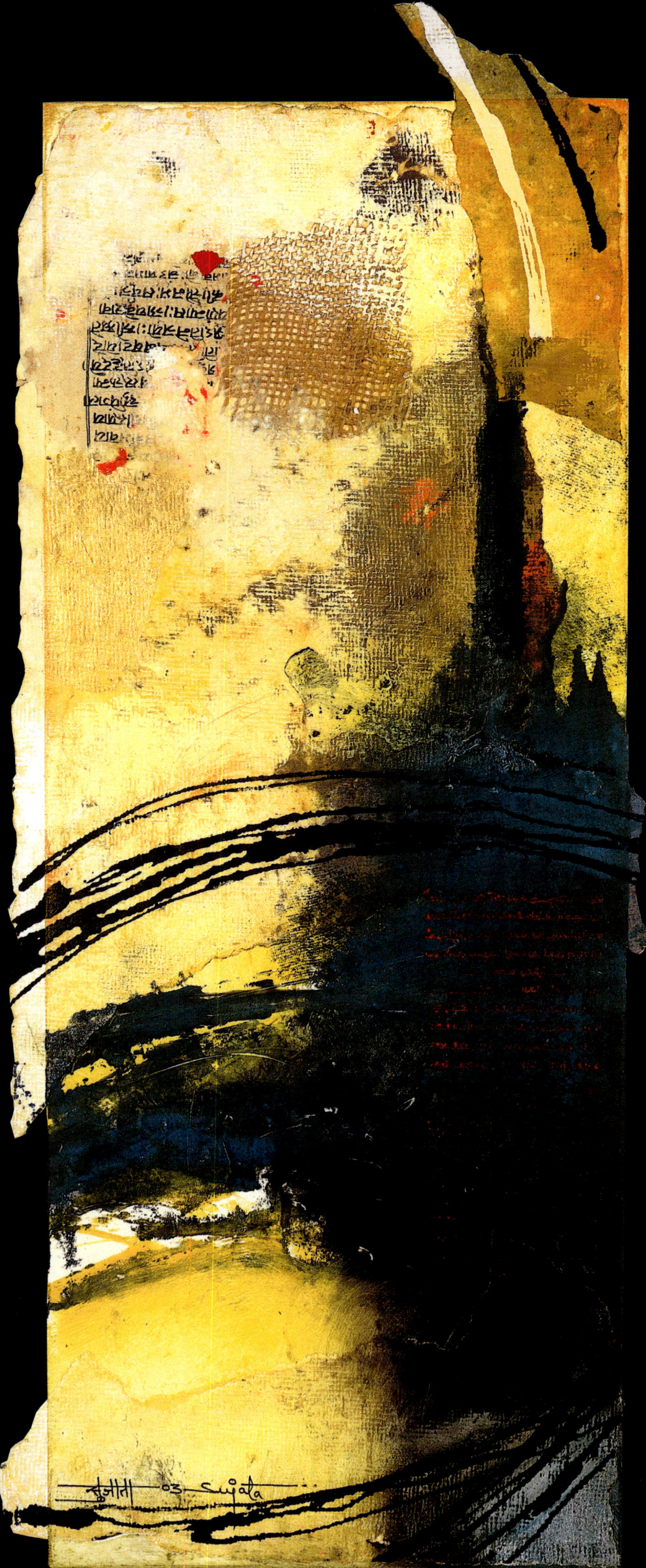

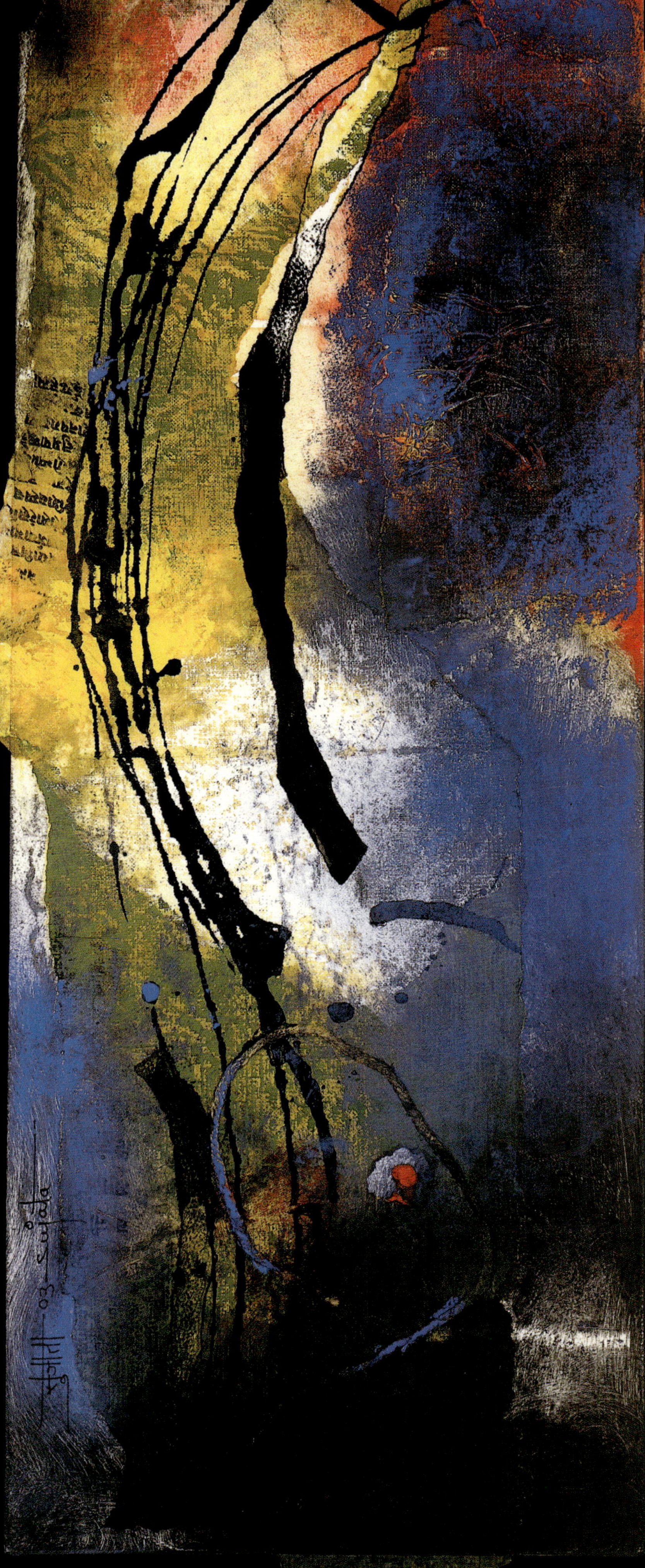

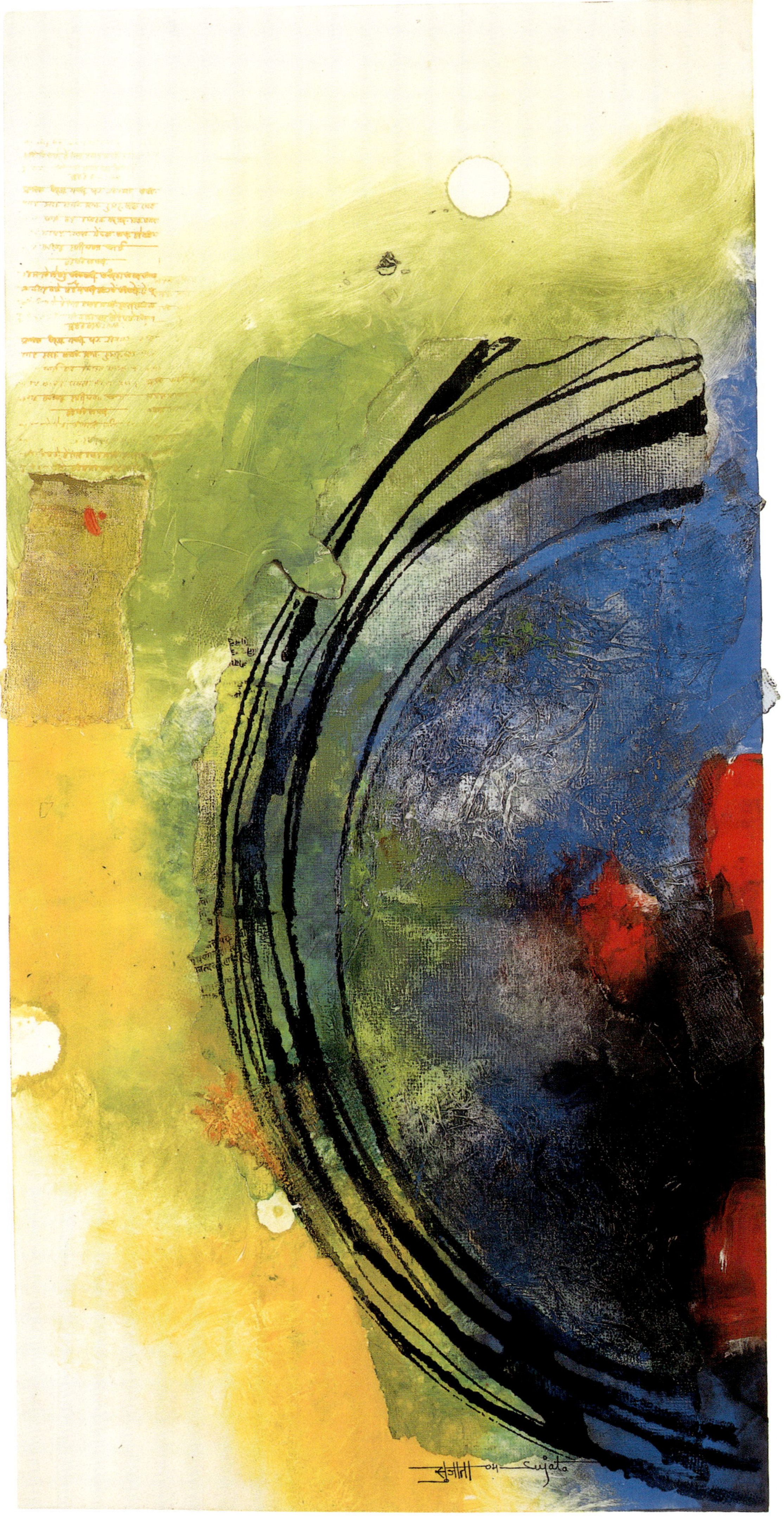

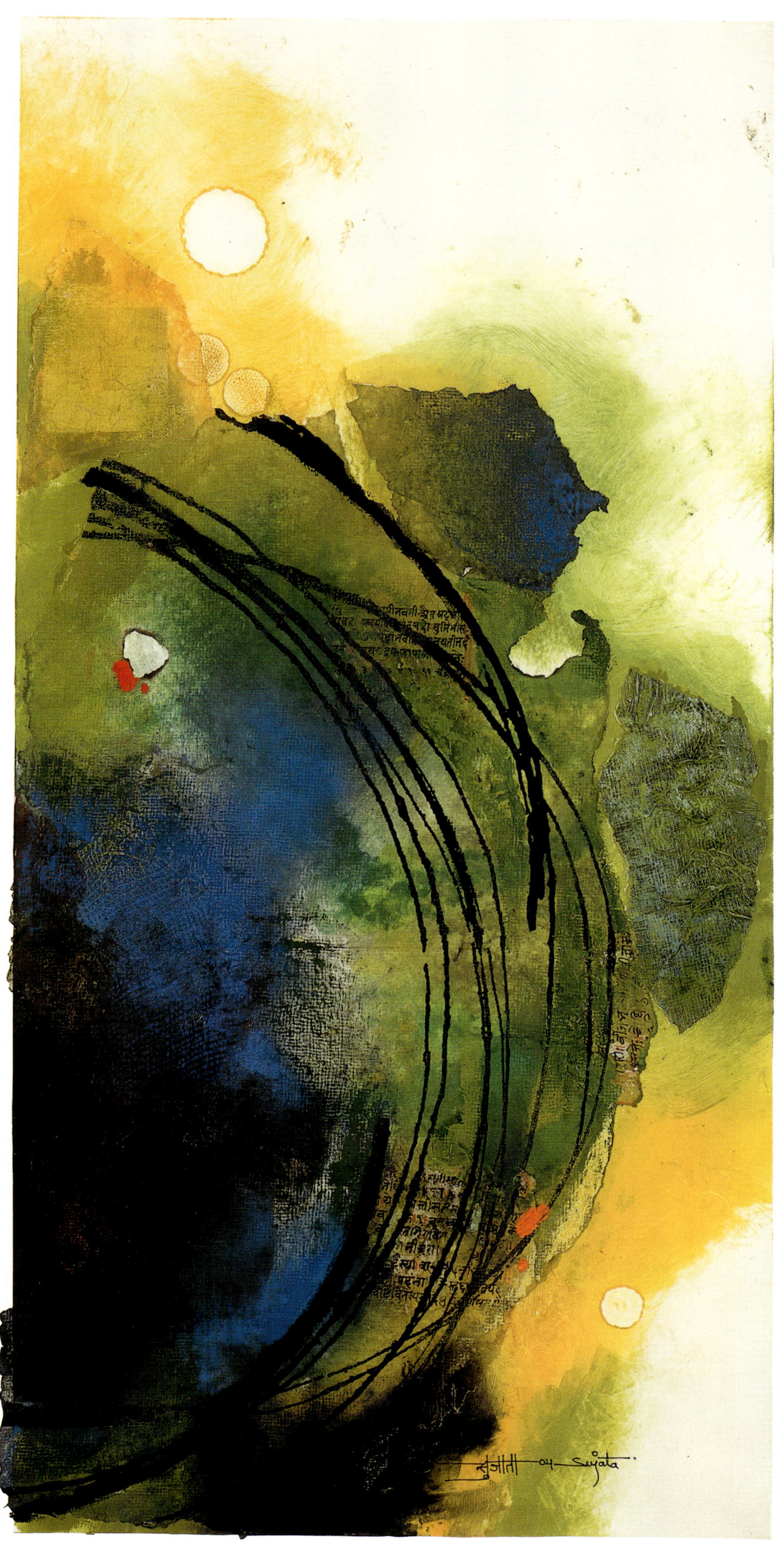
सुजाता 04 Sujata

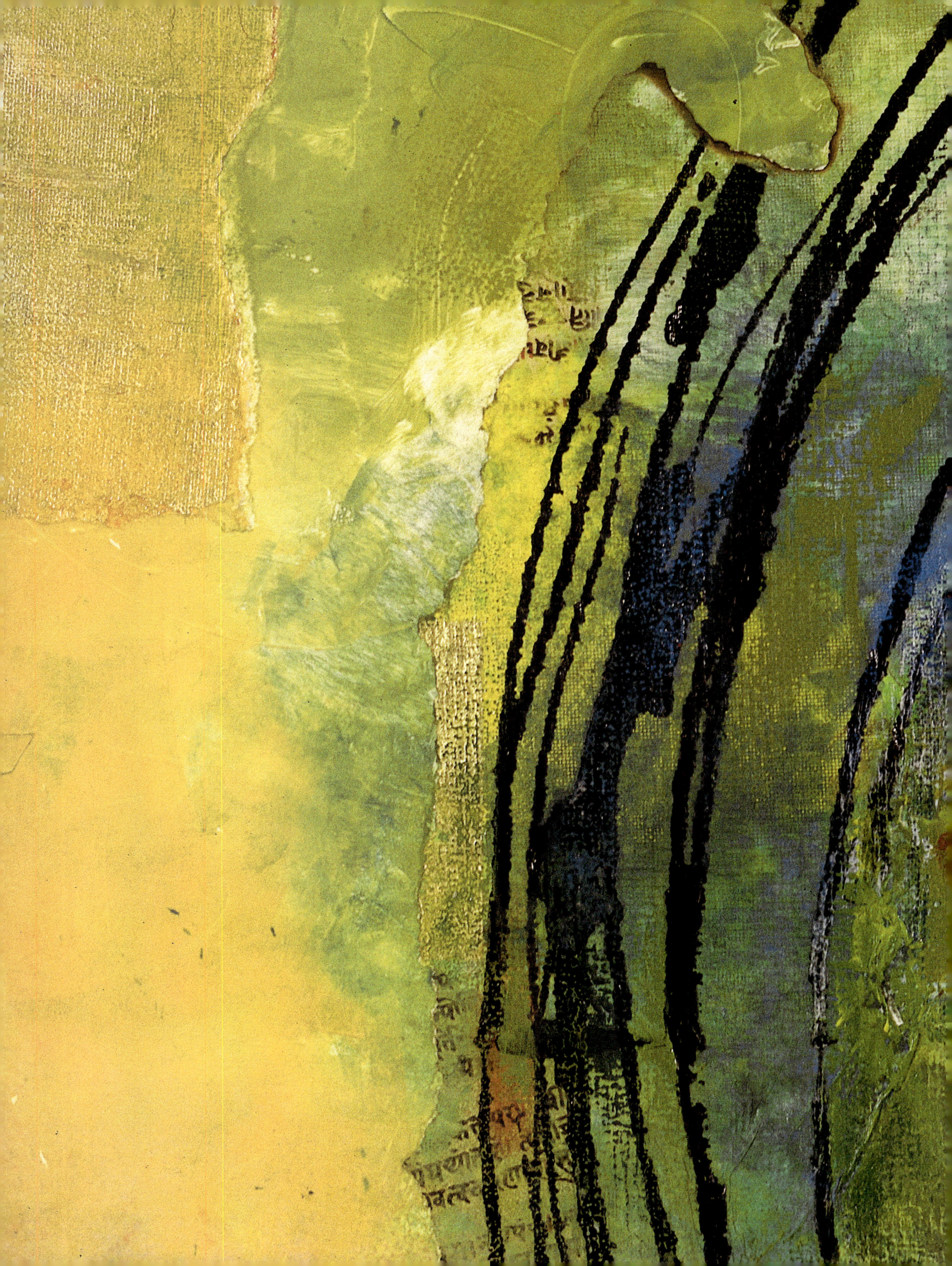

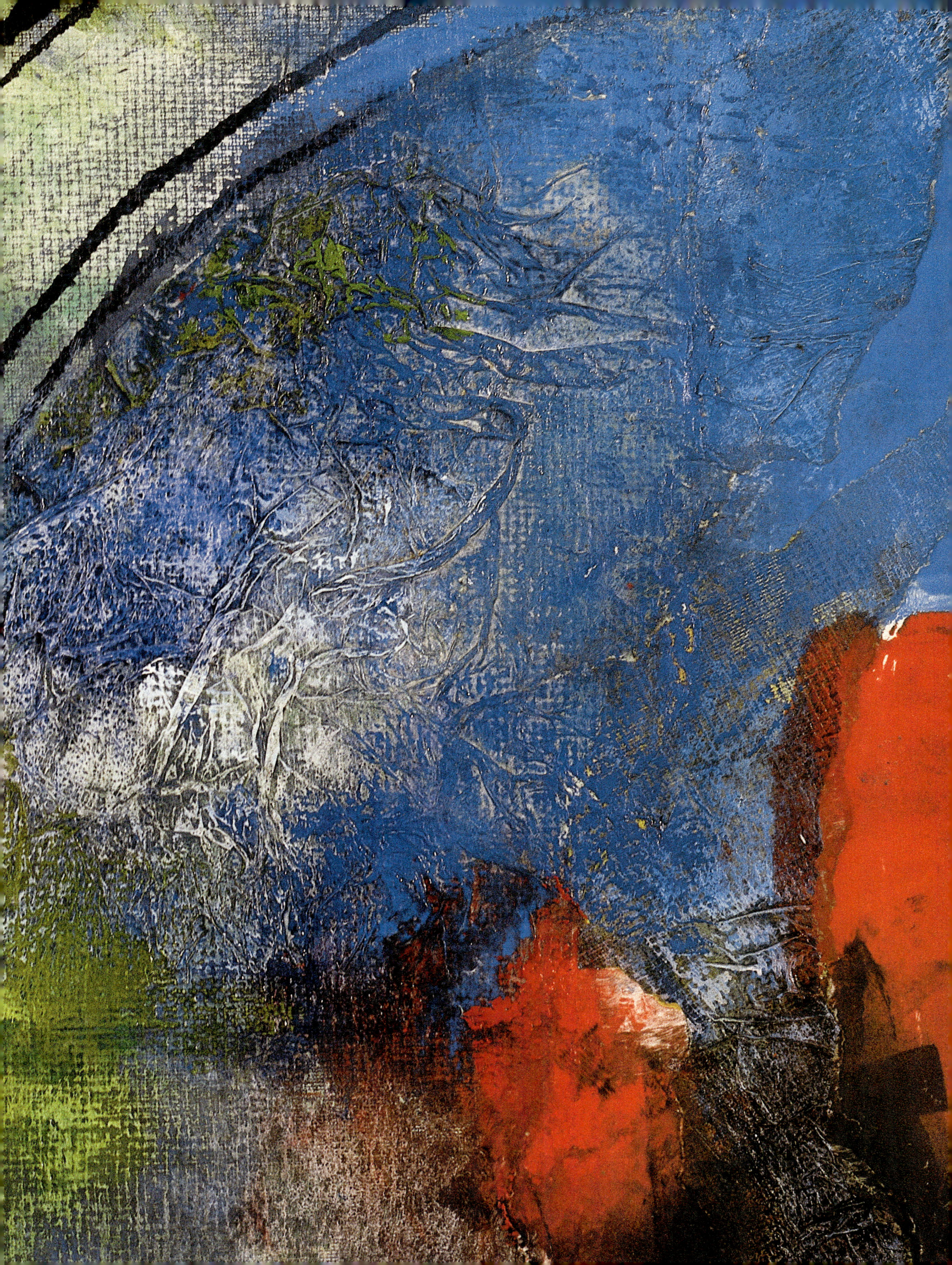

An old man and his young disciple walk side by side in the countryside.
Seeing a beautiful tree, the disciple asks:
– How many leaves does the tree have?
– Six hundred and forty-seven thousand, one hundred and twenty-six, replies the old man.
– Are you sure?
– If you don't believe me, climb the tree and count the leaves.

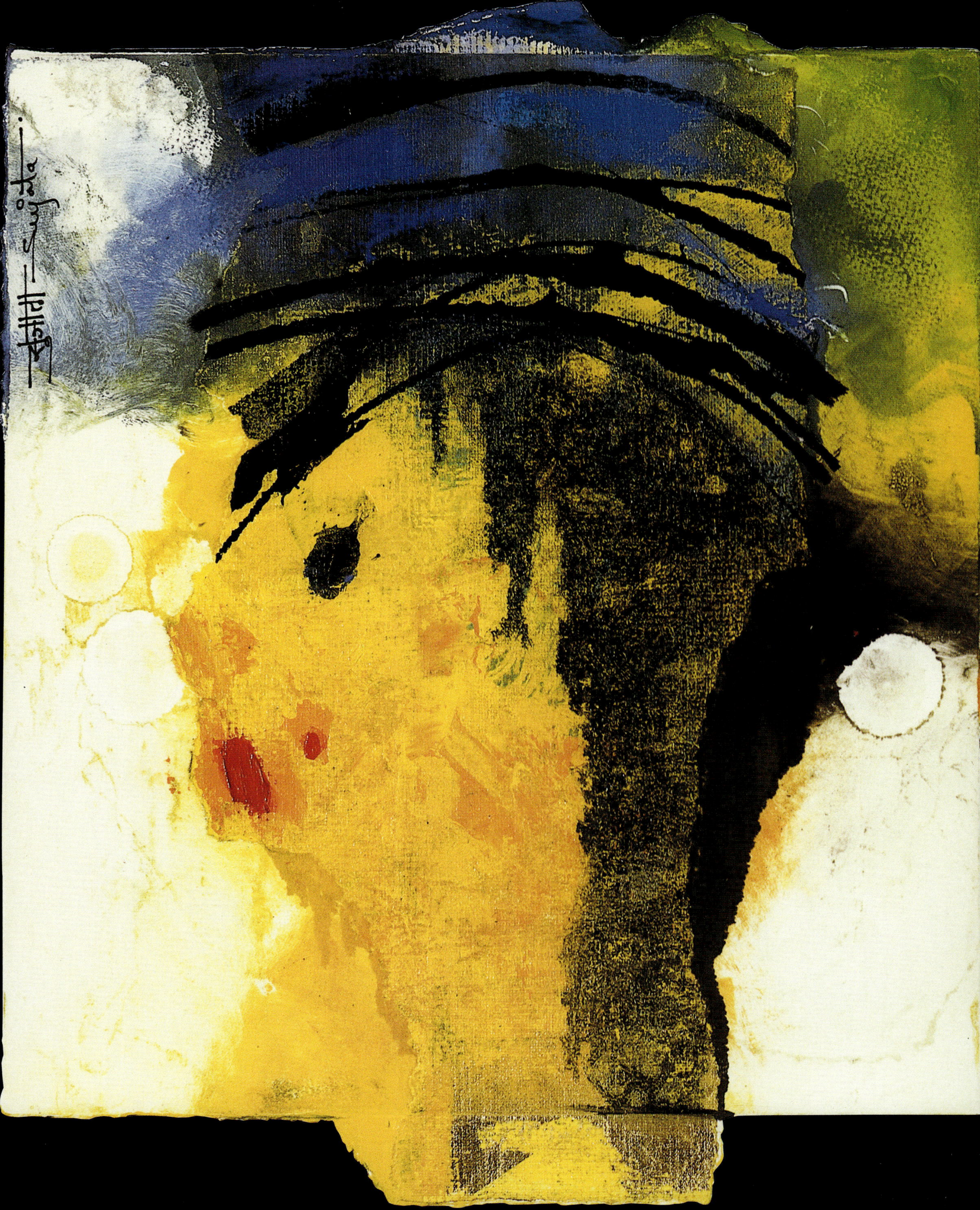

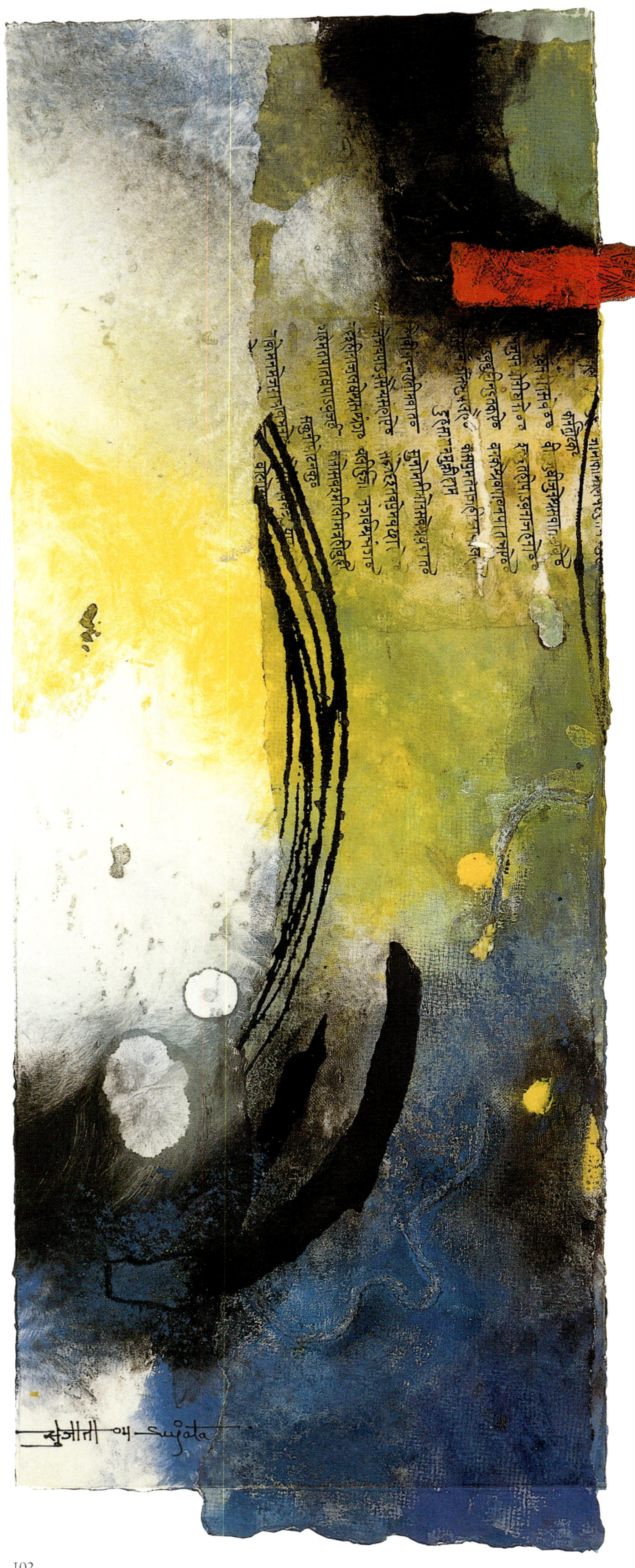
सुजाता 04 Sujata

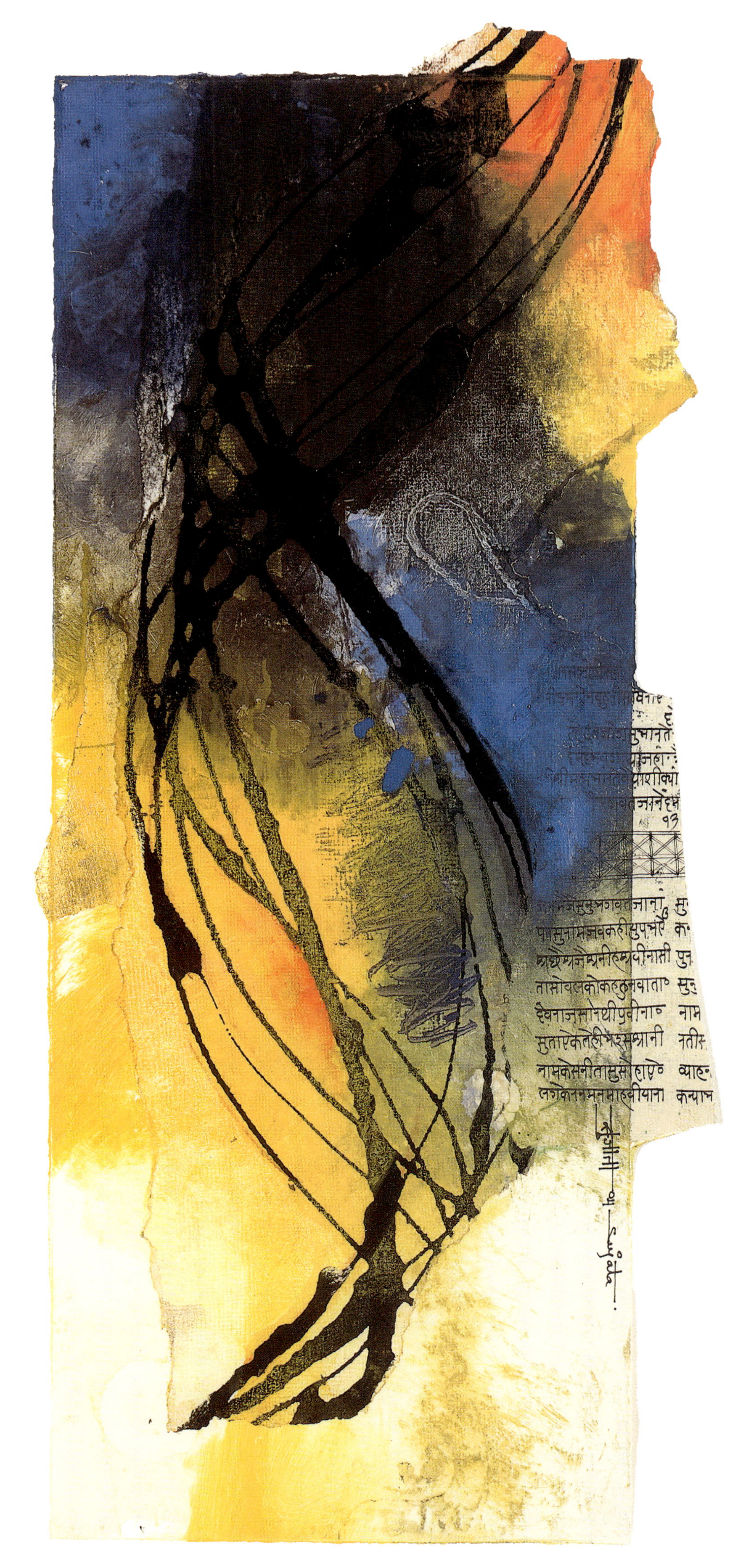

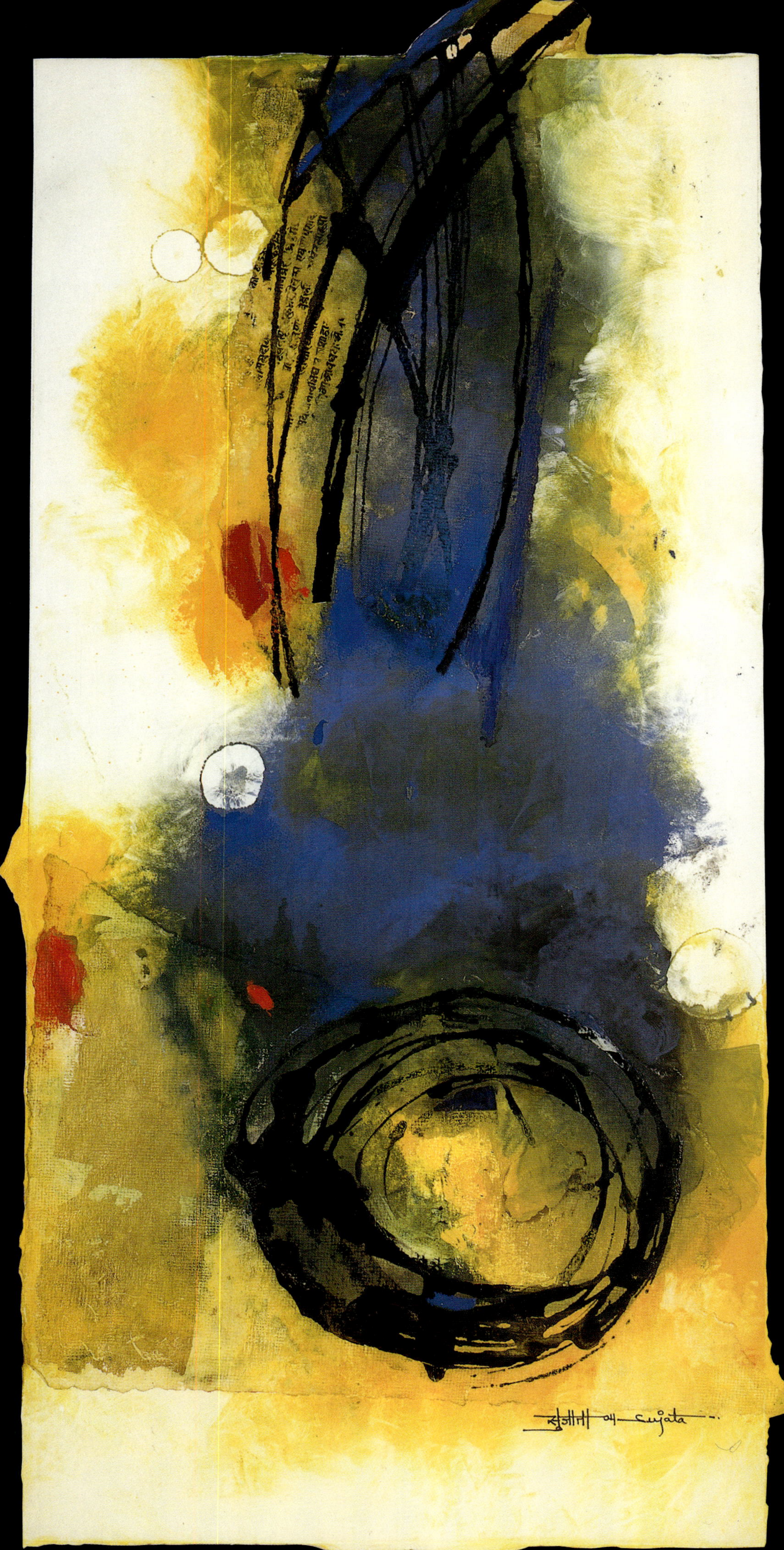
Sujata

– What is swifter than the wind?
– Thought.

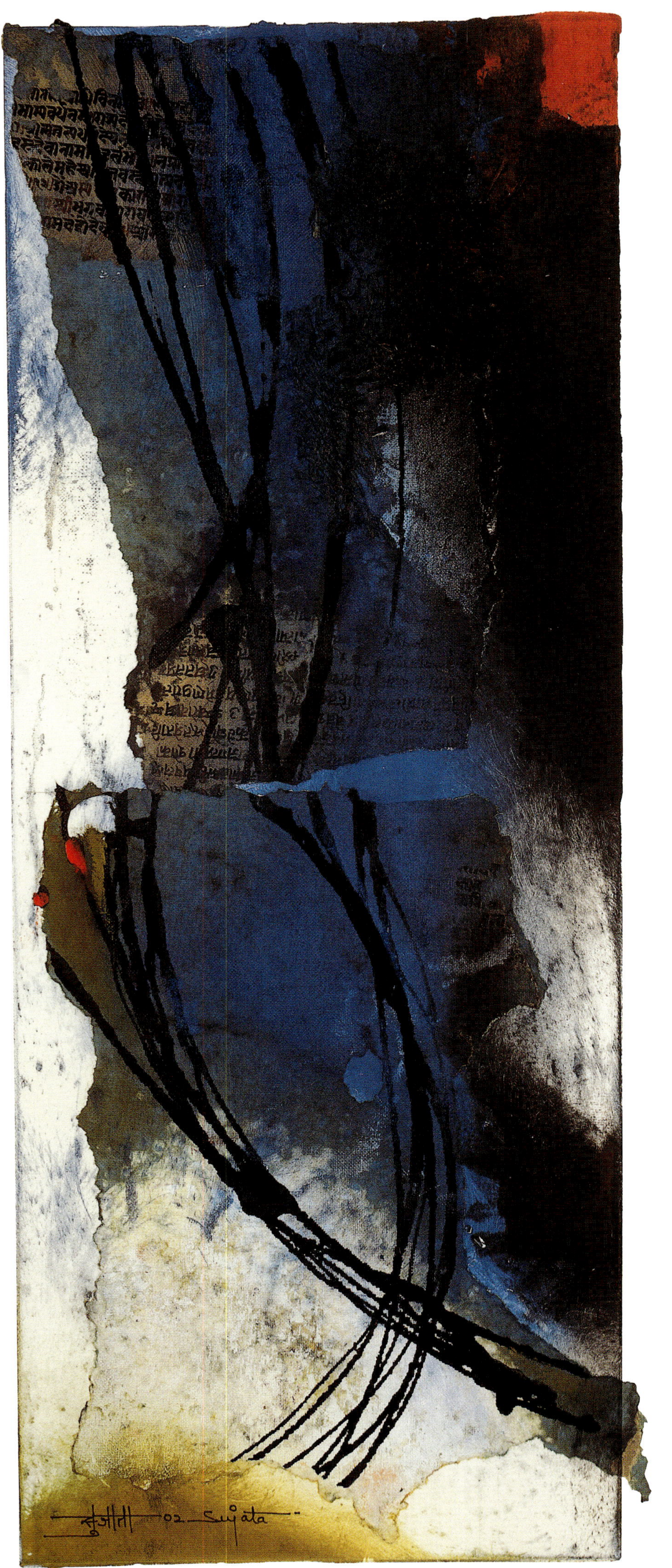
सुजाता ·02· Sujata

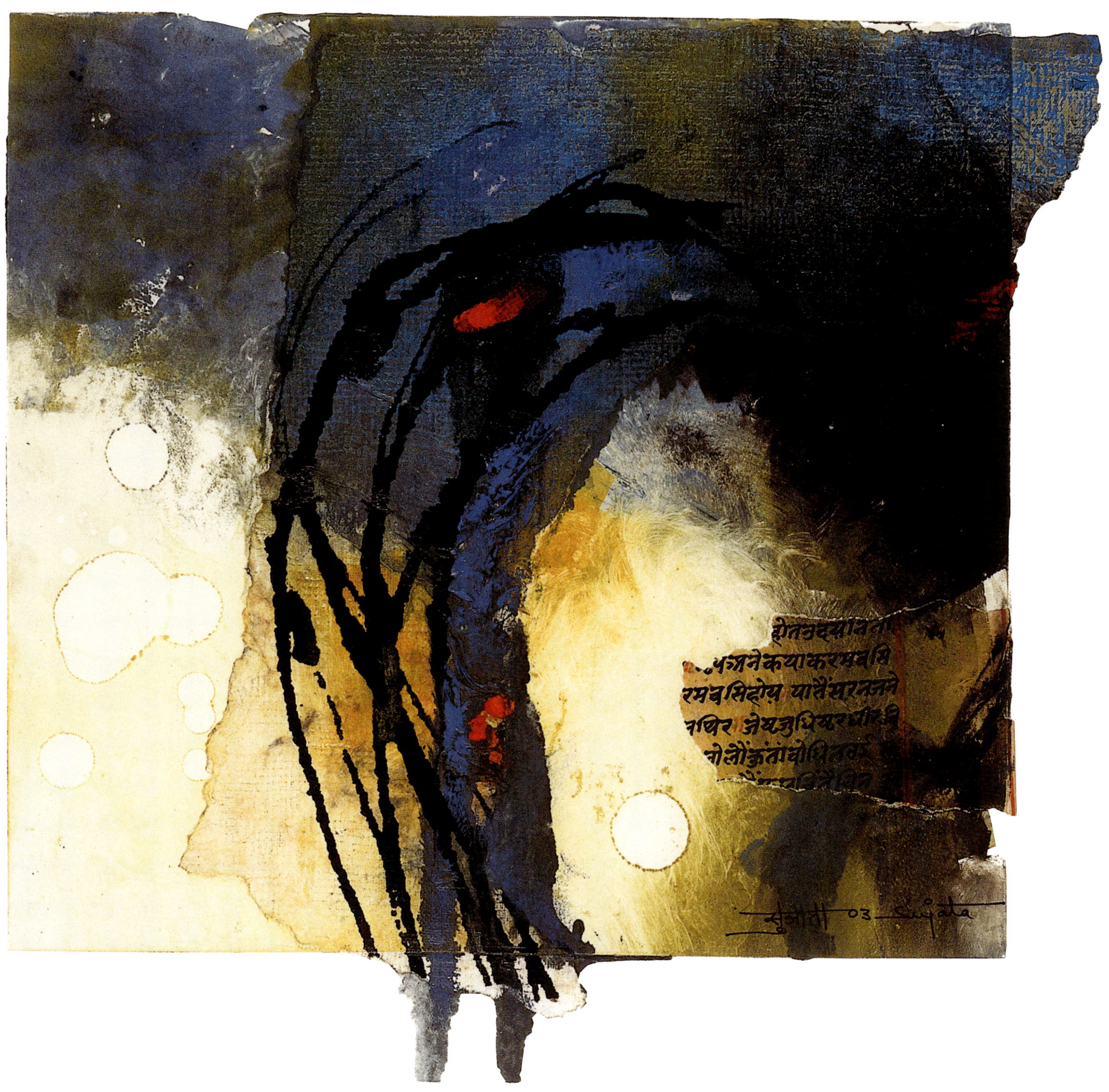
सुजाता 03 Sujata

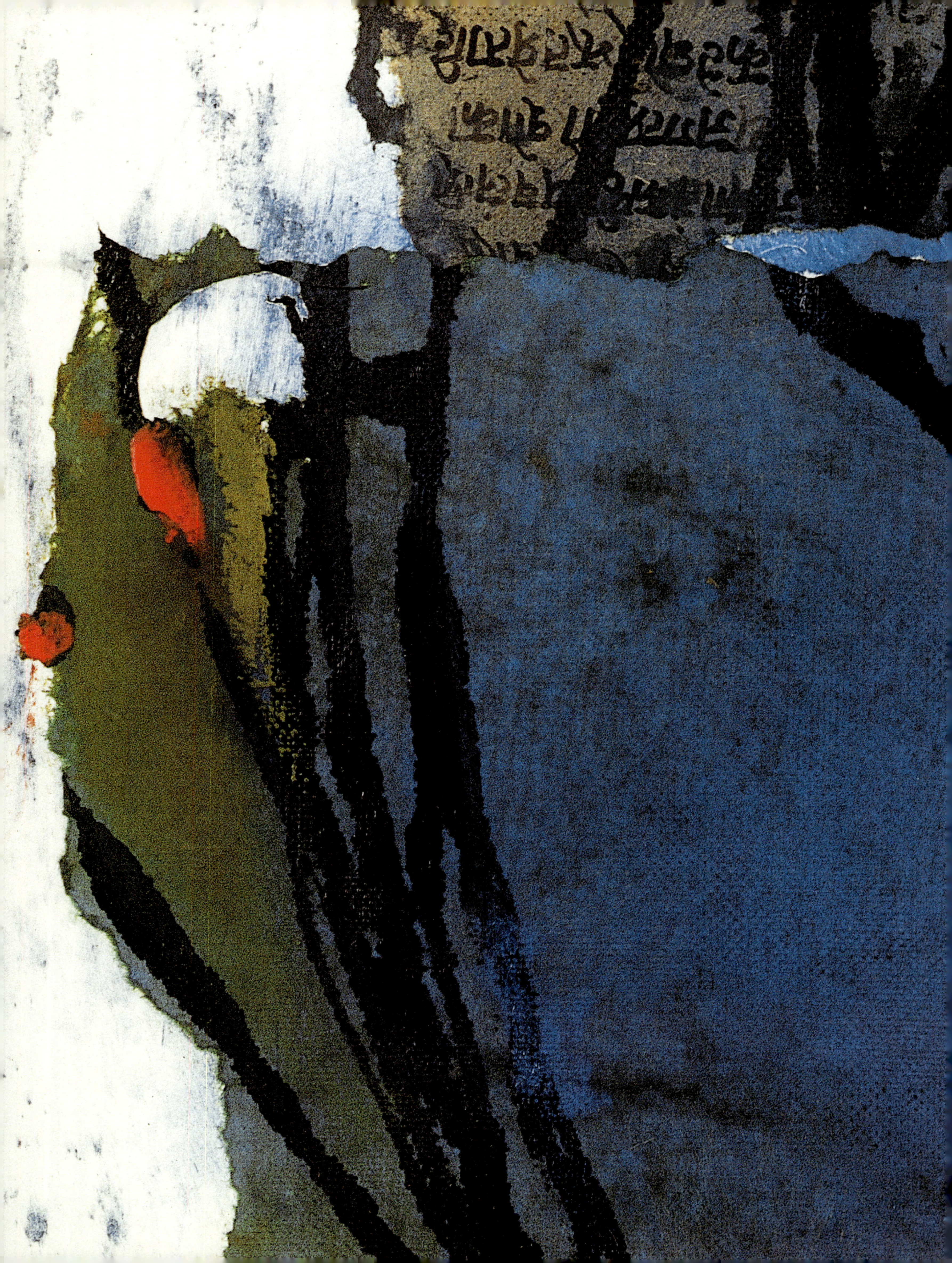

– What can cover the whole earth?
– Darkness.

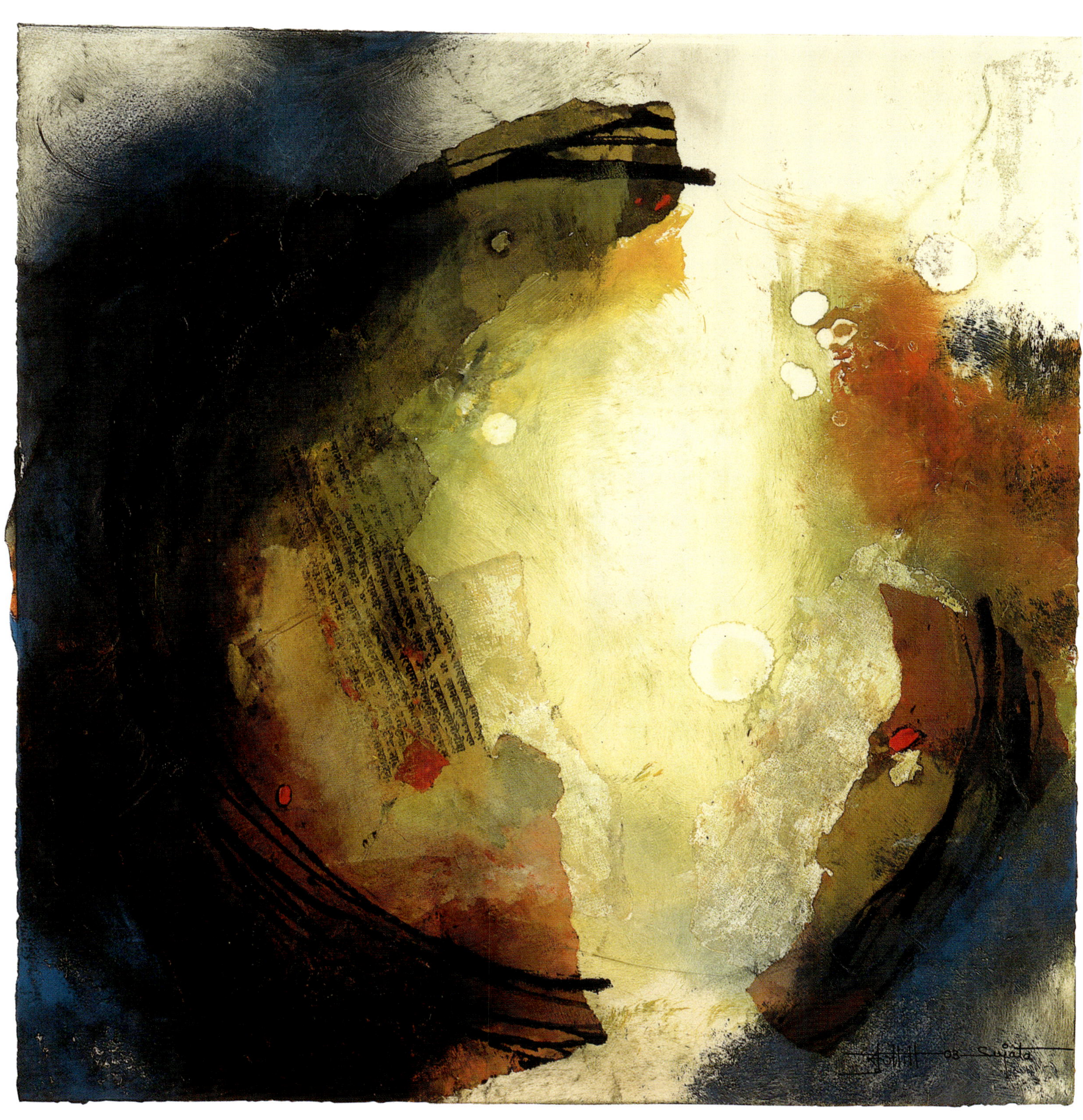
08 Sujata

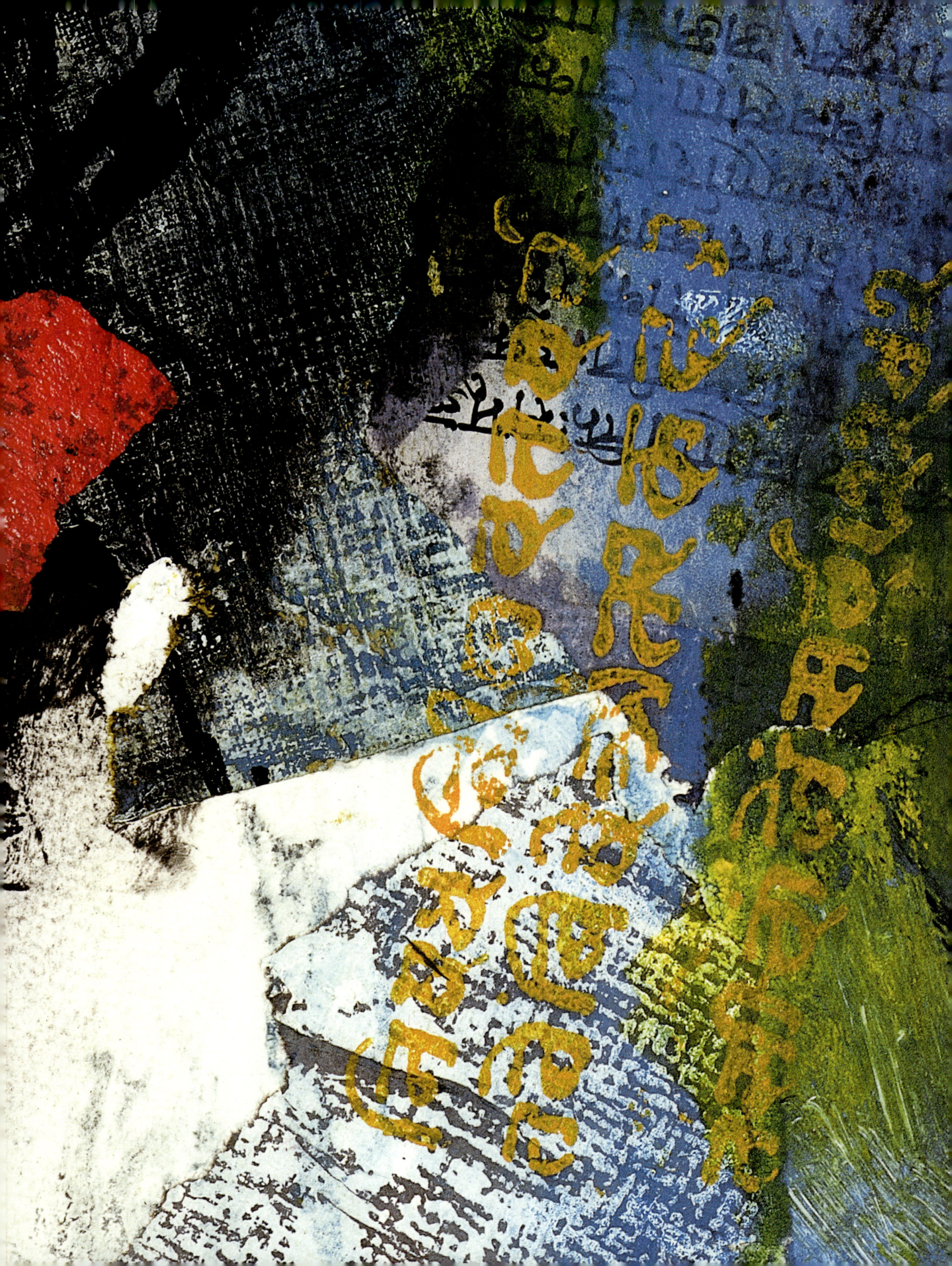

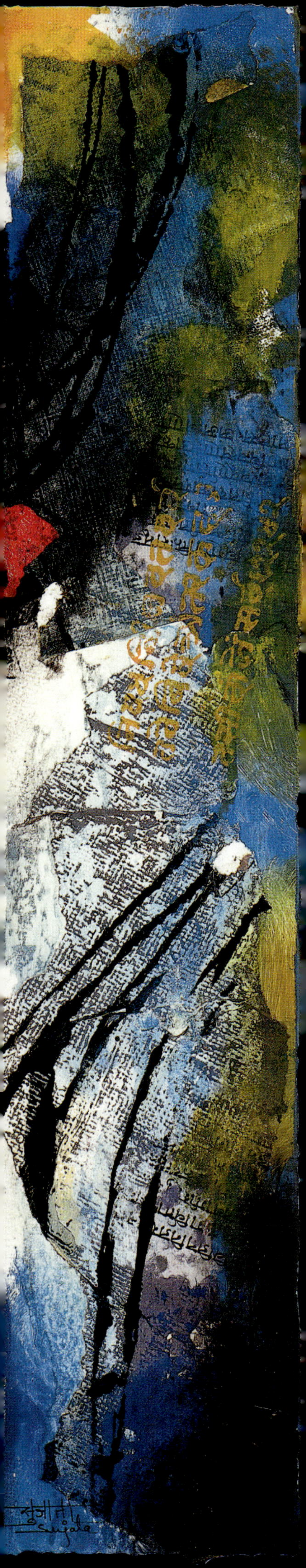

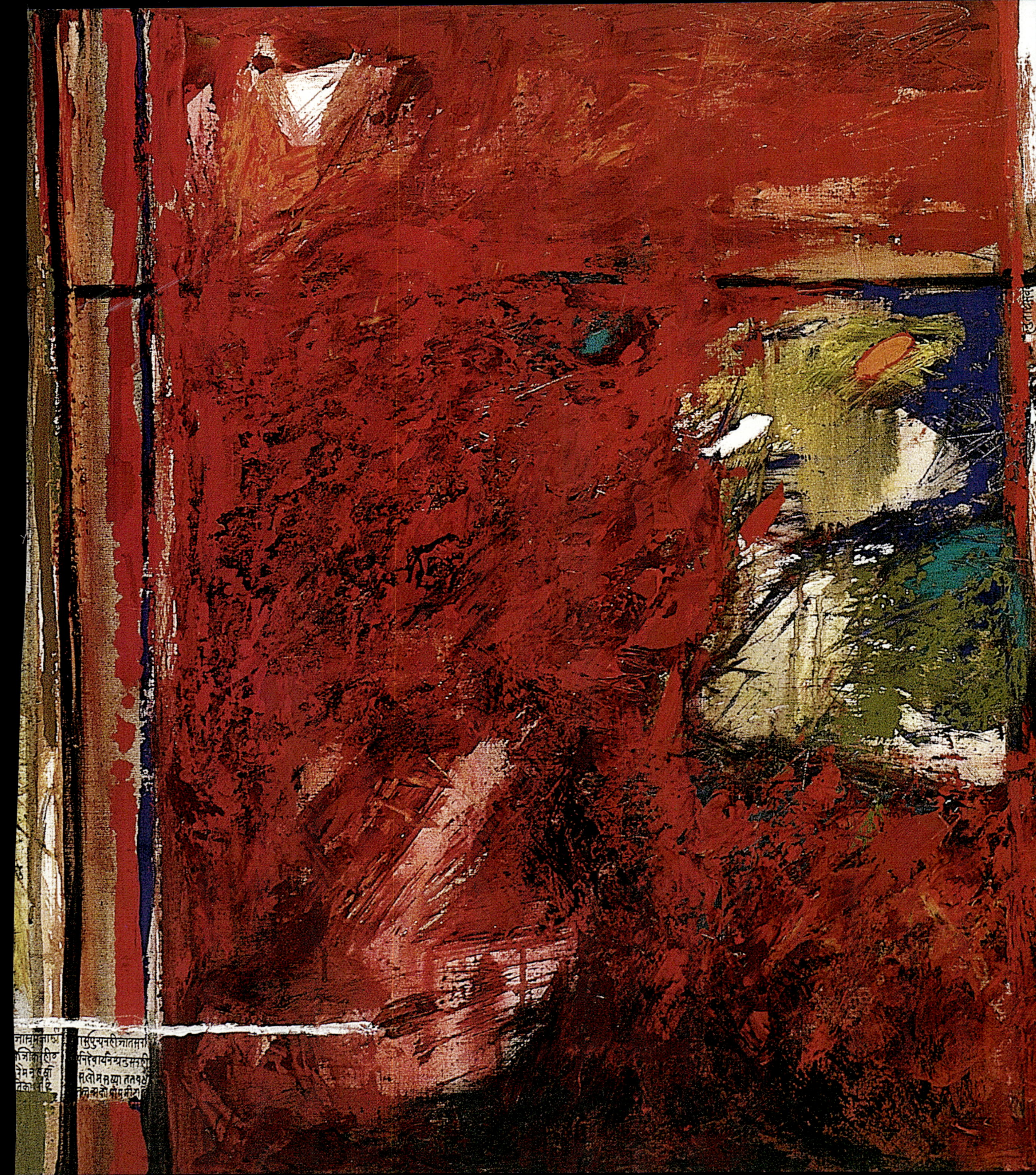

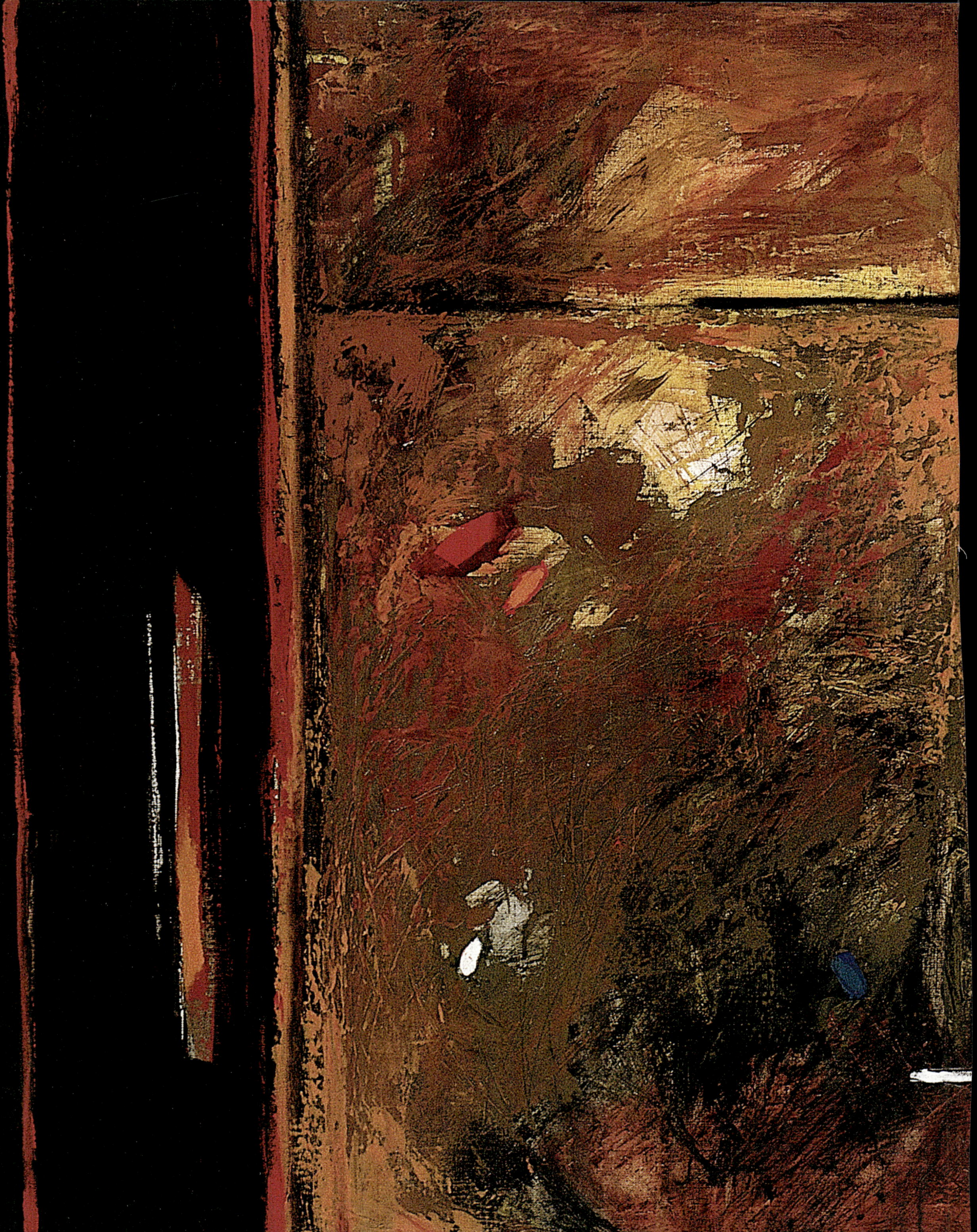

Acrylics on canvas

Acryliques sur toile

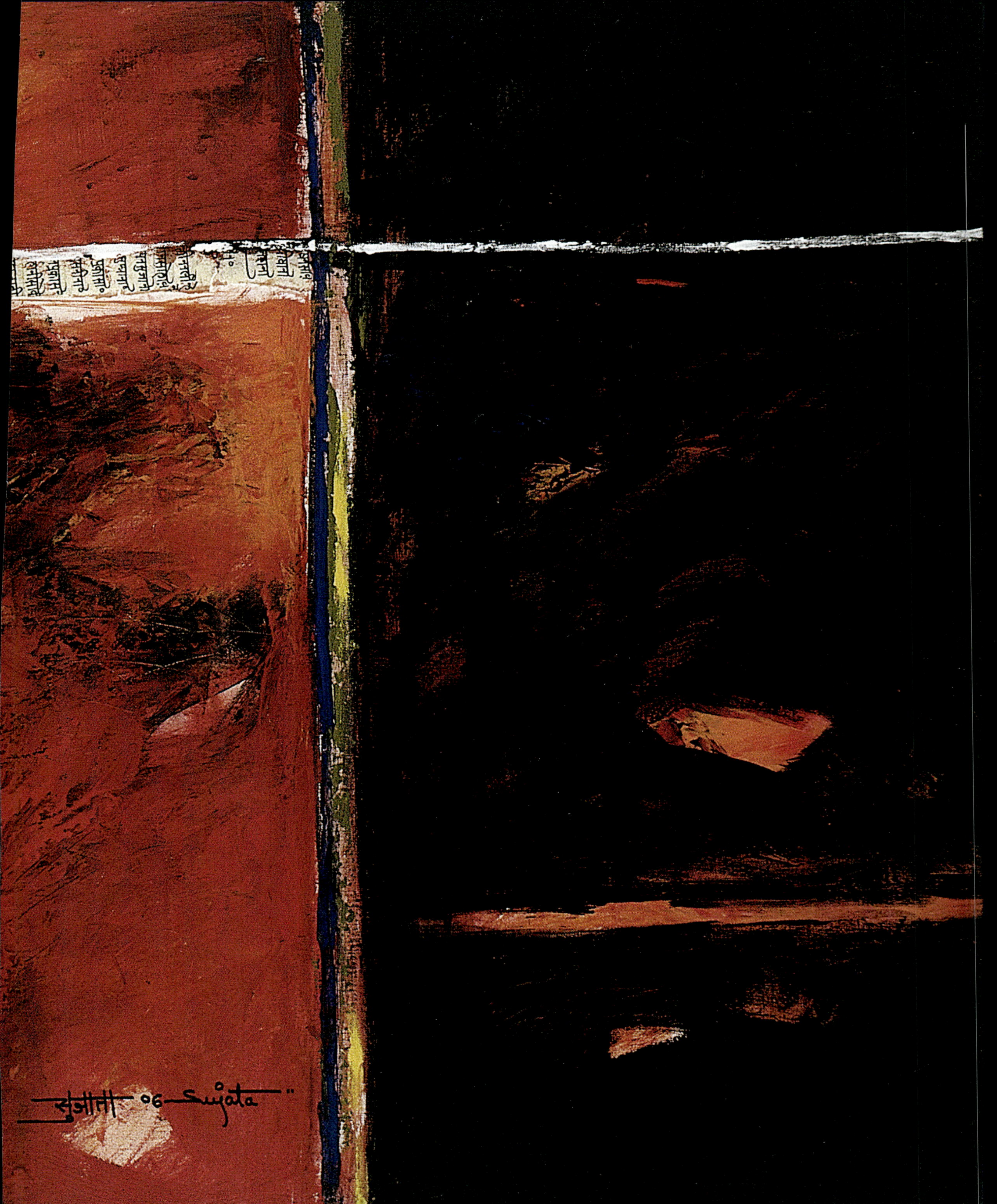
सुजाता '06 Sujata

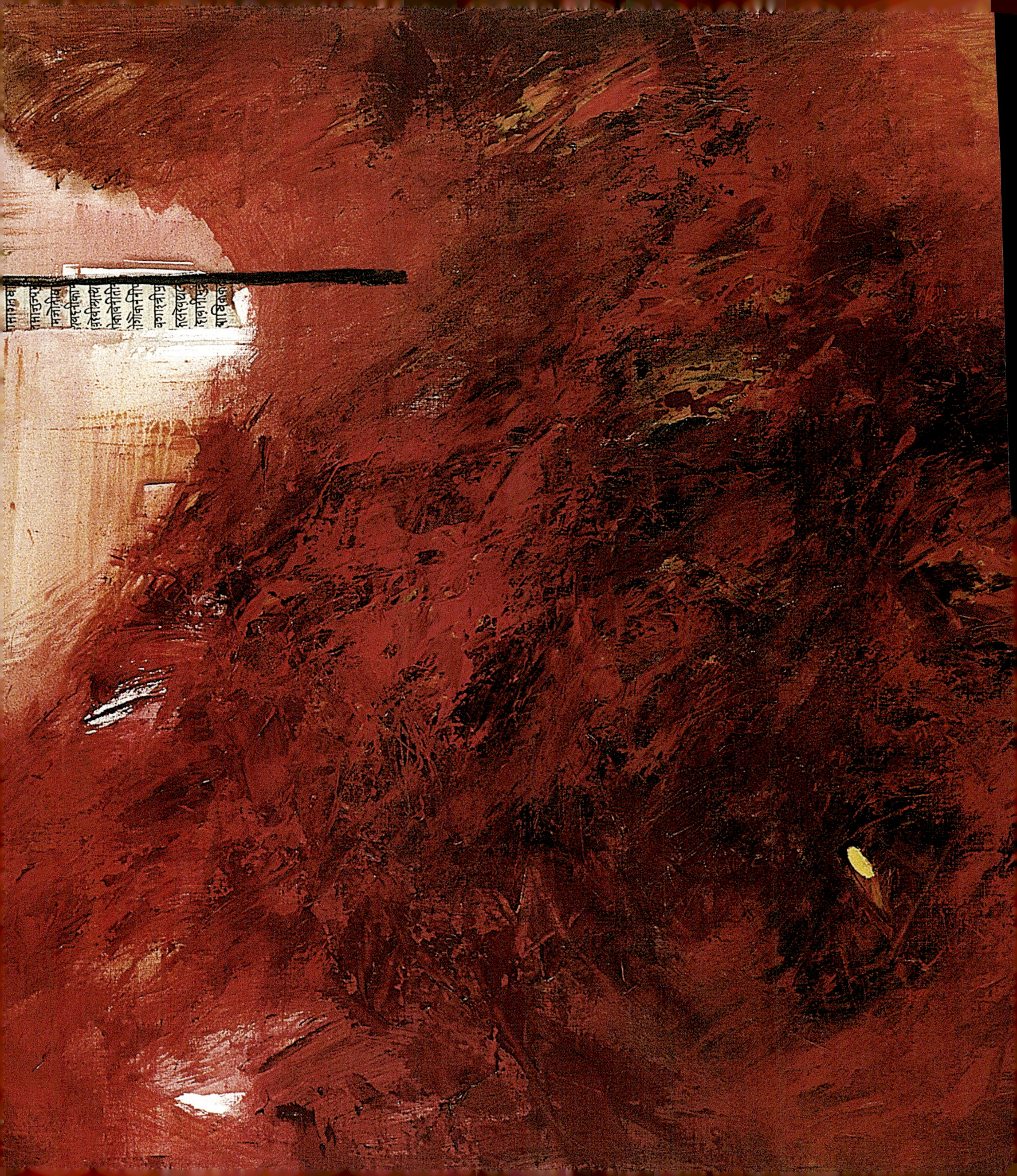

Yuddishthira possessed all the qualities necessary to be king.
But above all, he had the one most essential quality: he didn't desire to be one.

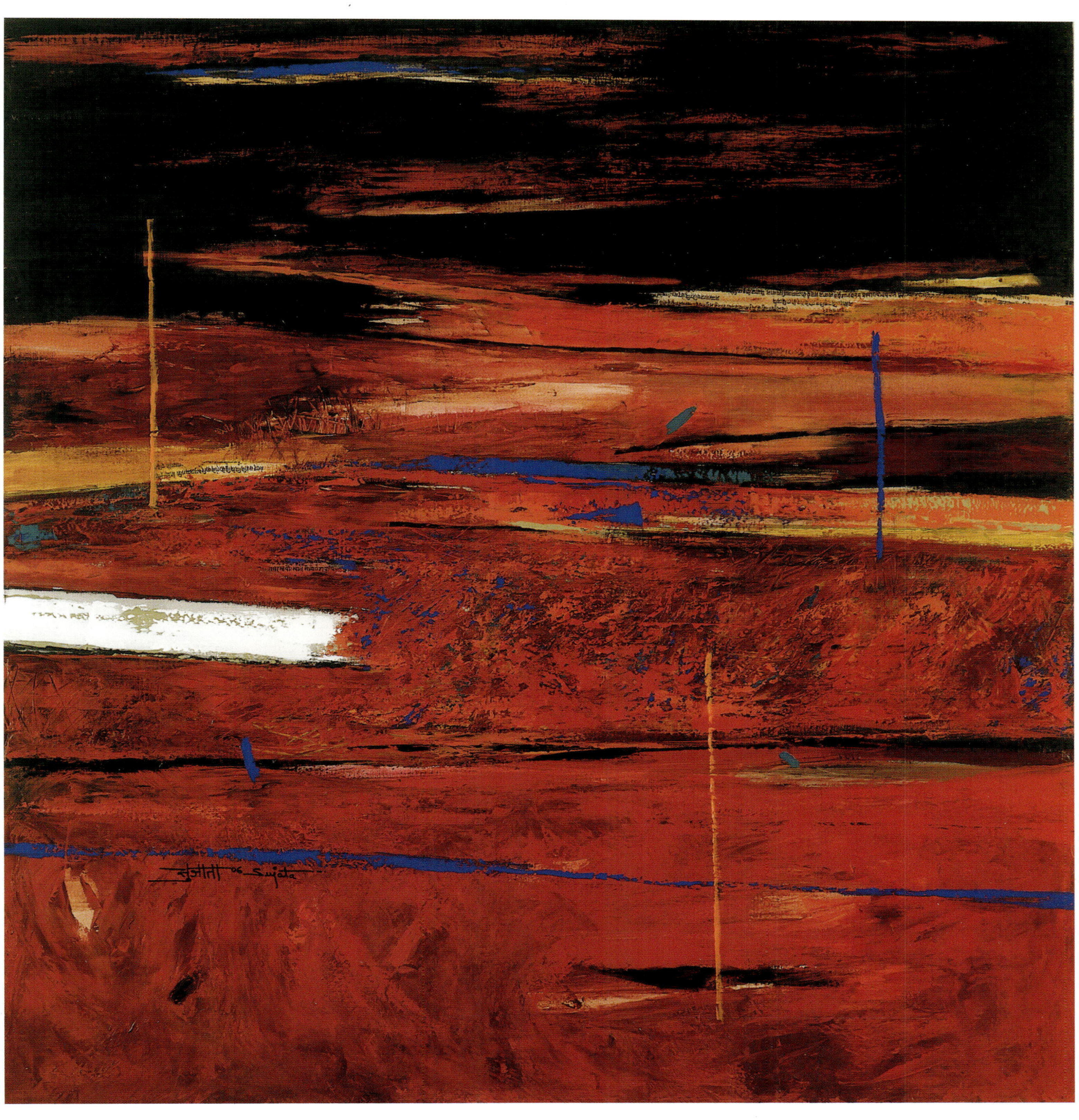

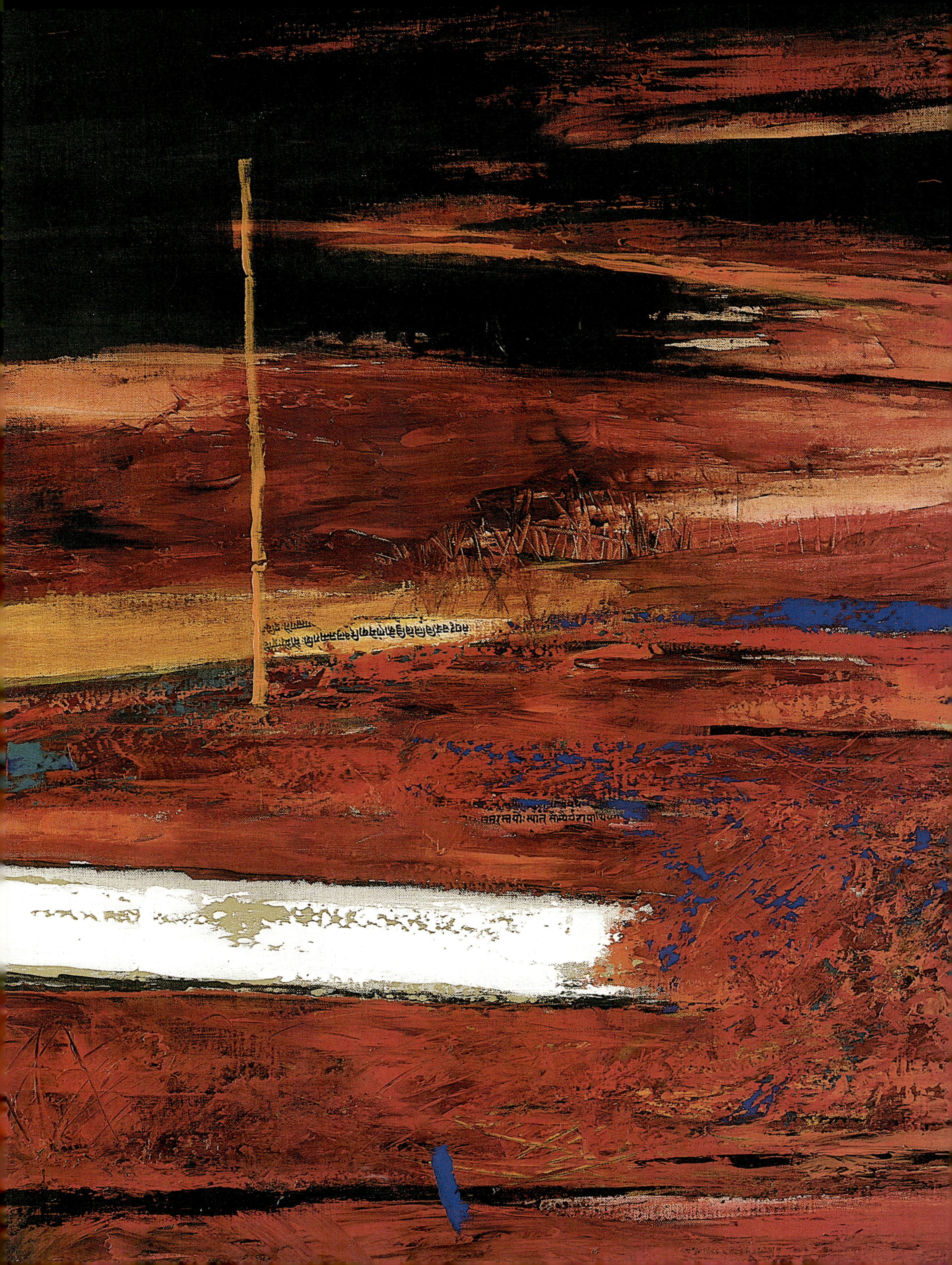

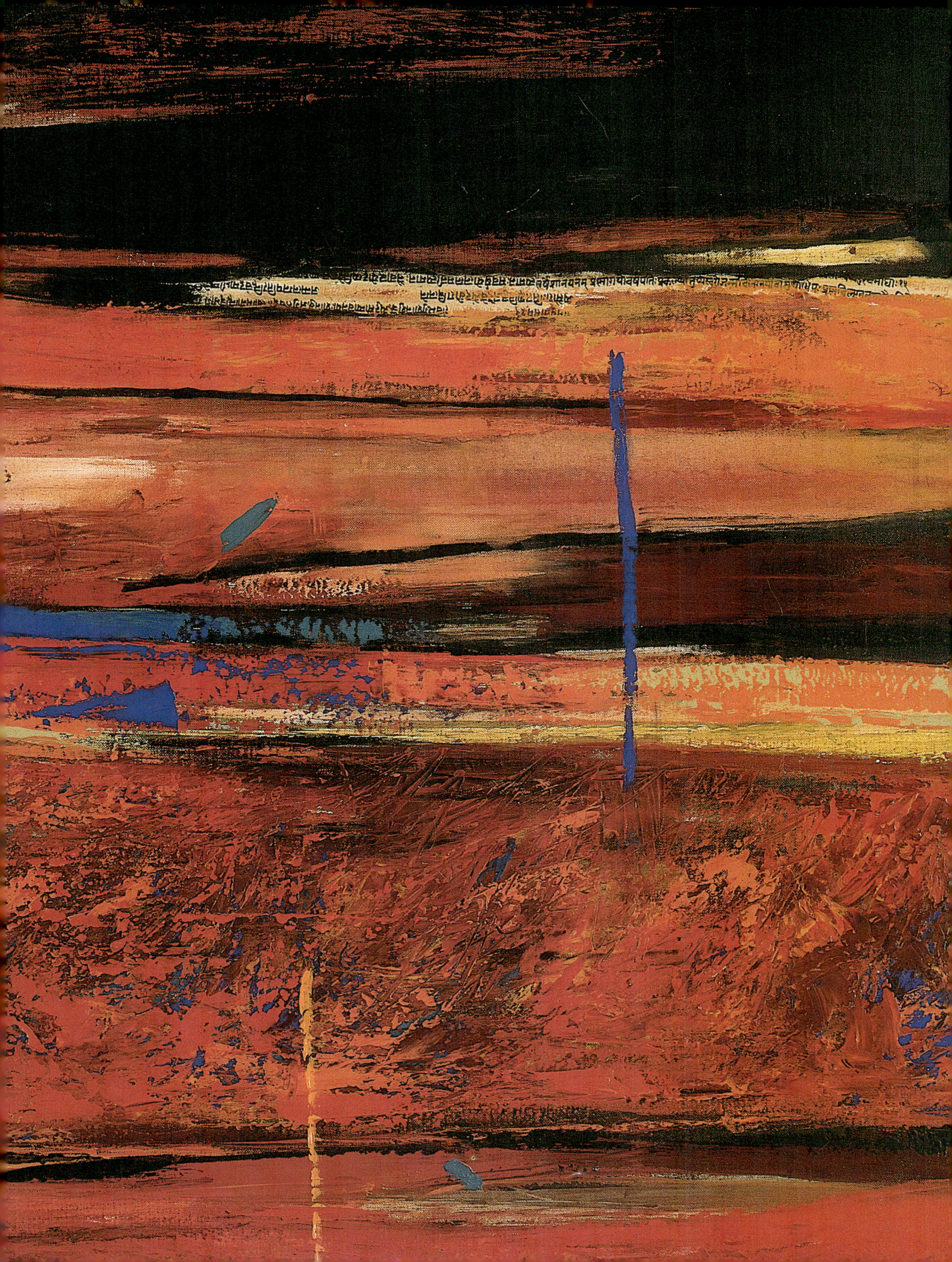

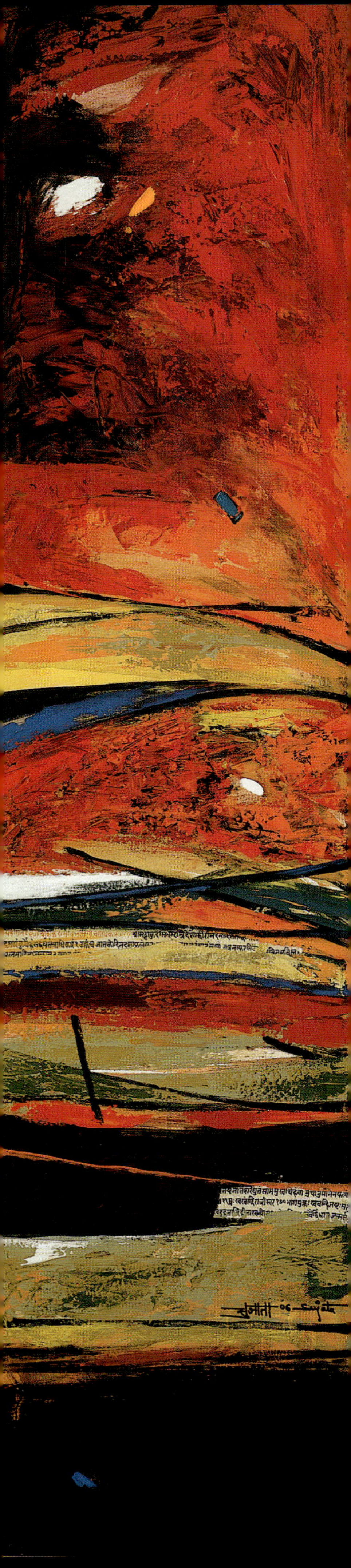

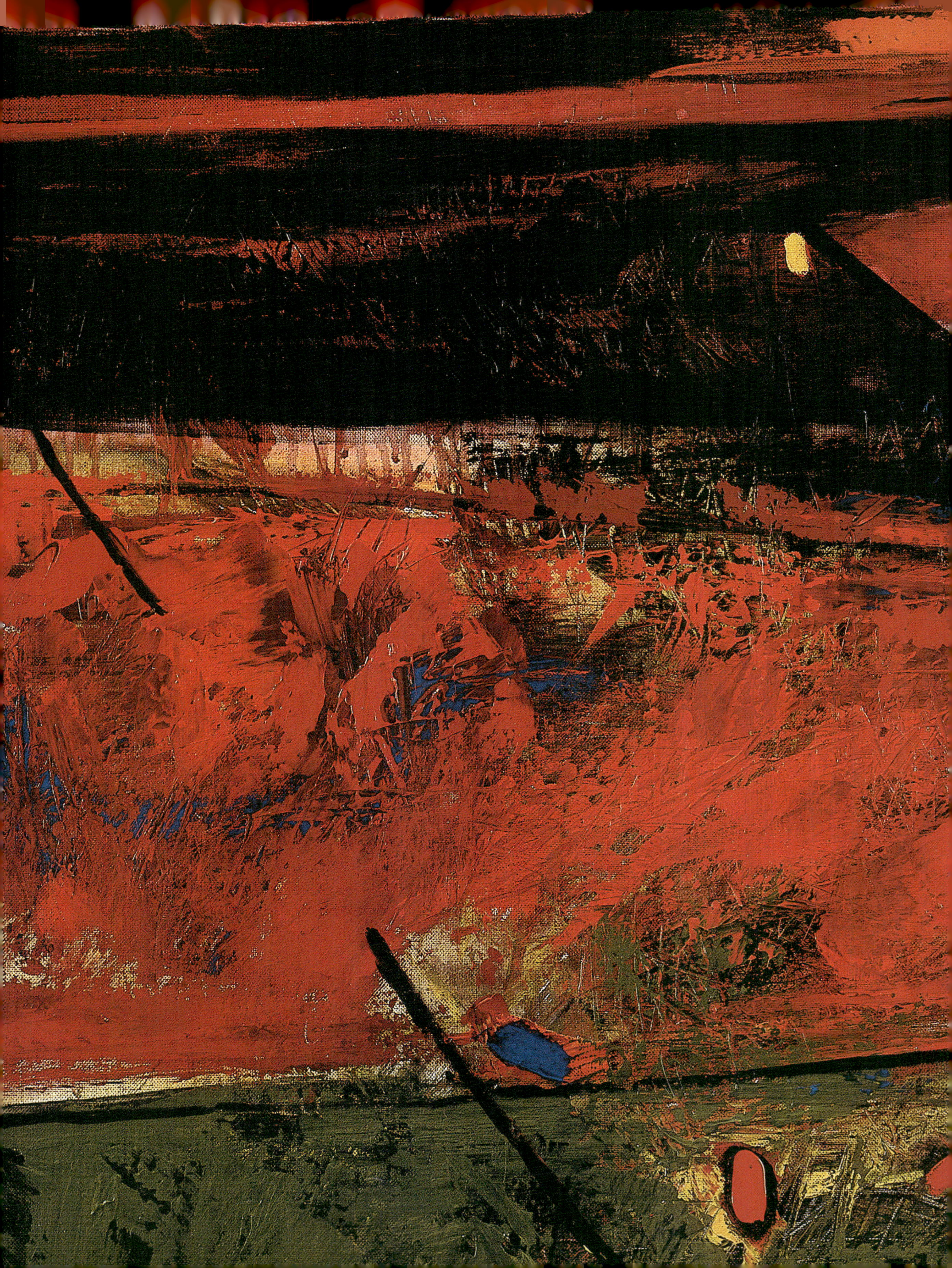

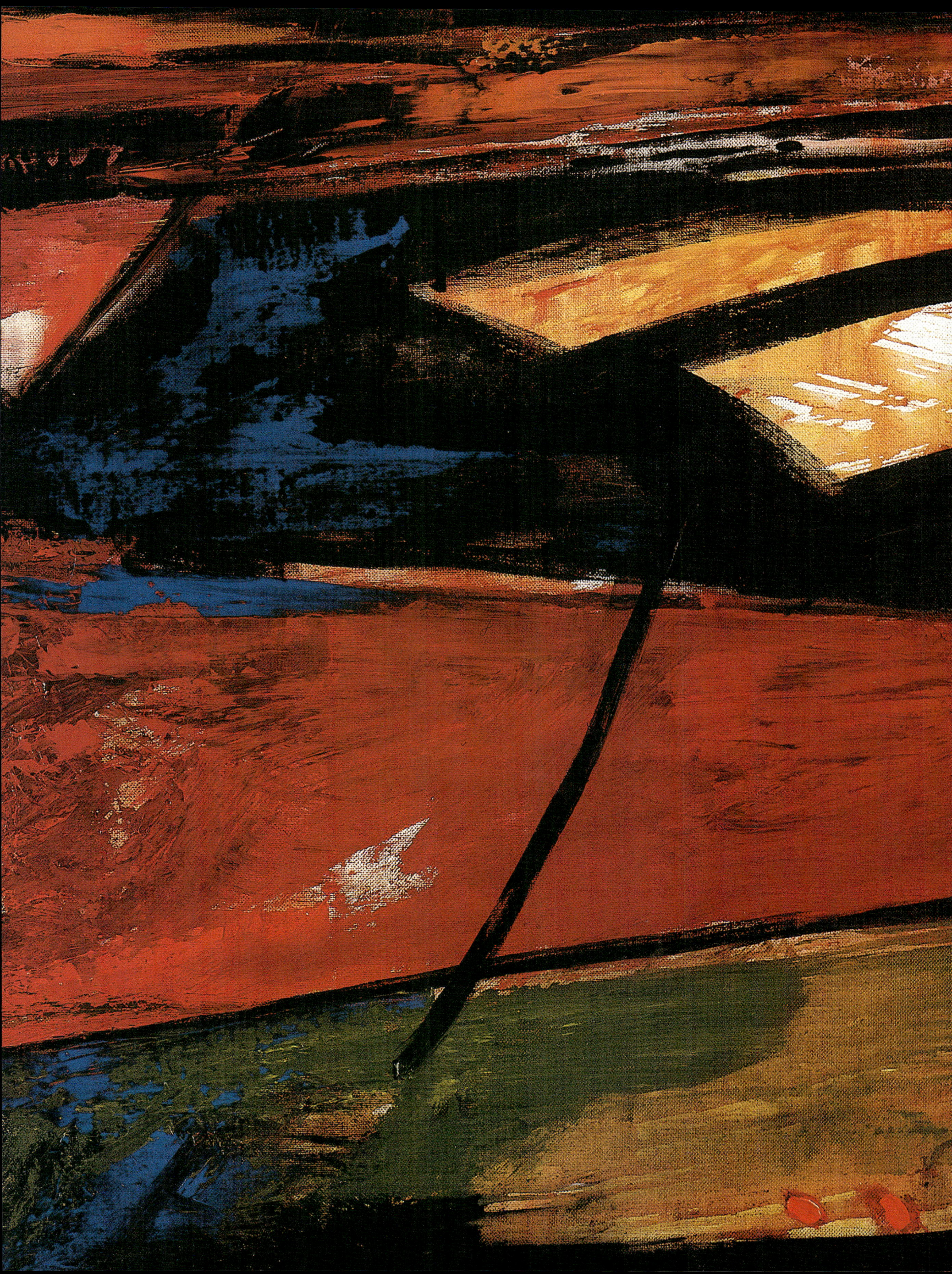

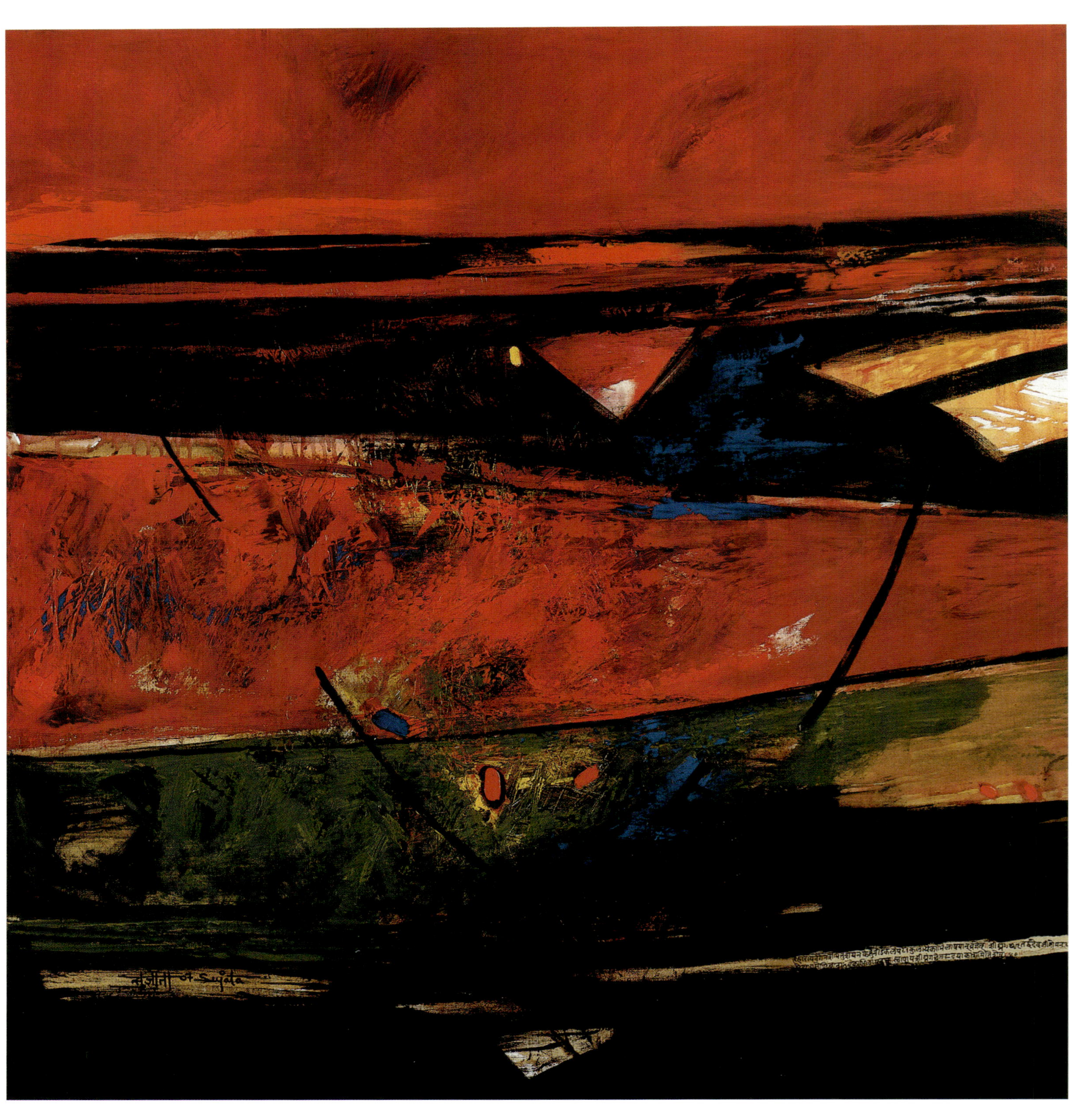

I heard a din in the sky like hundreds of thousands
of thunderclaps and, splitting the clouds, a huge chariot
appeared. Out of this chariot, which was shimmering
with sparks, with reflectors, vapours and unbearable light,
flew burning, screaming air.
The coachman's voice said to me: get in.
My heart beat hard. I climbed into this immense chariot.
Drawn by a colossal strength, it carried me away to luminous
regions which, when seen from the earth, looked like stars.

Yes, I saw thousands of worlds on fire, whistling in space.
I saw bodies shining with their own light, smoke, spirits,
fugitive creatures. I saw Ariavata, the great white elephant
with its four tusks. I went beyond the world of men,
I reached Amaravati, the centre of the universe, the city
which cannot be described, forever in motion in
limitless space.

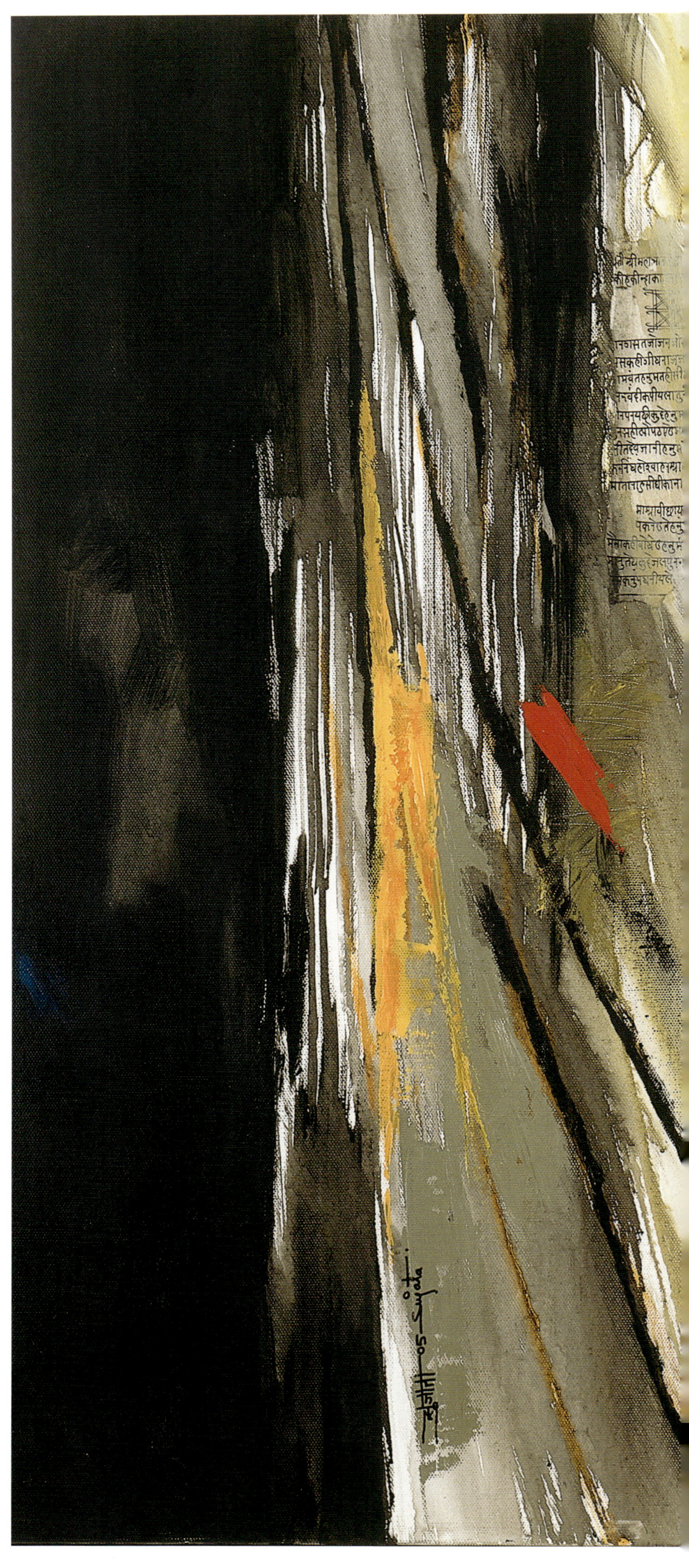

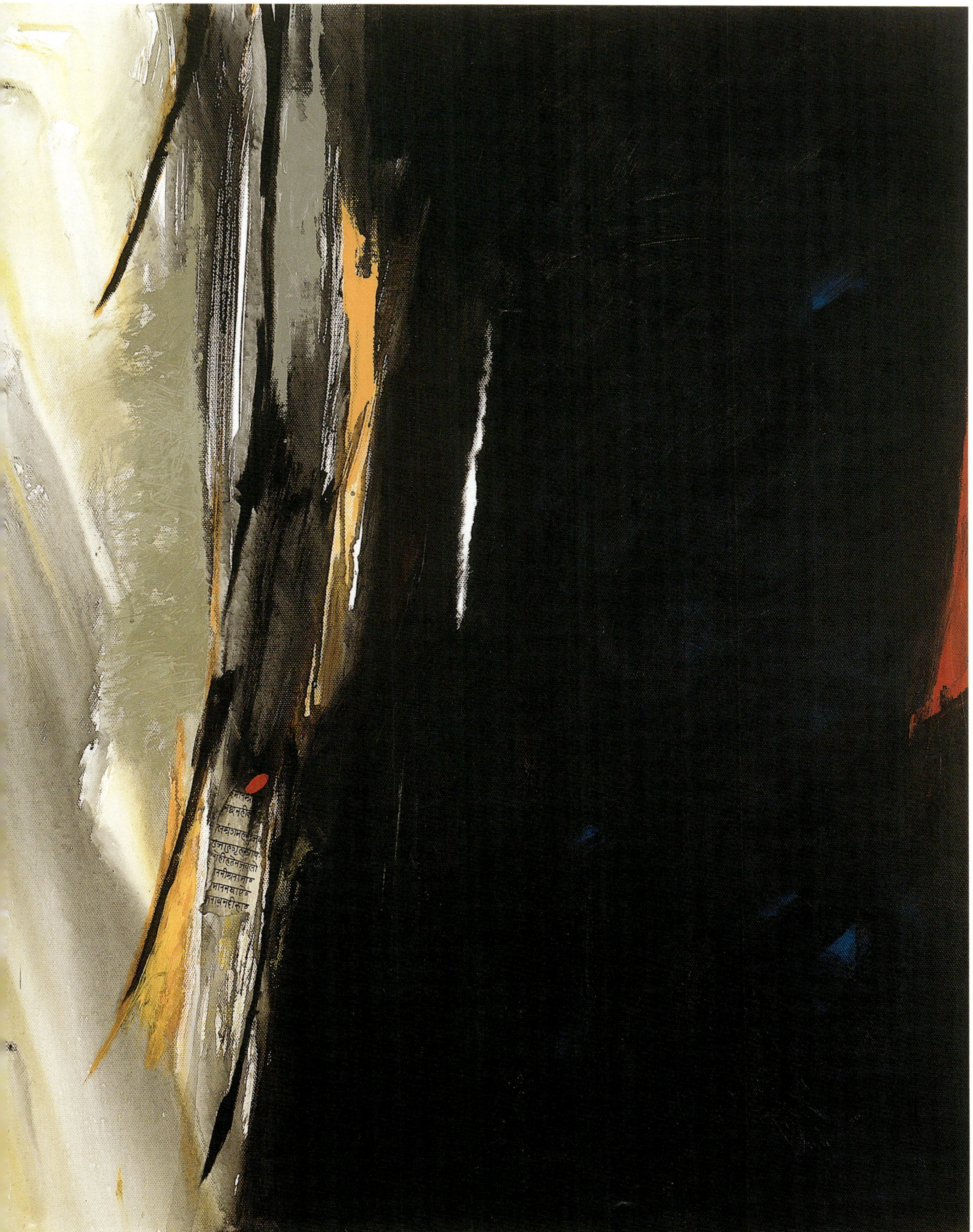

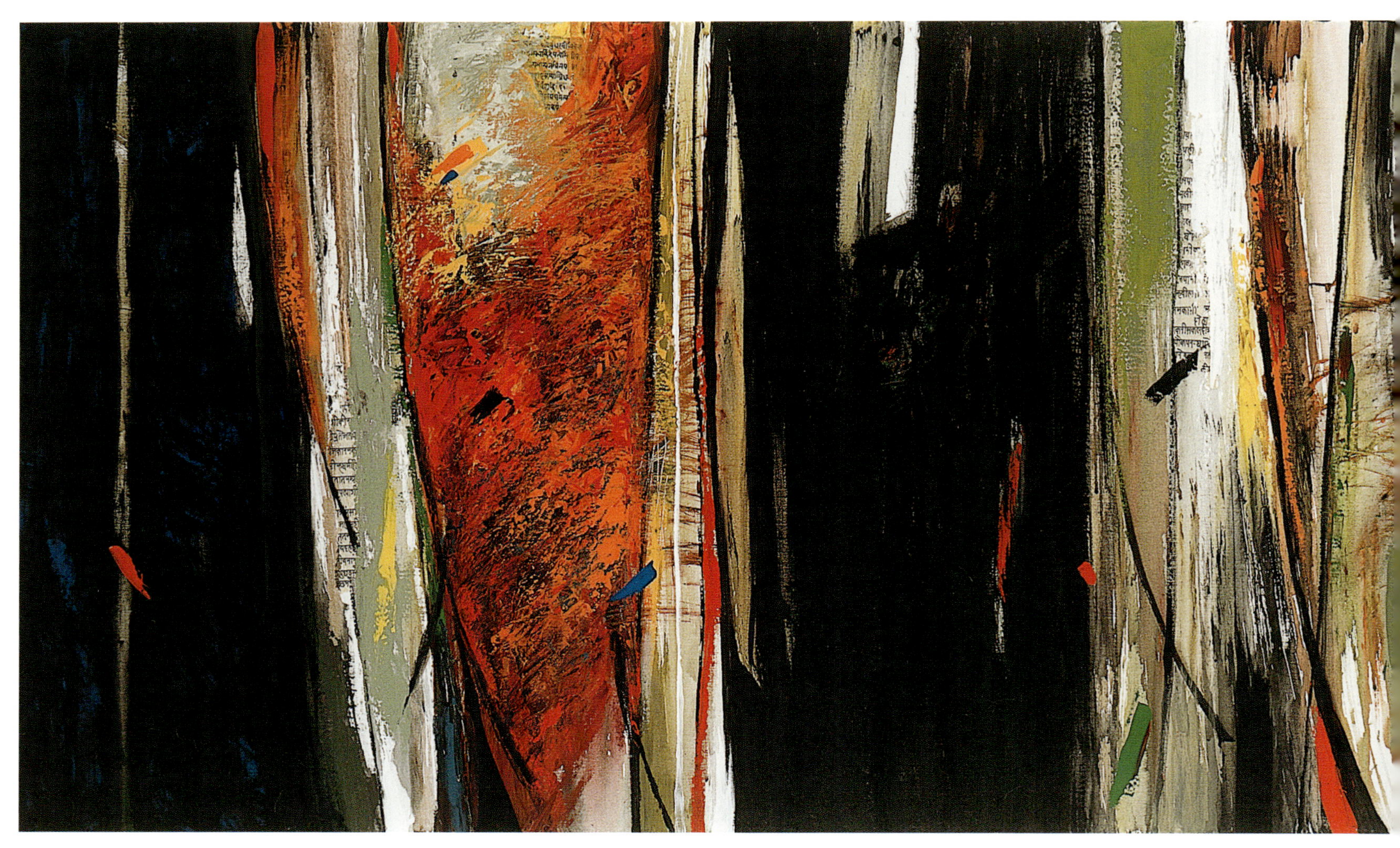

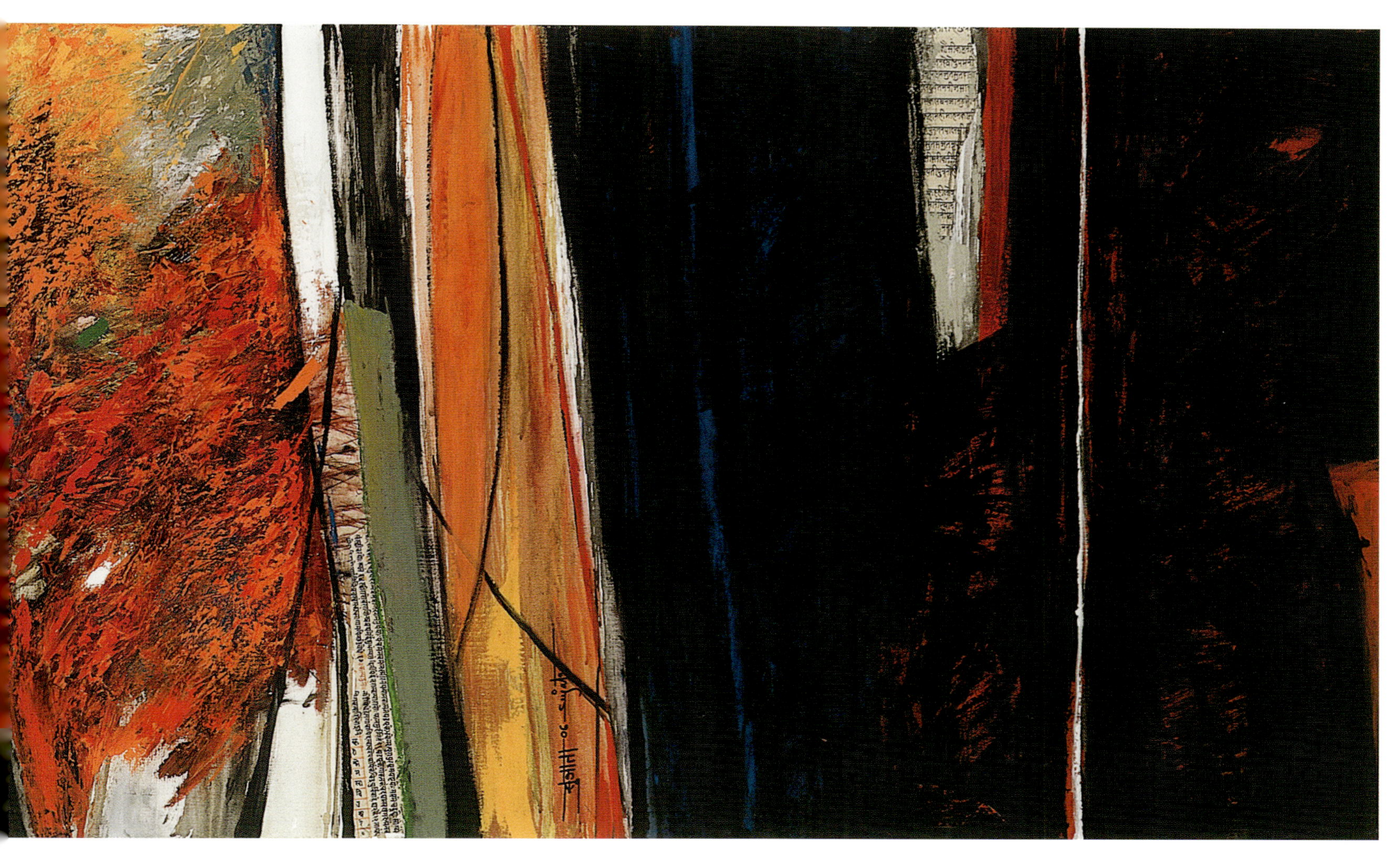

– Give me an example of grief.
– Ignorance.
– Of poison.
– Desire.
– An example of defeat.
– Victory.

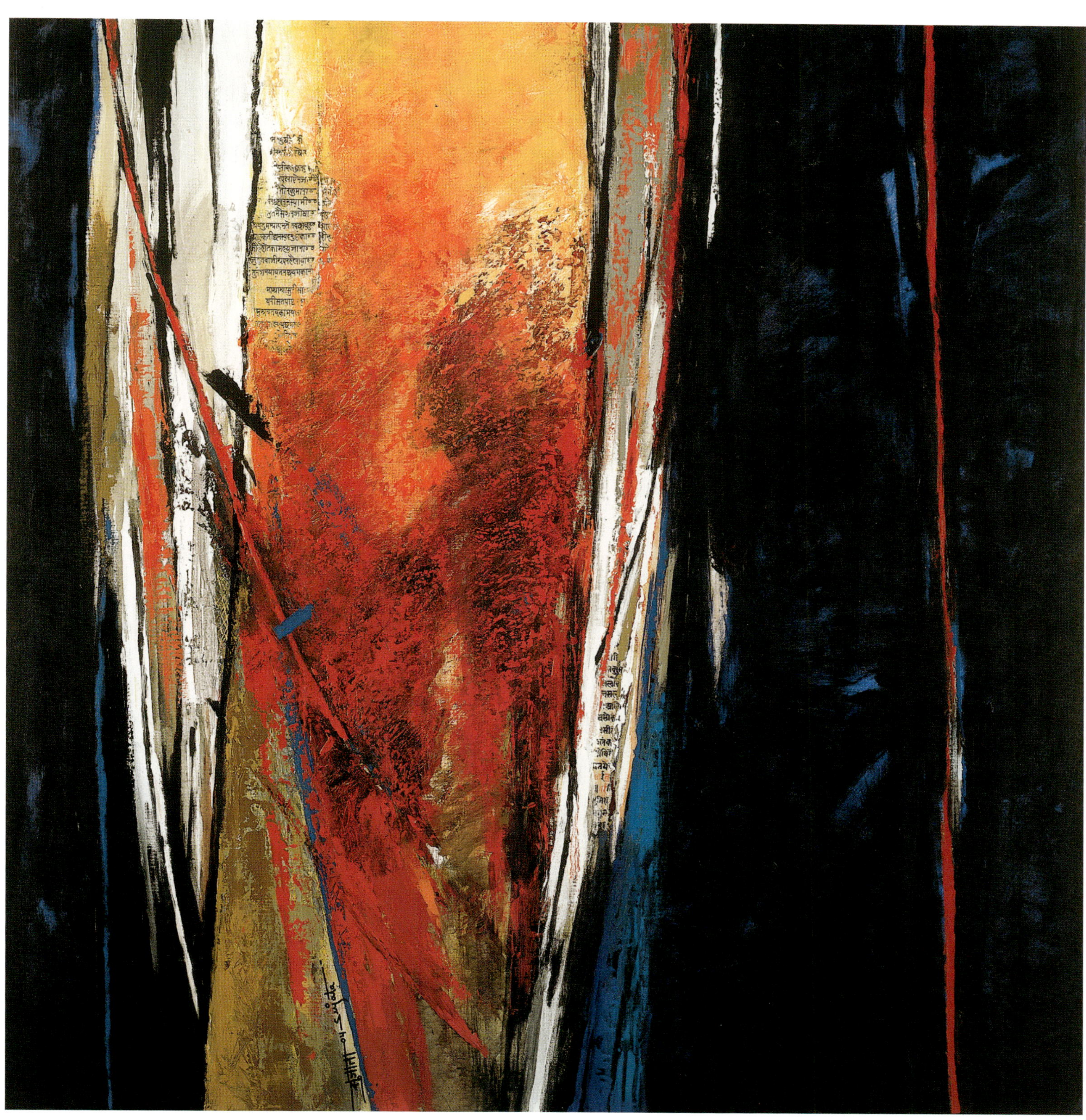

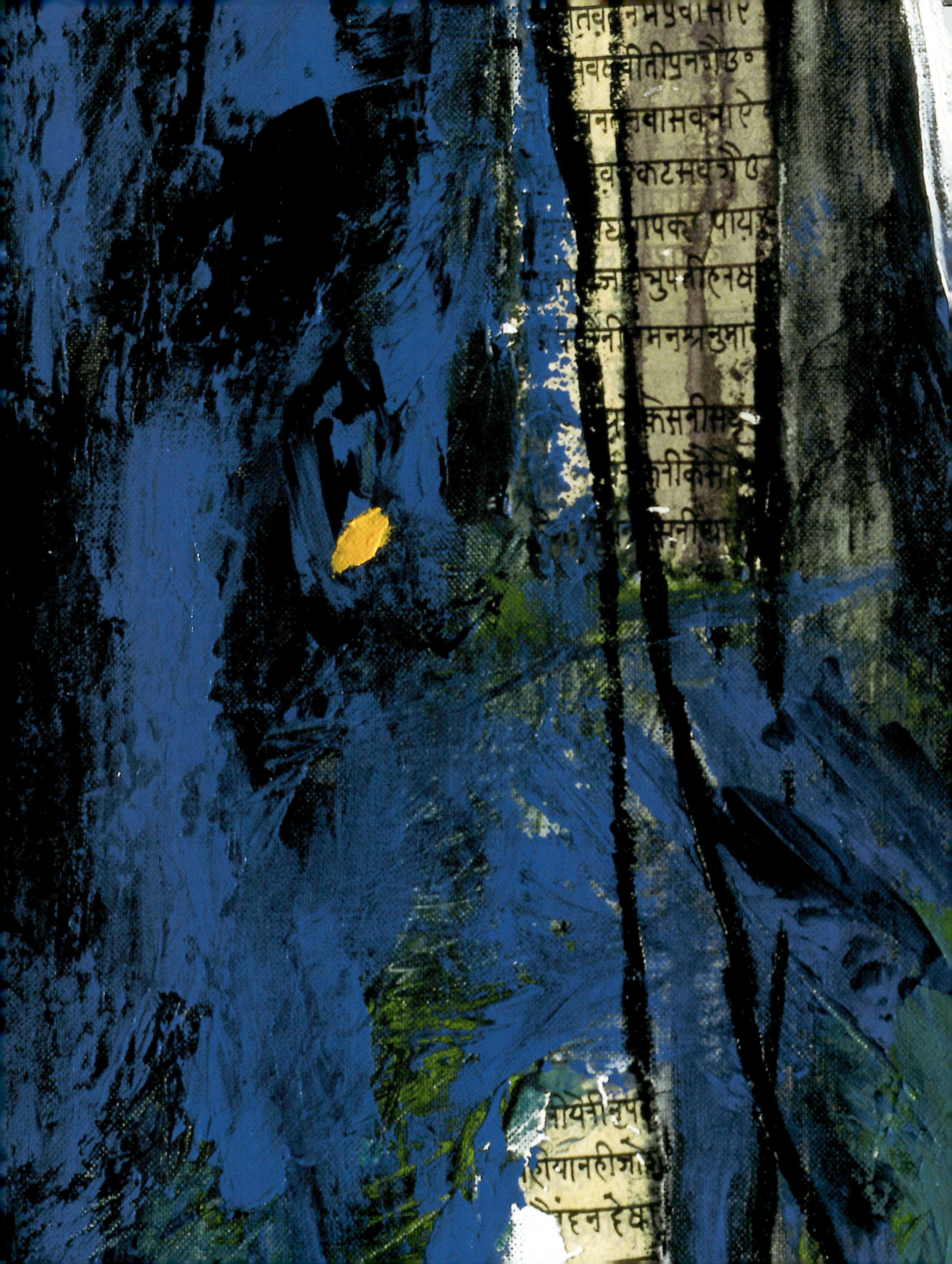

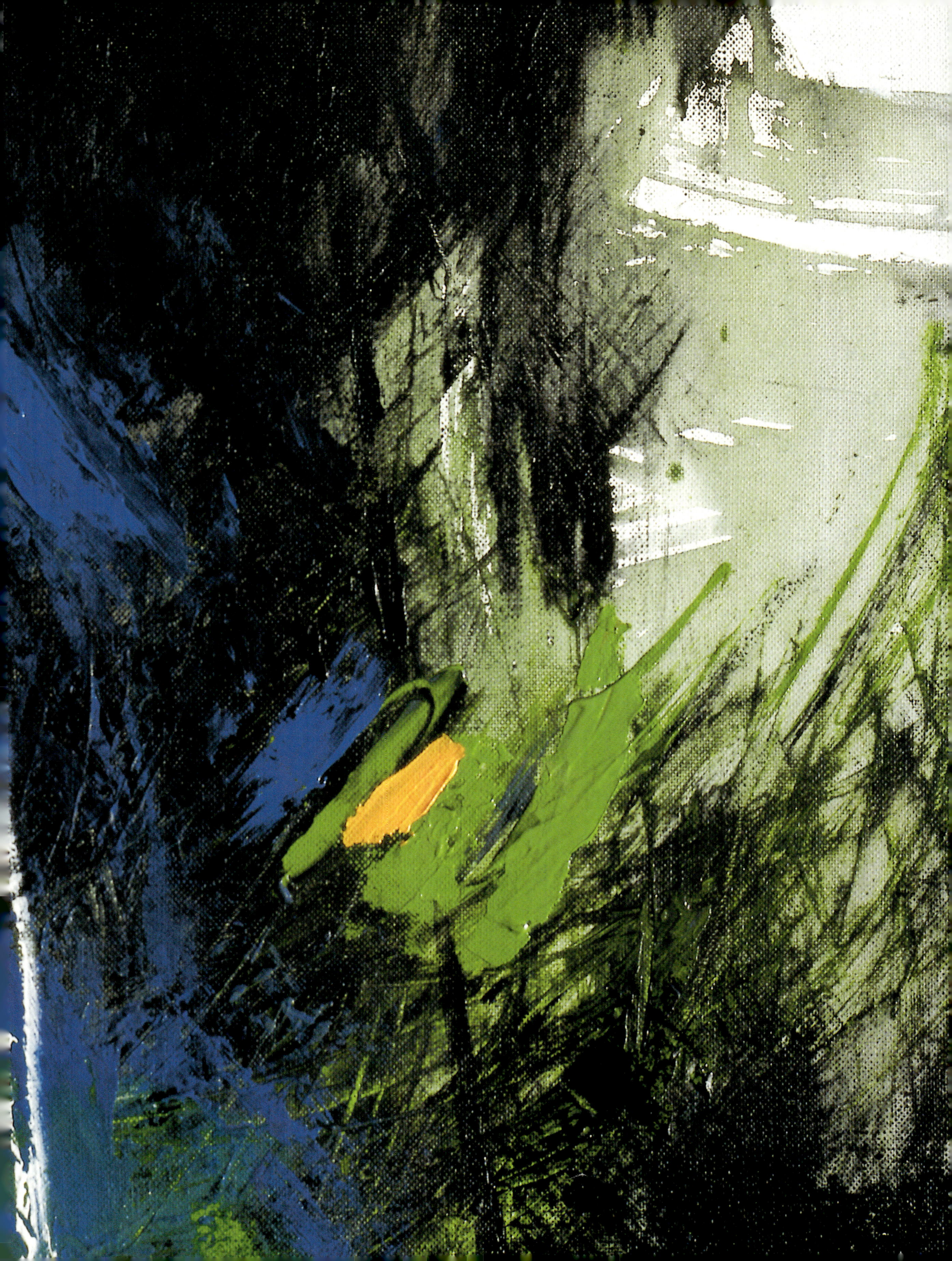

A man is walking through a dark forest full of ferocious beasts. The forest is surrounded by a huge net. The man is scared, he runs to escape the animals, he falls into a dark well.

Miraculously, he clings on to blades of grass, to tangled roots. He feels the warm breath of a great serpent which opens its mouth at the bottom of the well; he is going to fall into its mouth; at the edge of the hole a giant elephant is going to crush him; white and black mice are gnawing at the roots from which he dangles; dangerous bees fly above the hole and dribble droplets of honey…

Then the man extends his finger, softly, cautiously, he extends his finger to collect the drops of honey. Threatened by so many dangers, faced by several deaths, he knows not indifference, the taste of honey still arouses him.

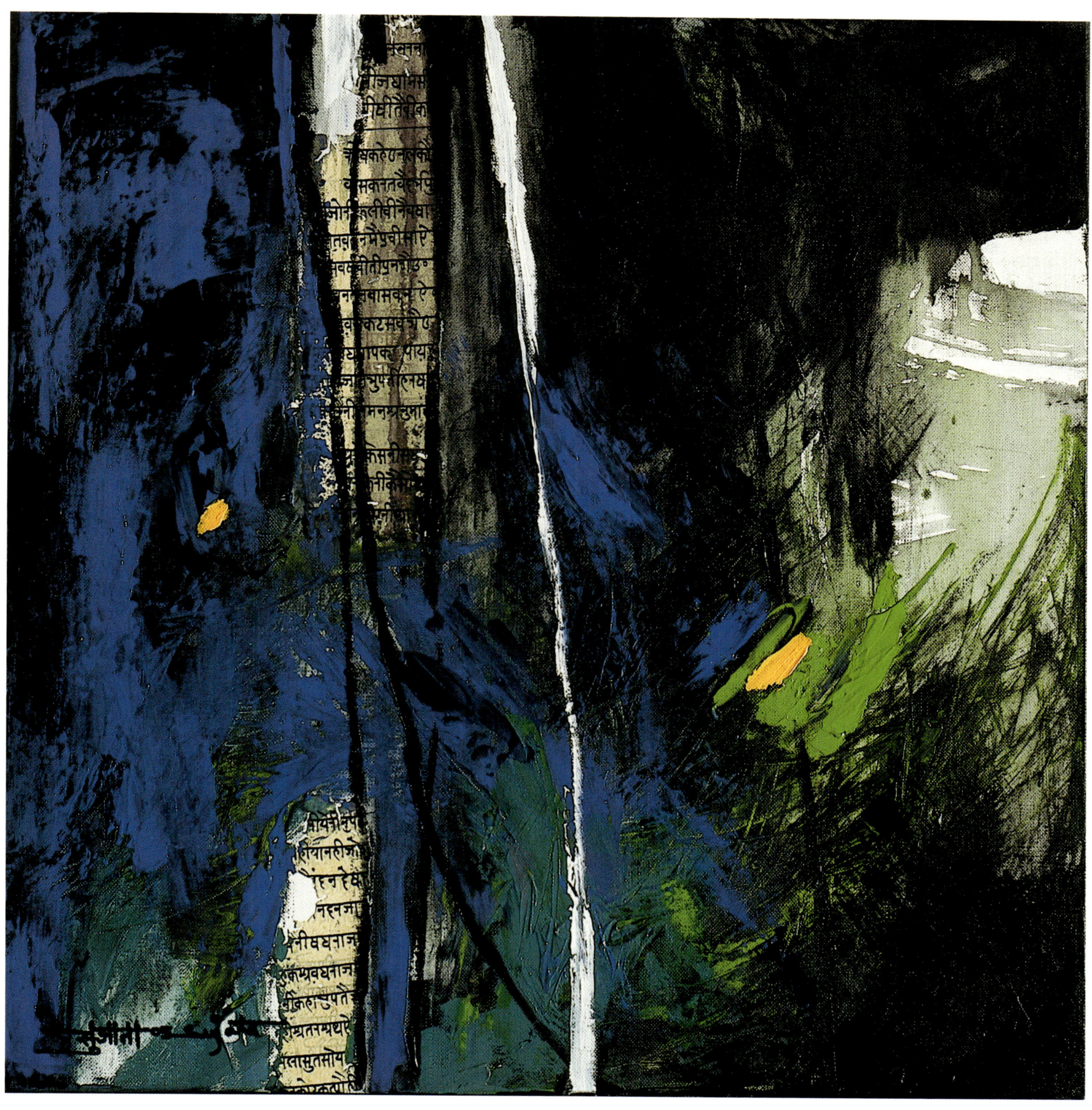

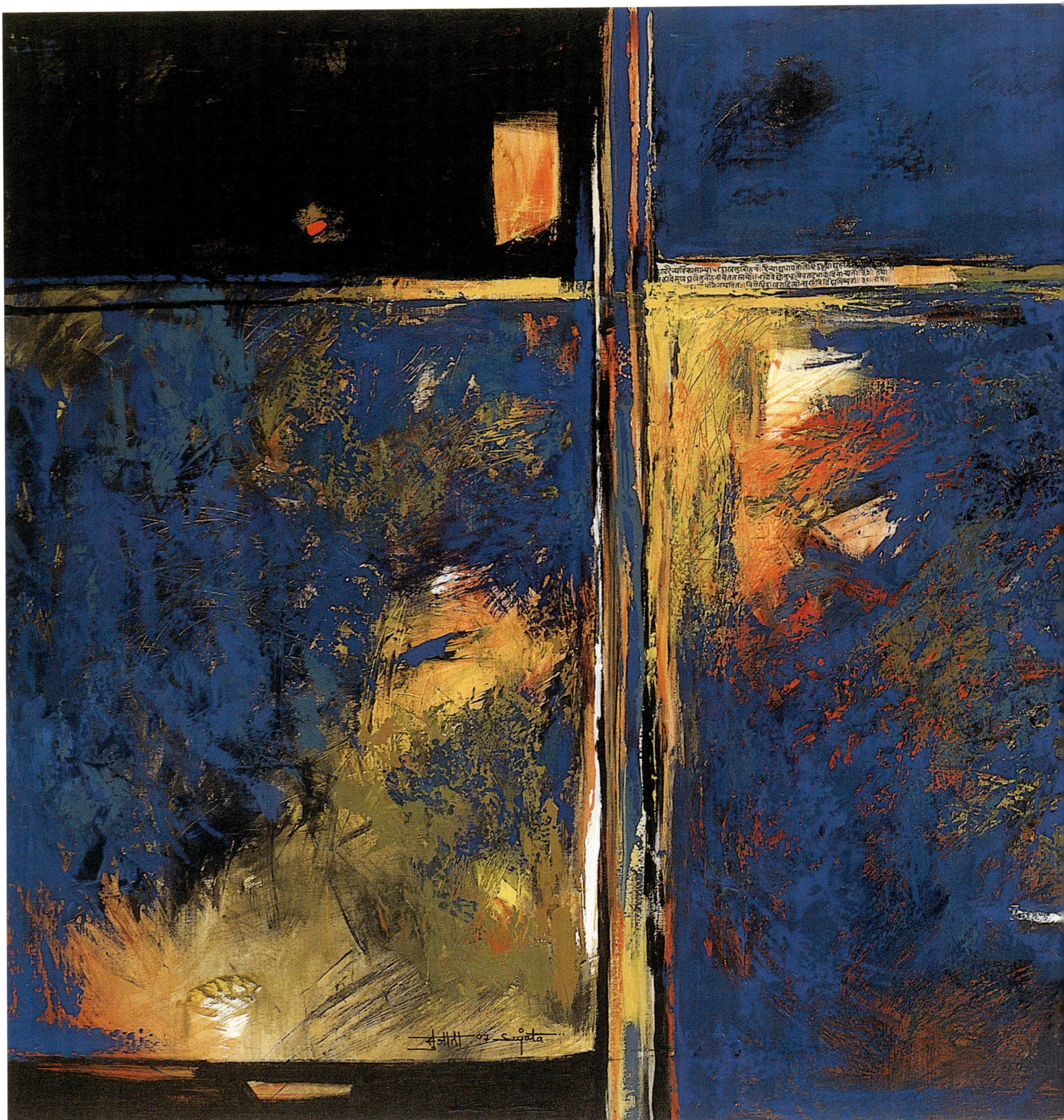

07 Sujata

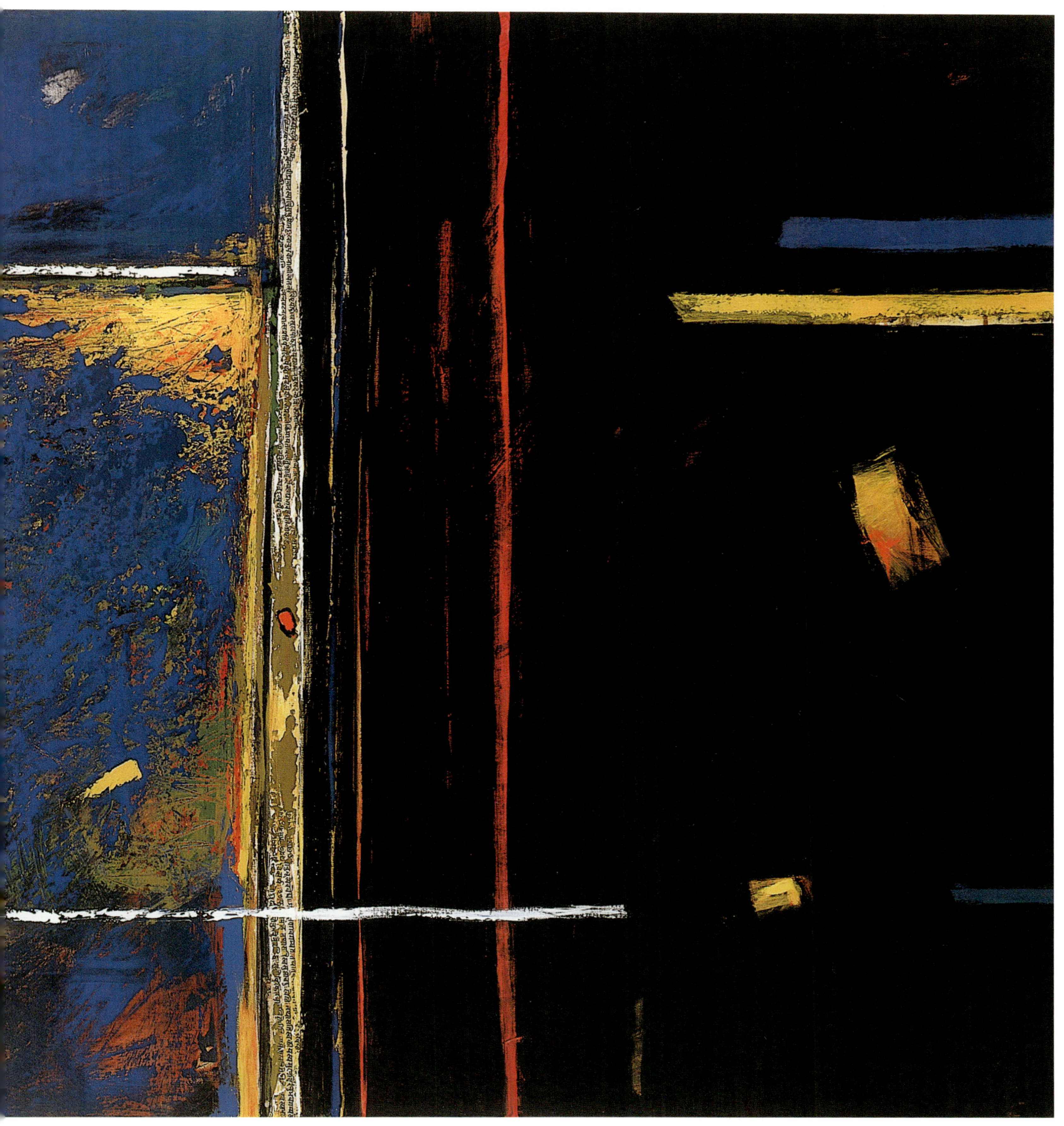

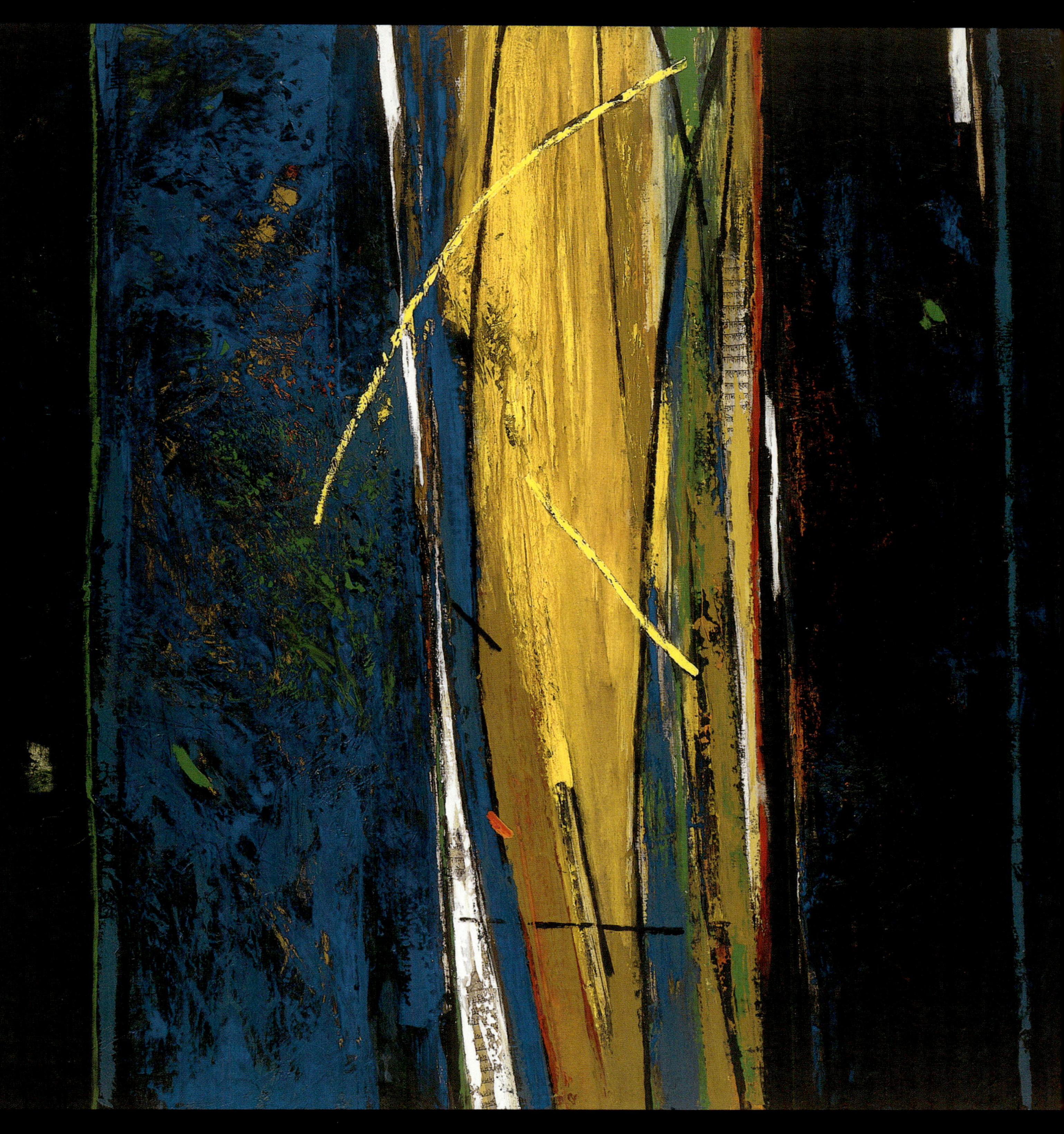

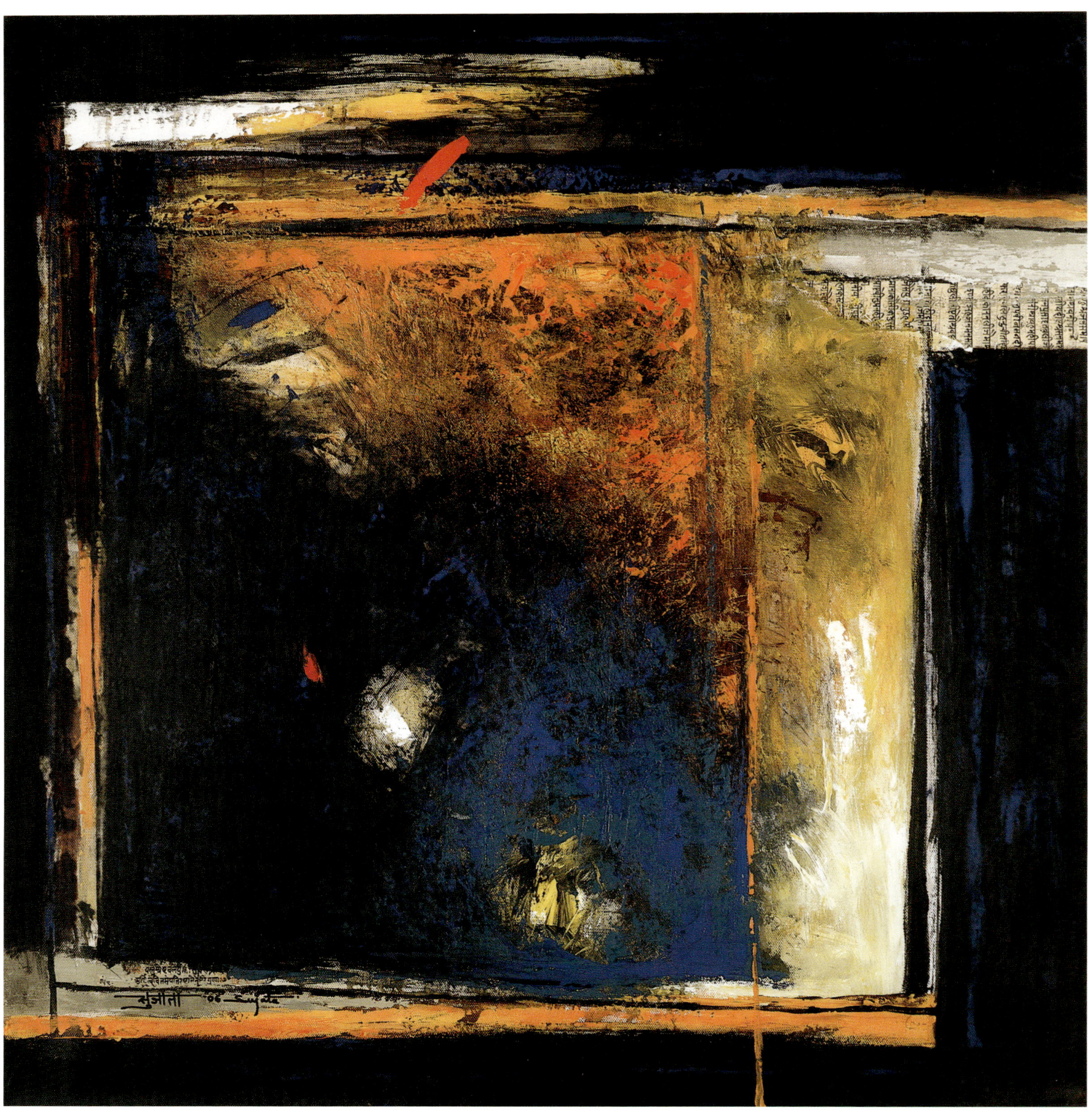

Oppose the subtle with the subtler still and the dark with the even darker.

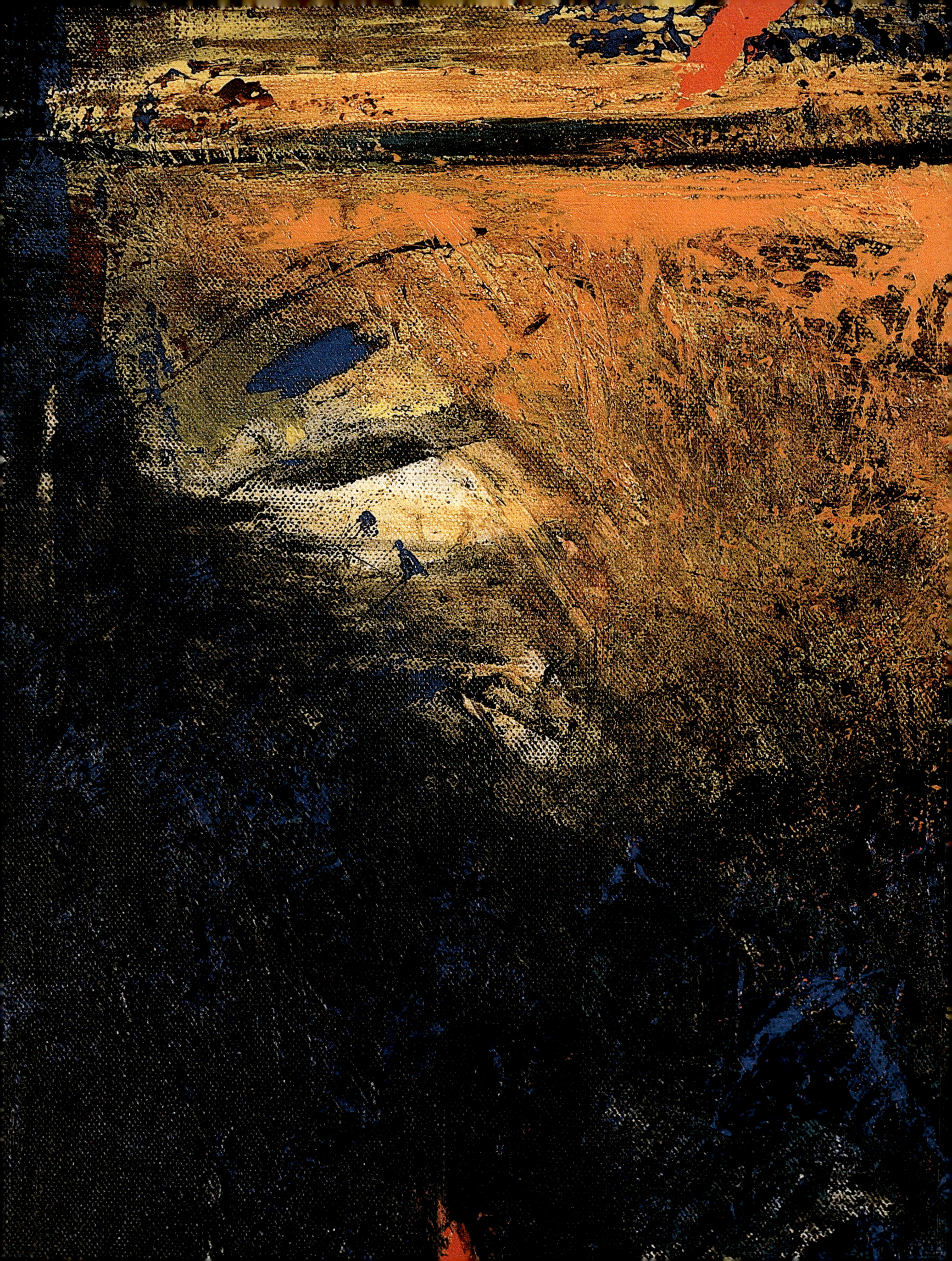

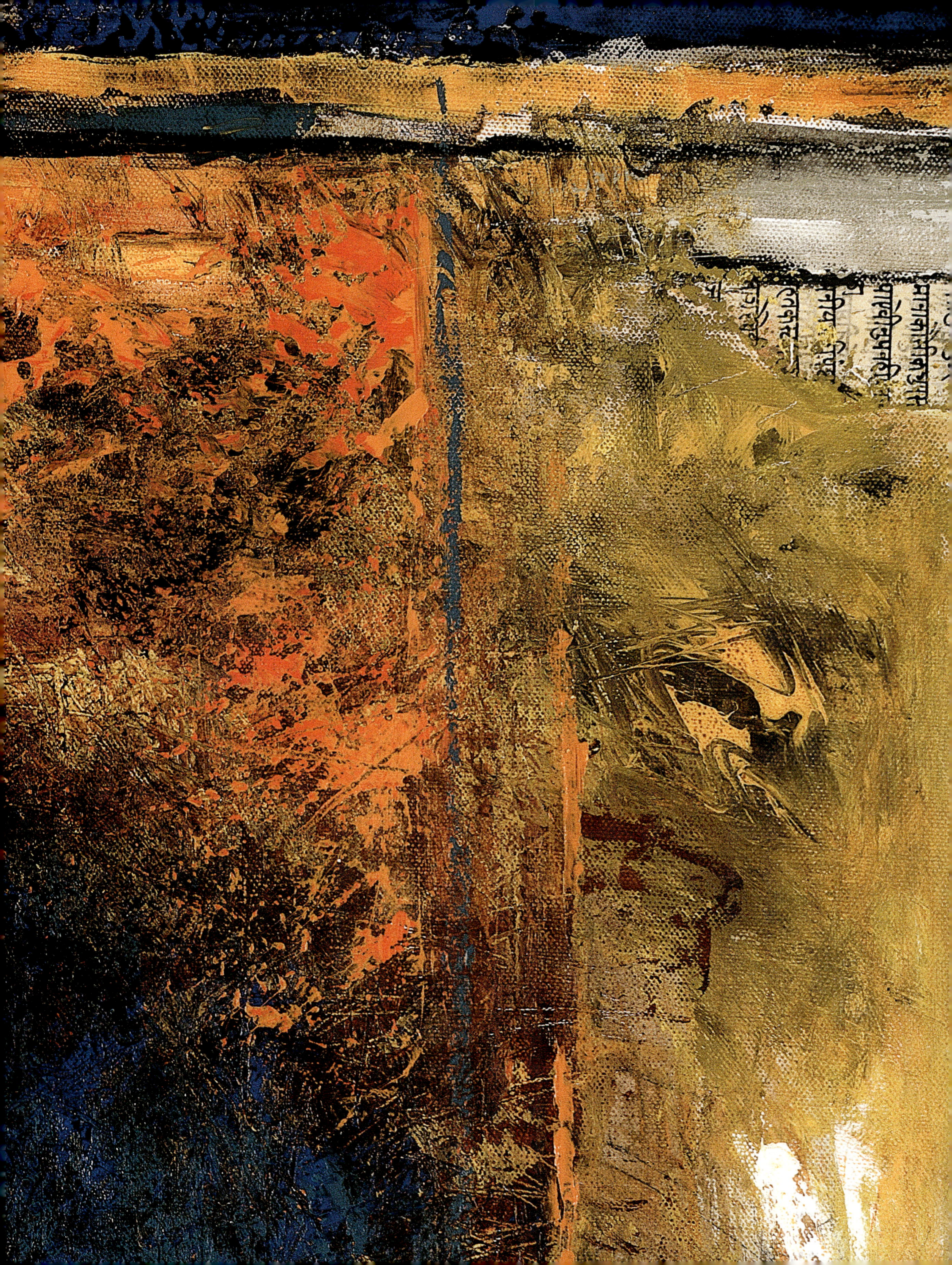

The spirit is whimsical and unstable, it is fleeting, febrile, turbulent and tenacious.
To subjugate it seems to me more difficult than taming the wind.

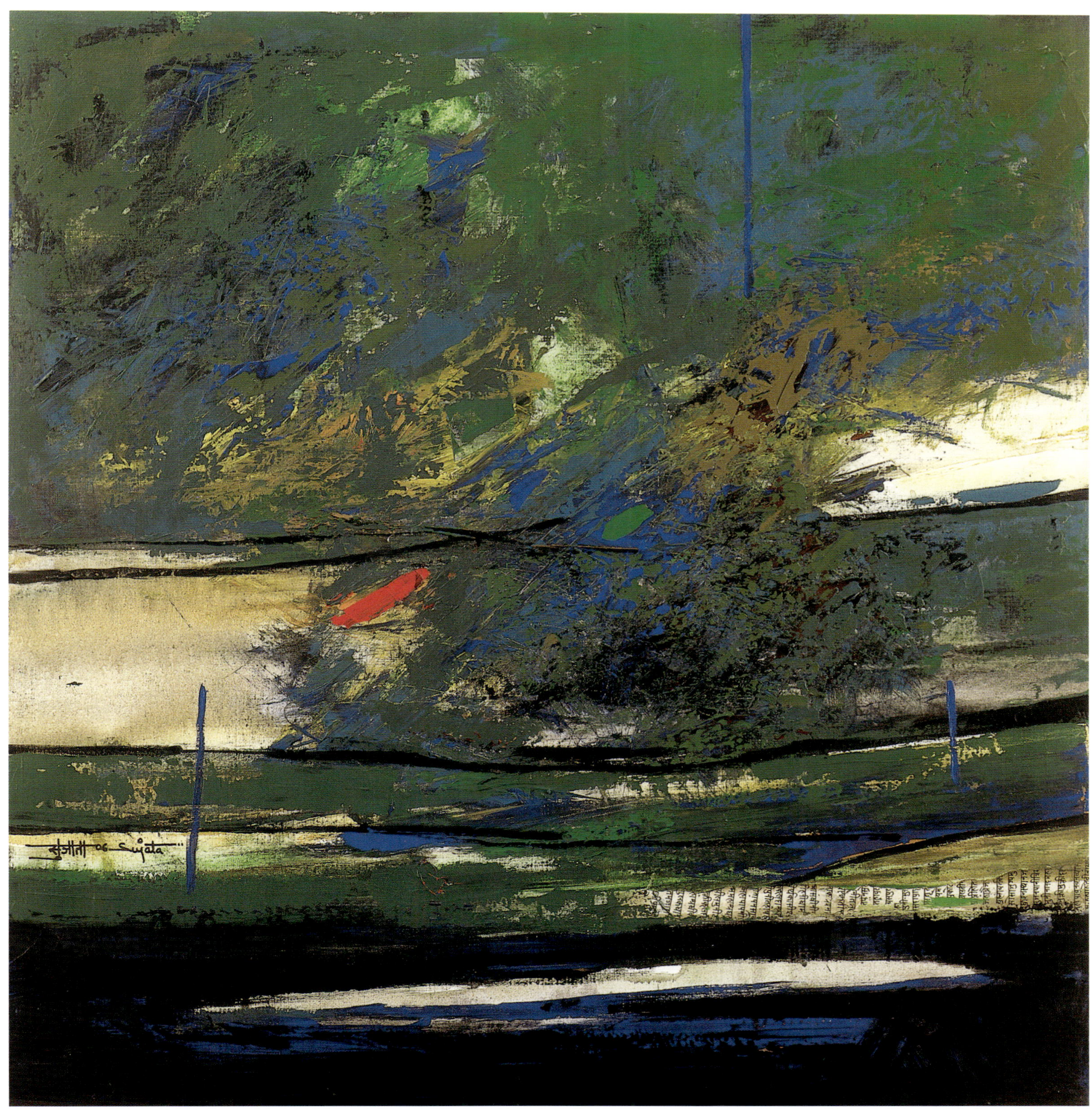
06 Sujata

Love is the same in every world.

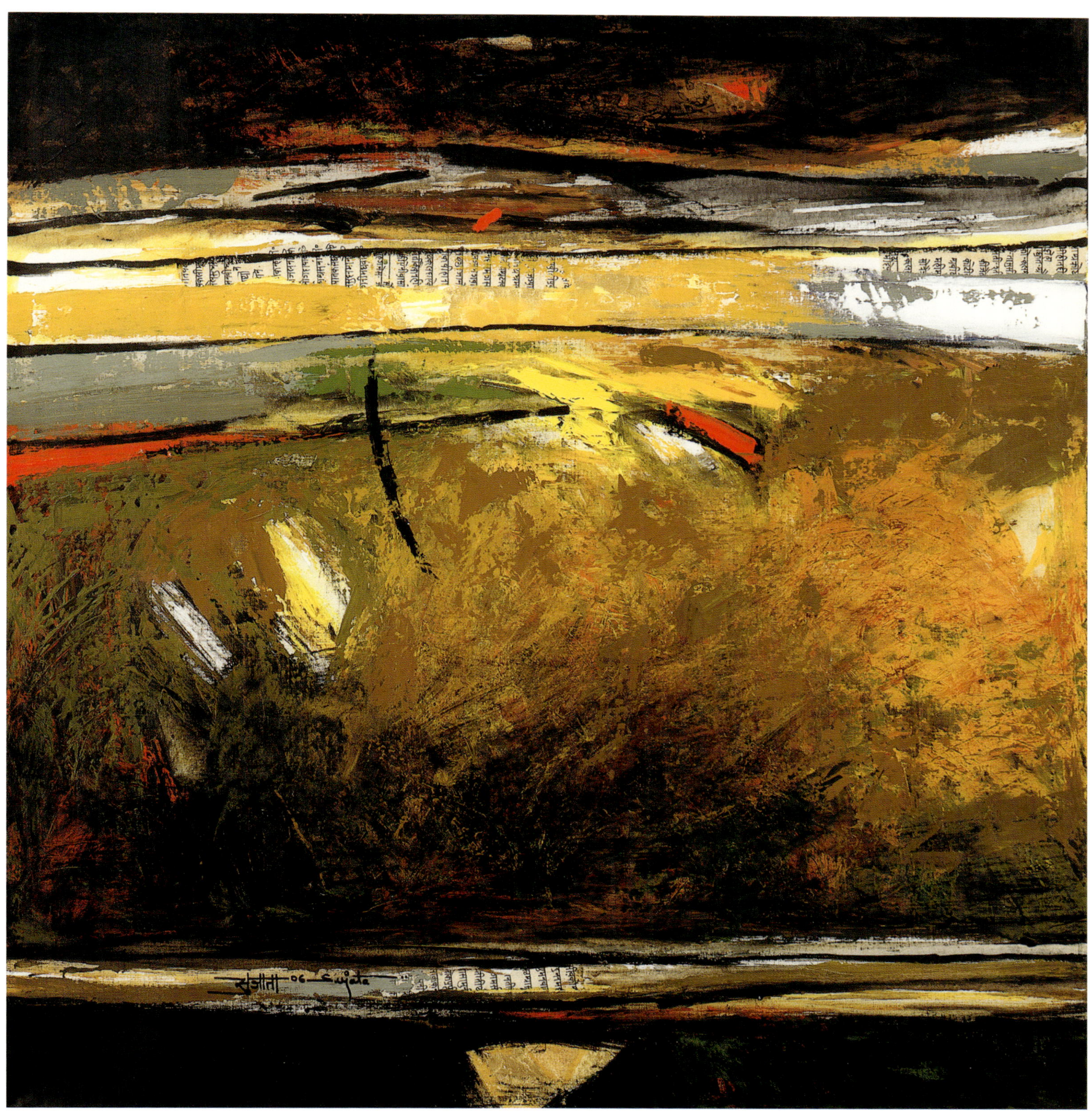

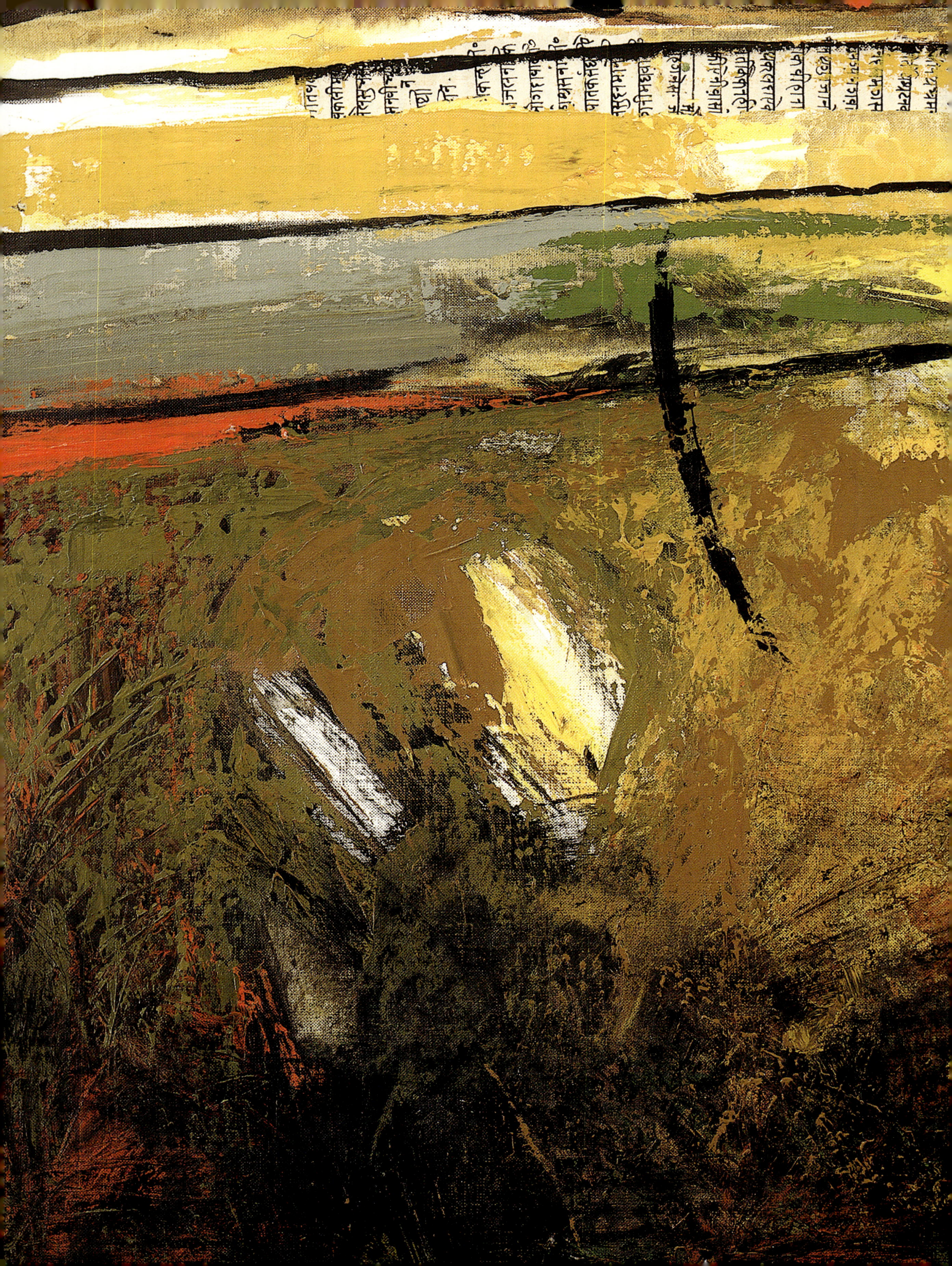

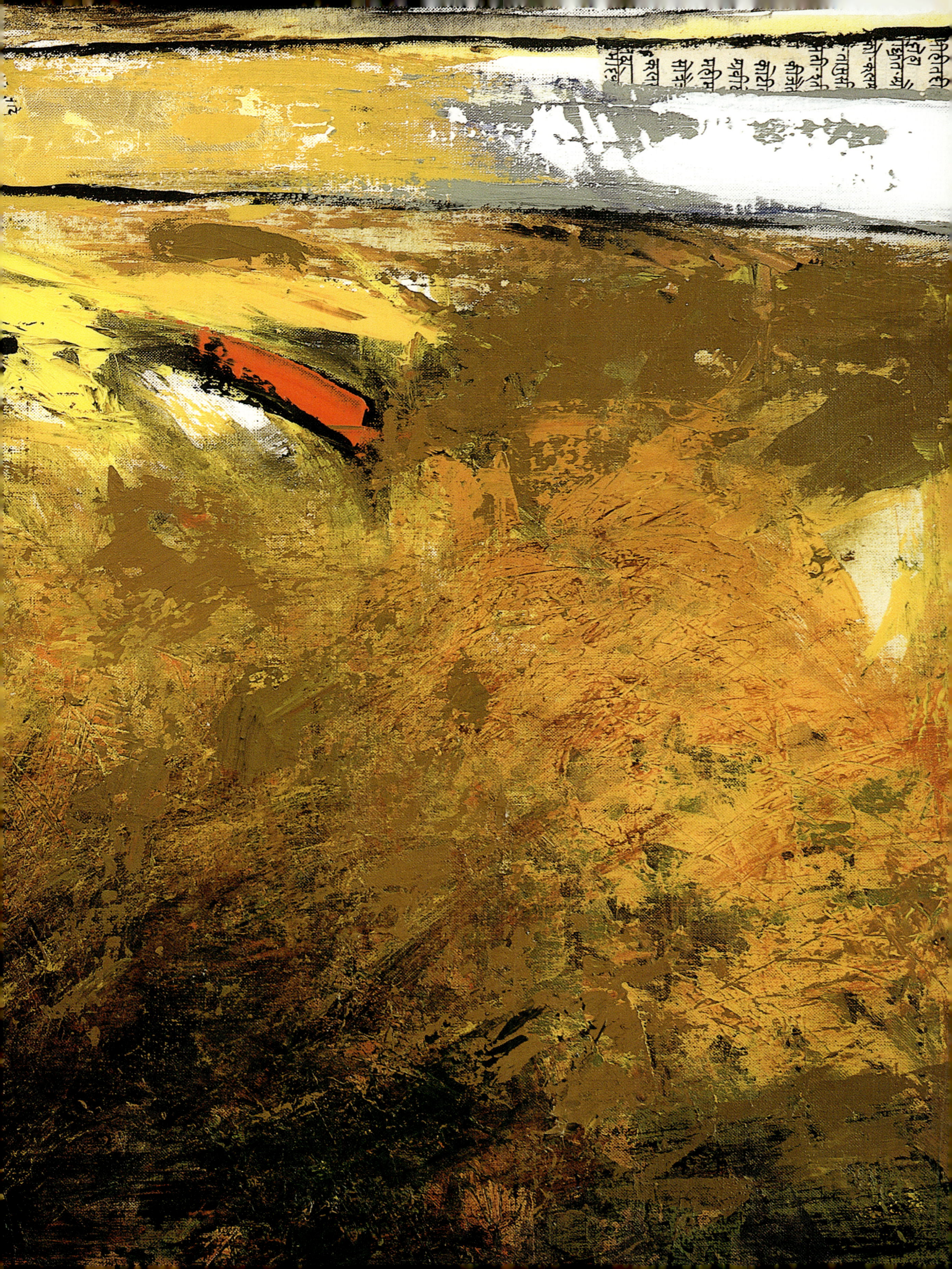

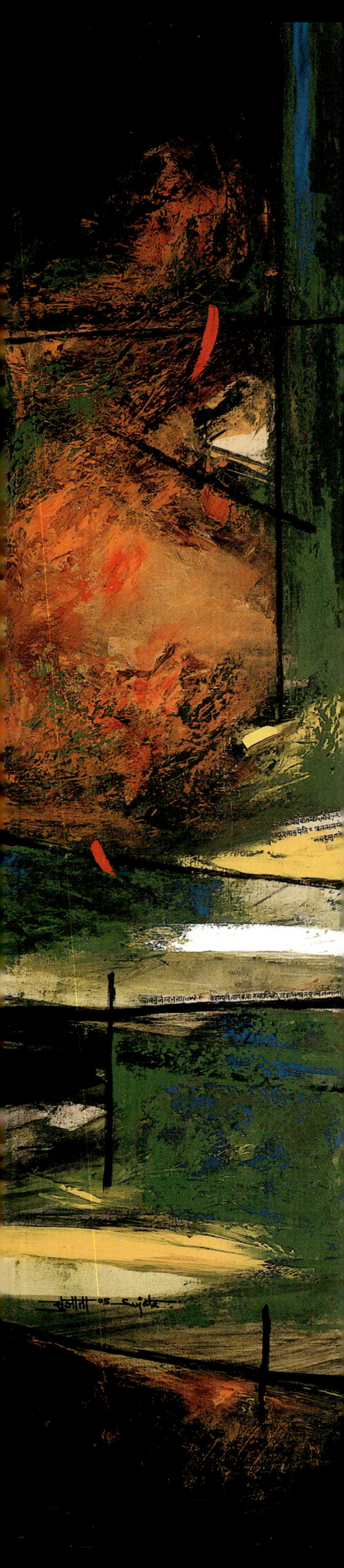

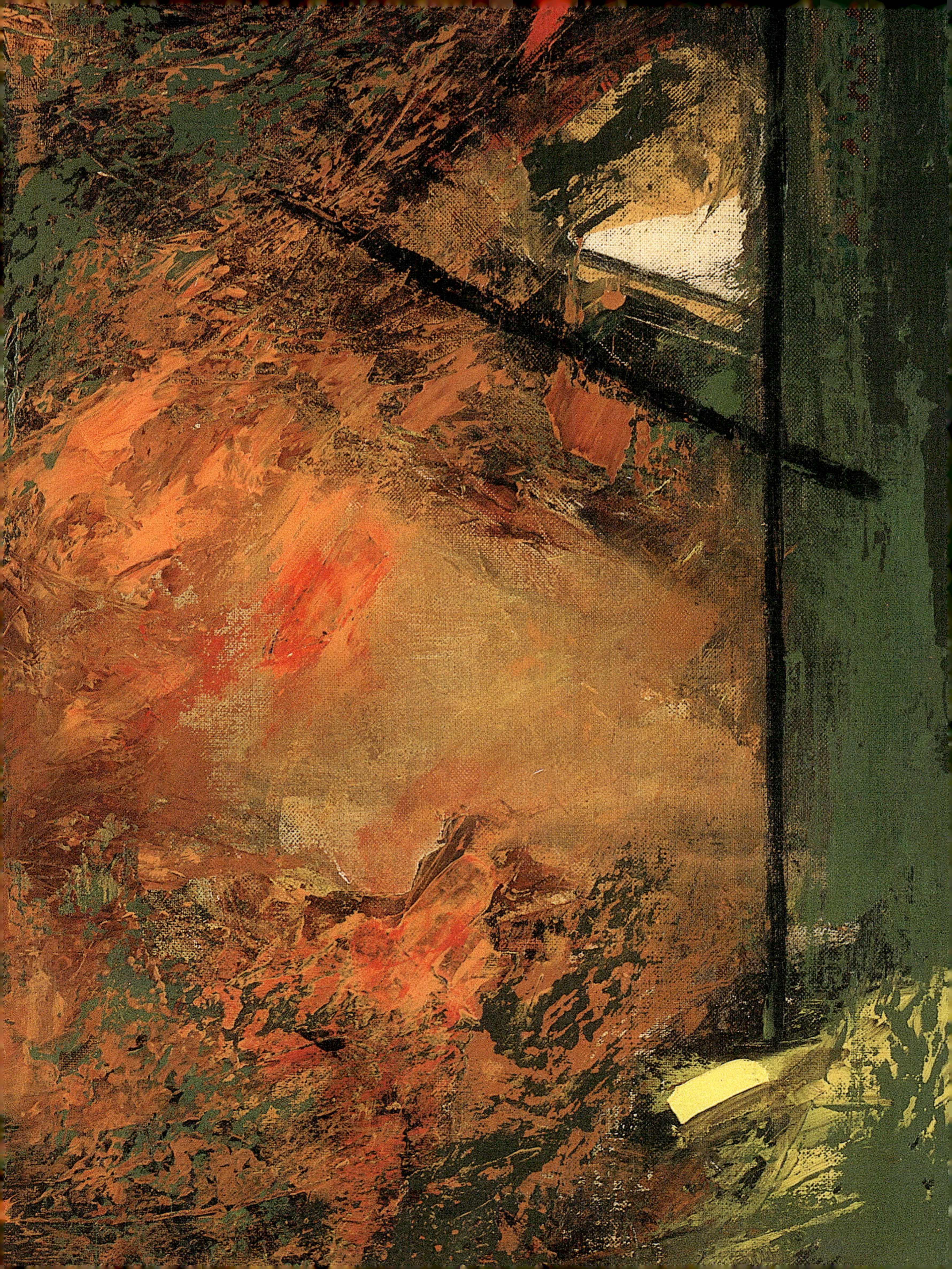

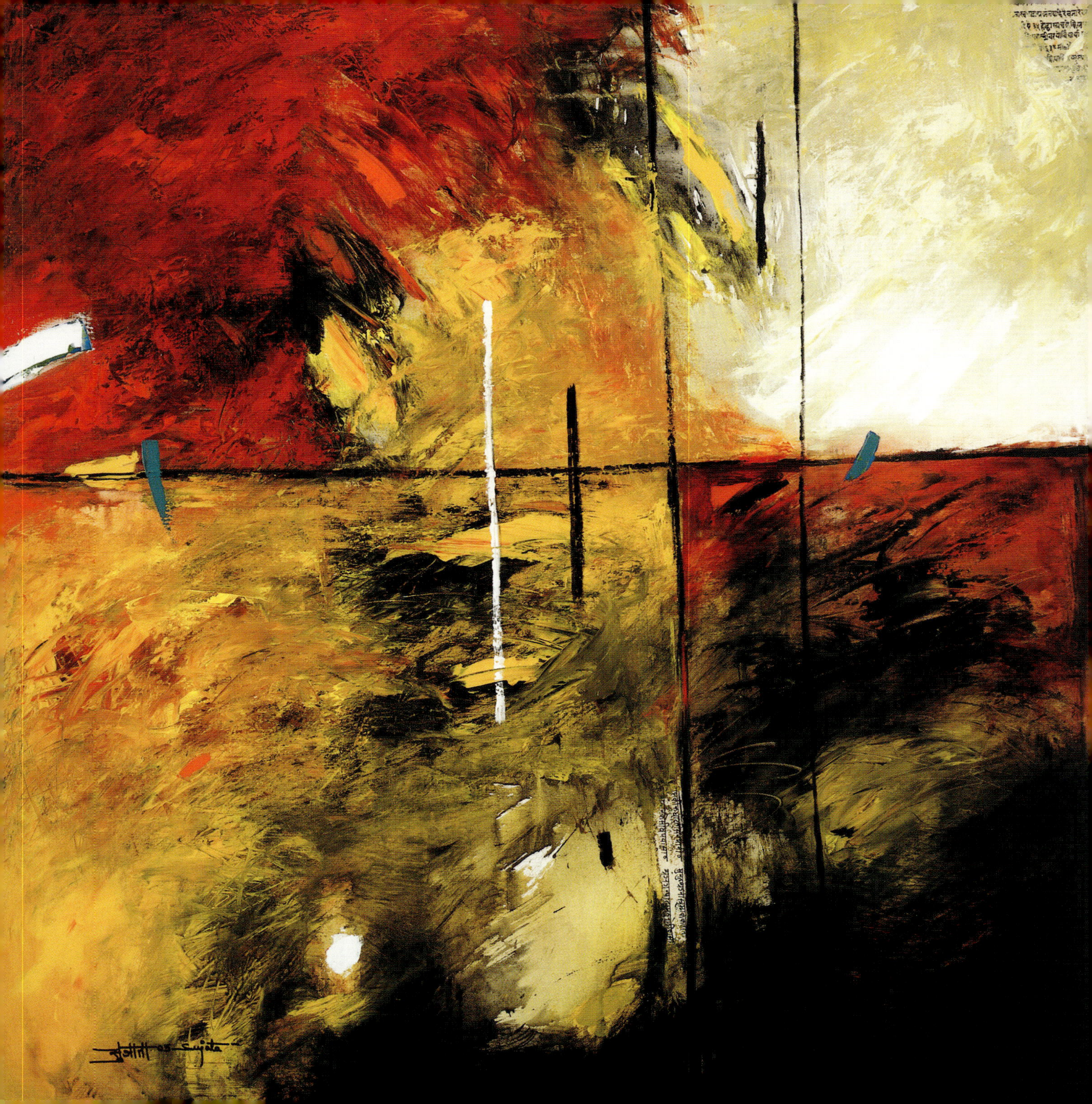

To lies, silence brings no response.

It's wrong to believe that the world was created for eternity. The world we know will last a long time, but not forever. It will be destroyed, inevitably. Shiva the destroyer is already at work, and we carry within us the indelible mark of this destruction.

Thereafter, we will drift into a long, very long sleep, the sleep of Vishnu. The God is asleep on the limitless ocean. In his stomach sleeps the creative principle, Brahma, who will one day rise again and recreate the world in an instant.
Brahma sleeps inside Vishnu, who sleeps. But Brahma dreams long dreams; he dreams for millions of years, he dreams so as never to forget the beauties of the vanished world.

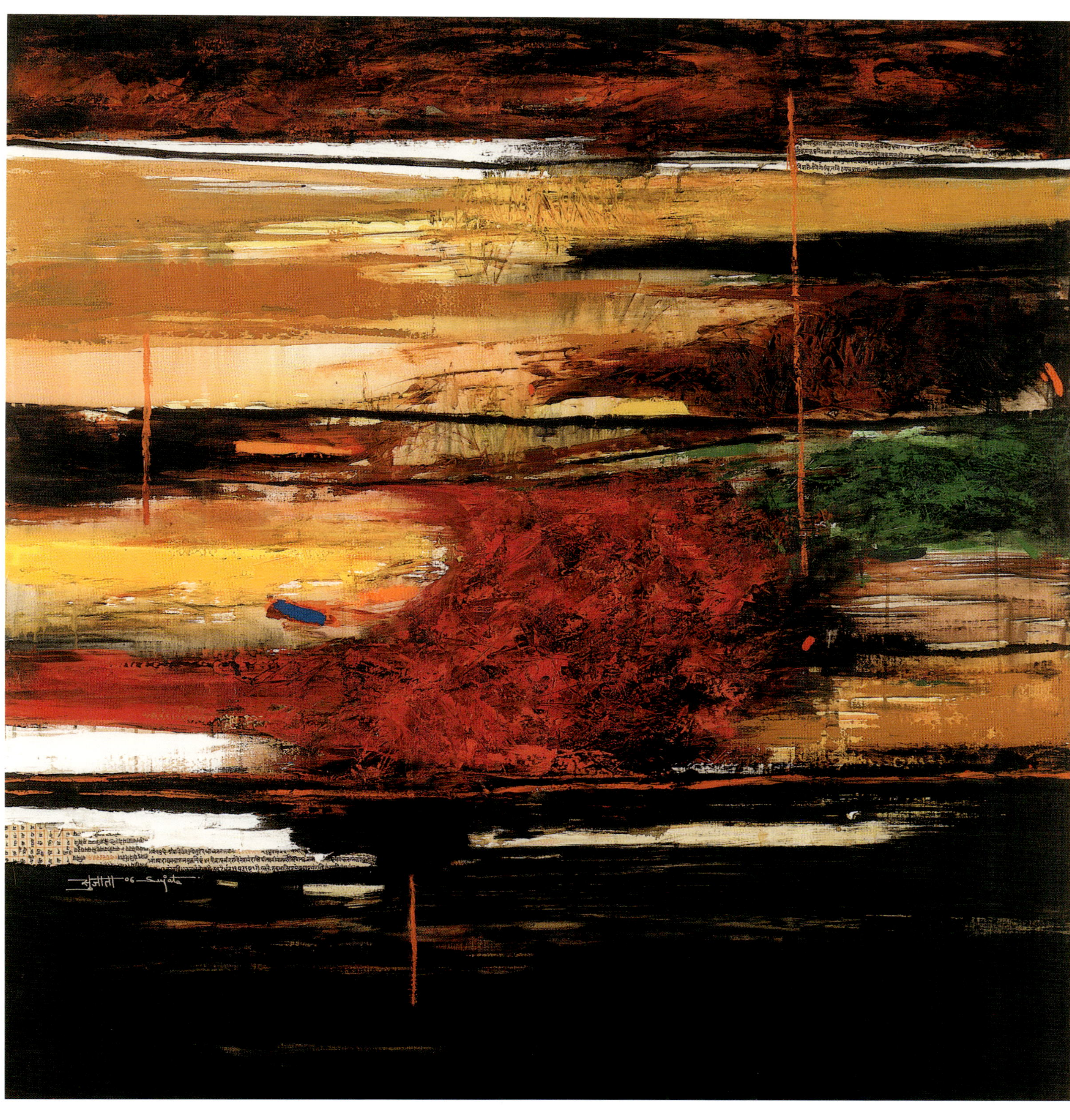
सुजाता '06 Sujata

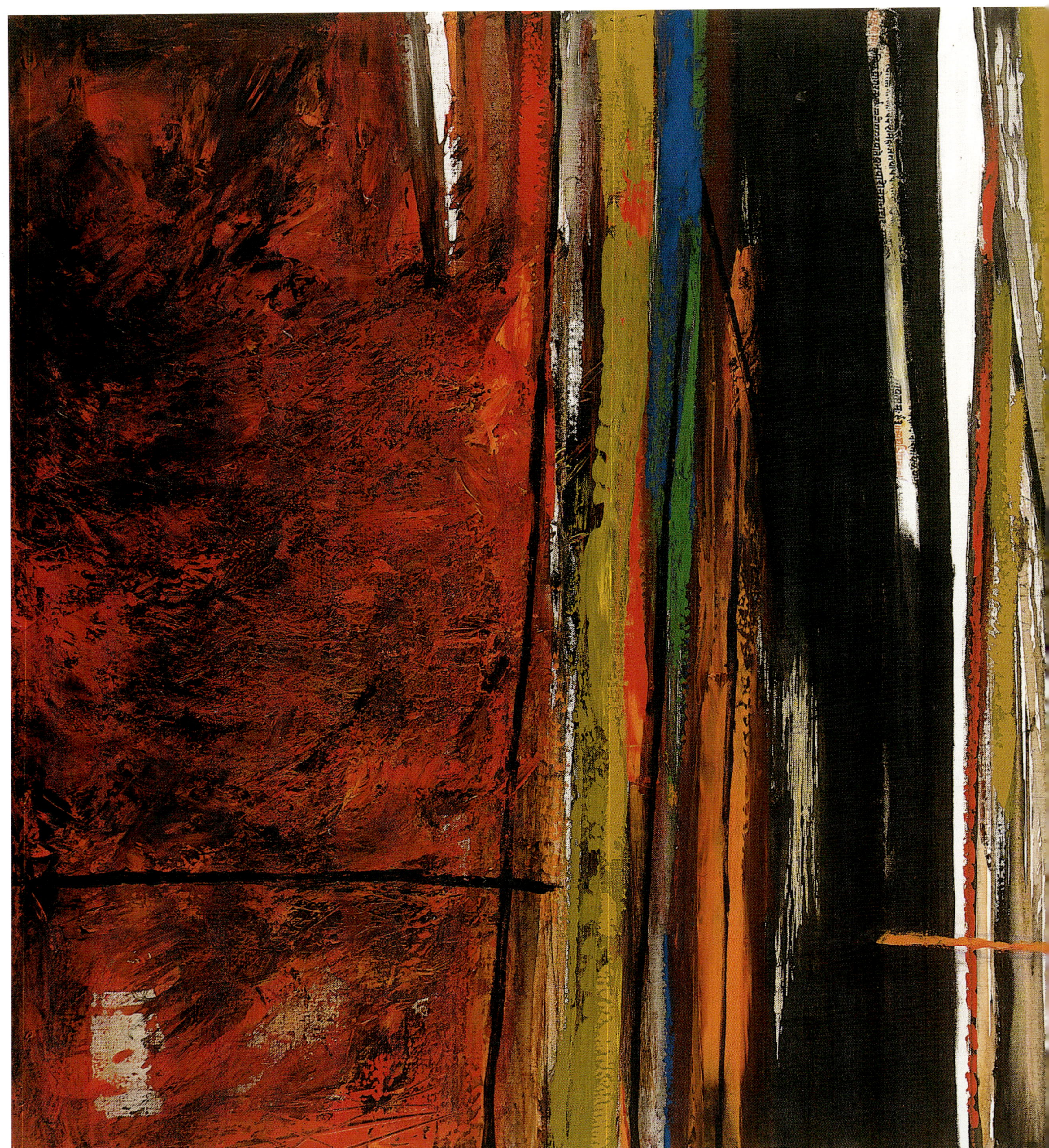

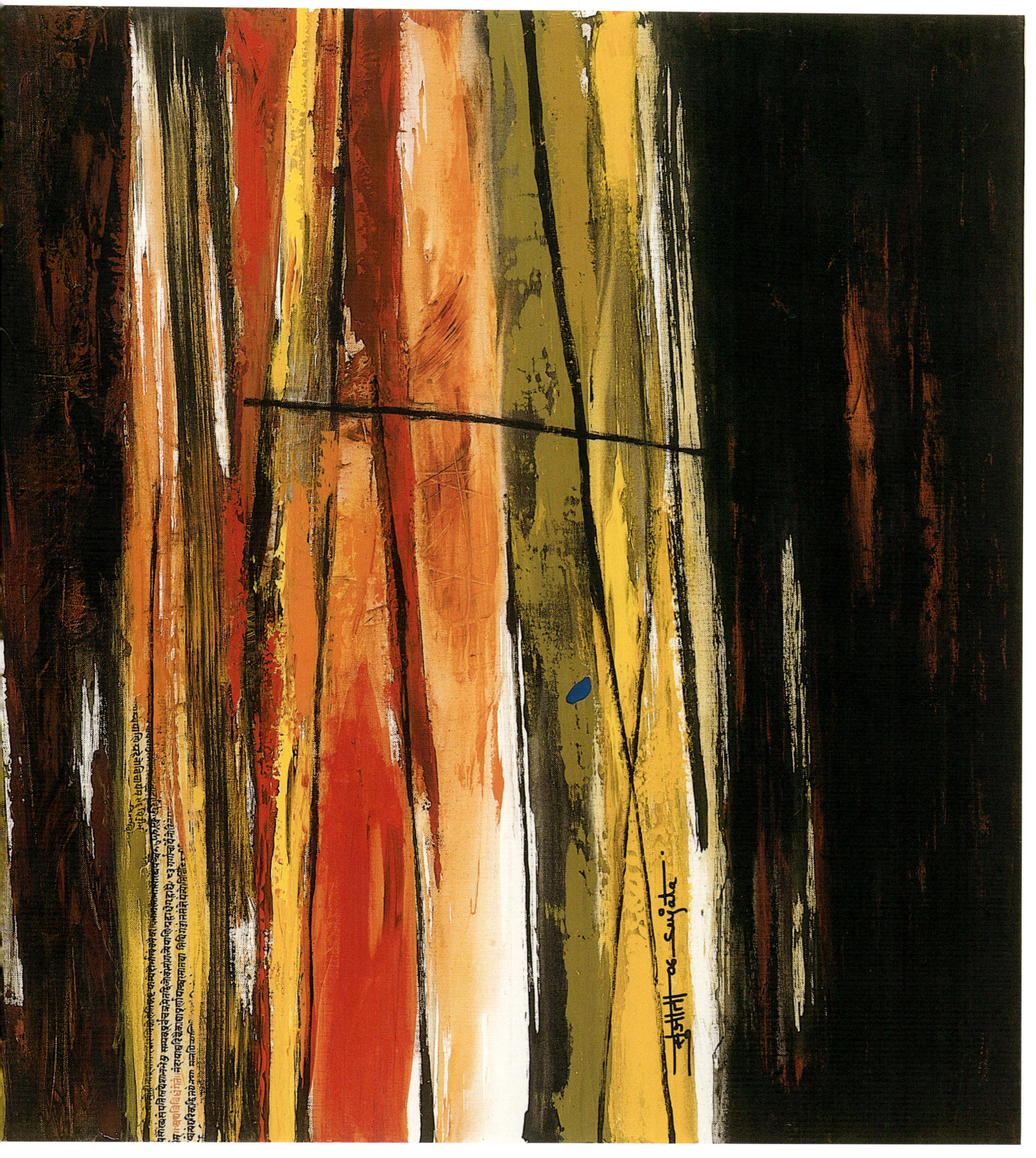

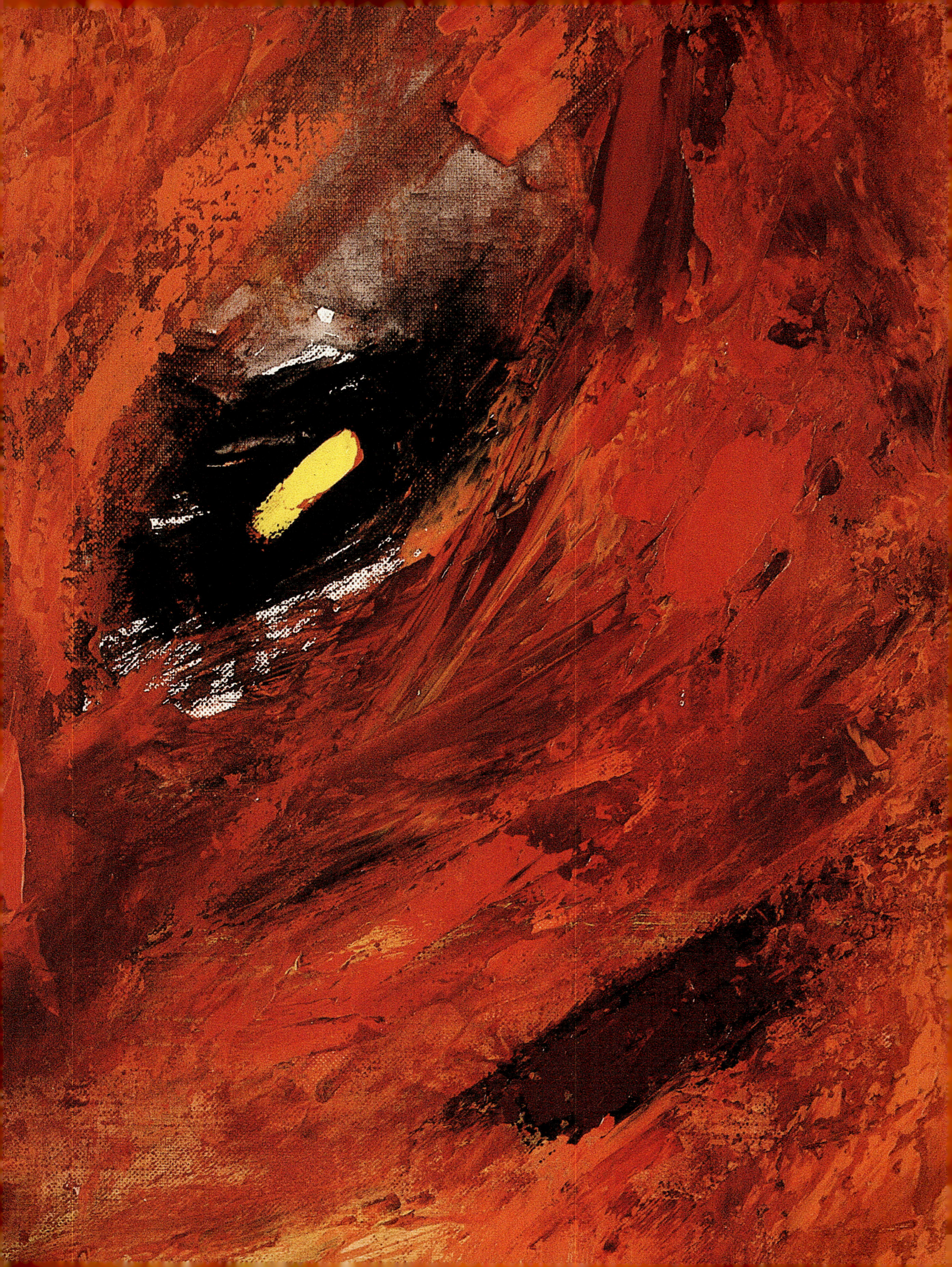

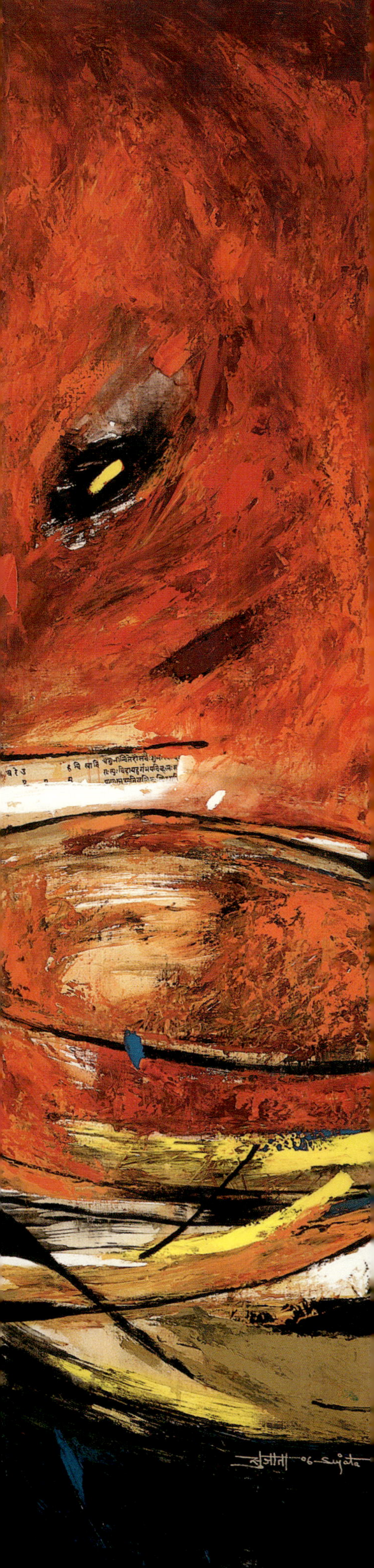

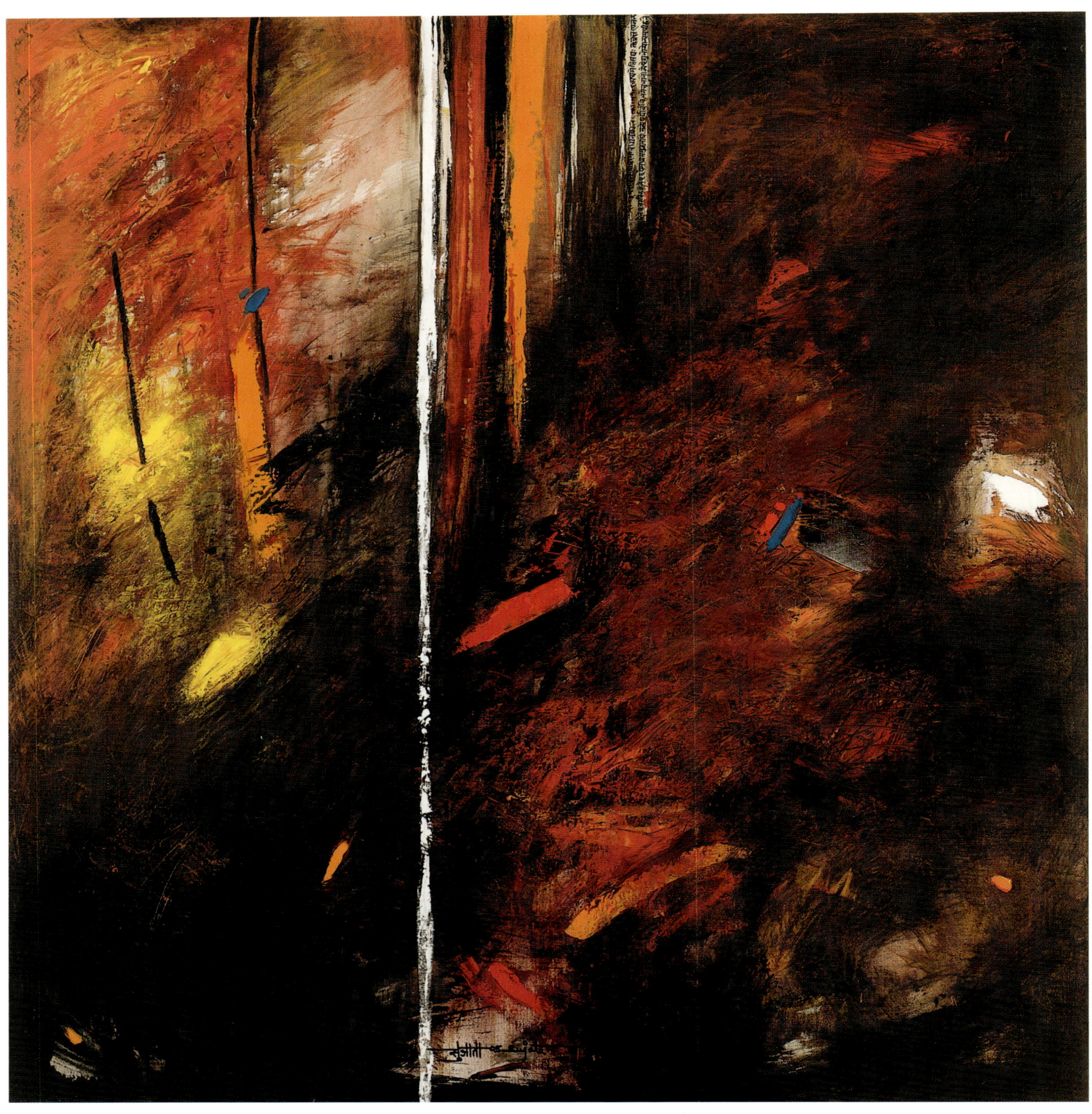

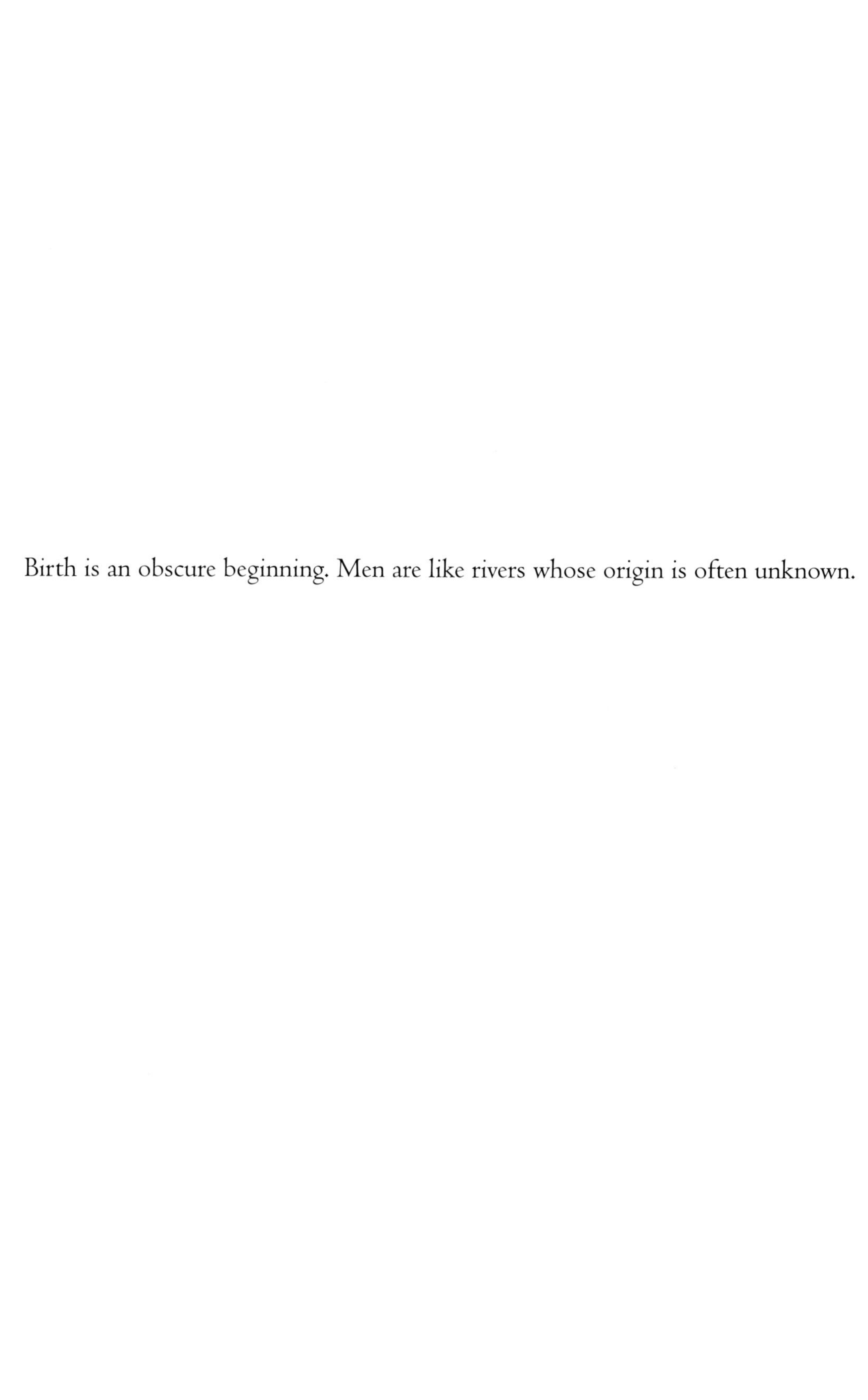

Birth is an obscure beginning. Men are like rivers whose origin is often unknown.

I see you. I see all the worlds in a single point.

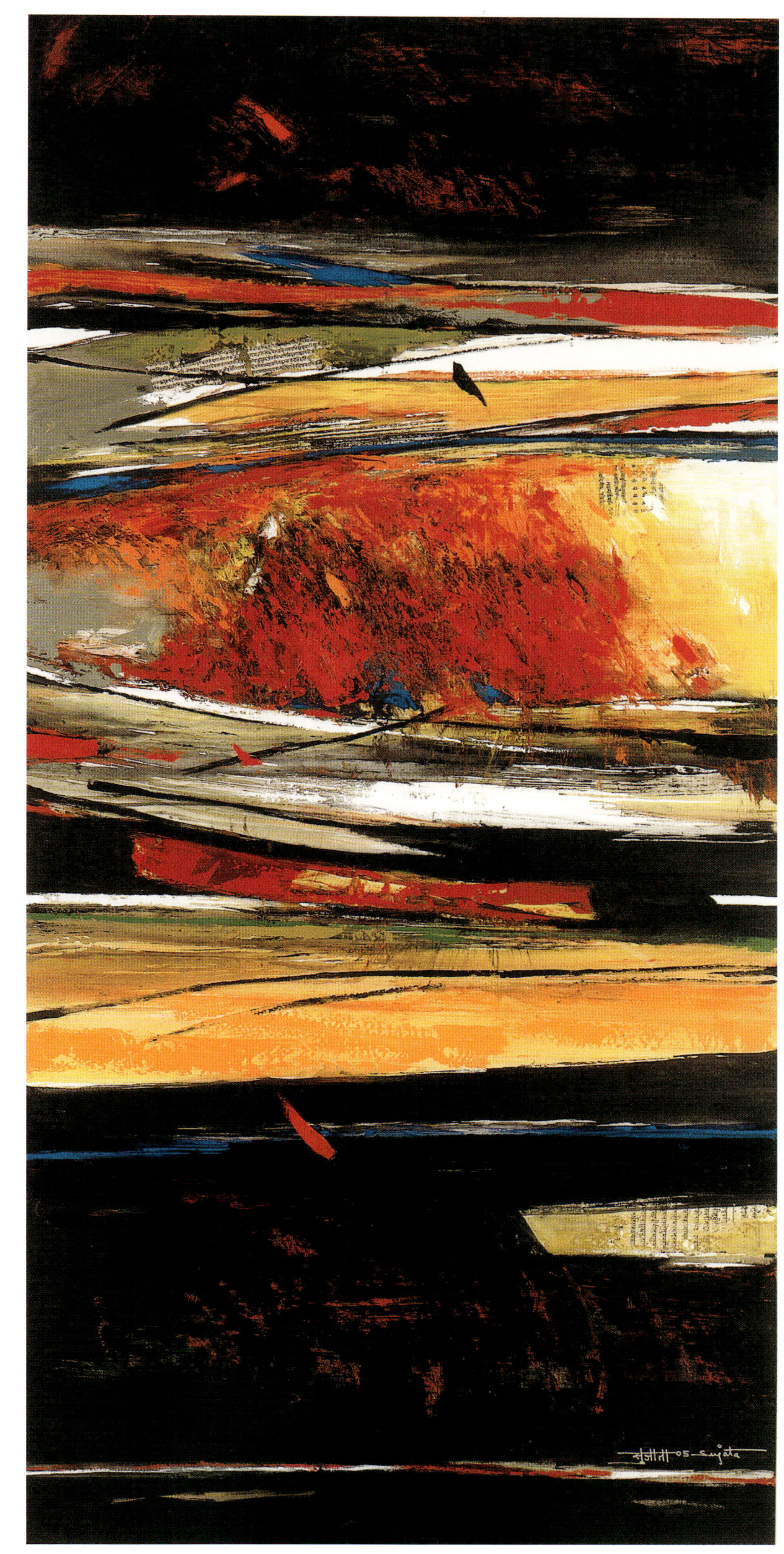
05 Sujata

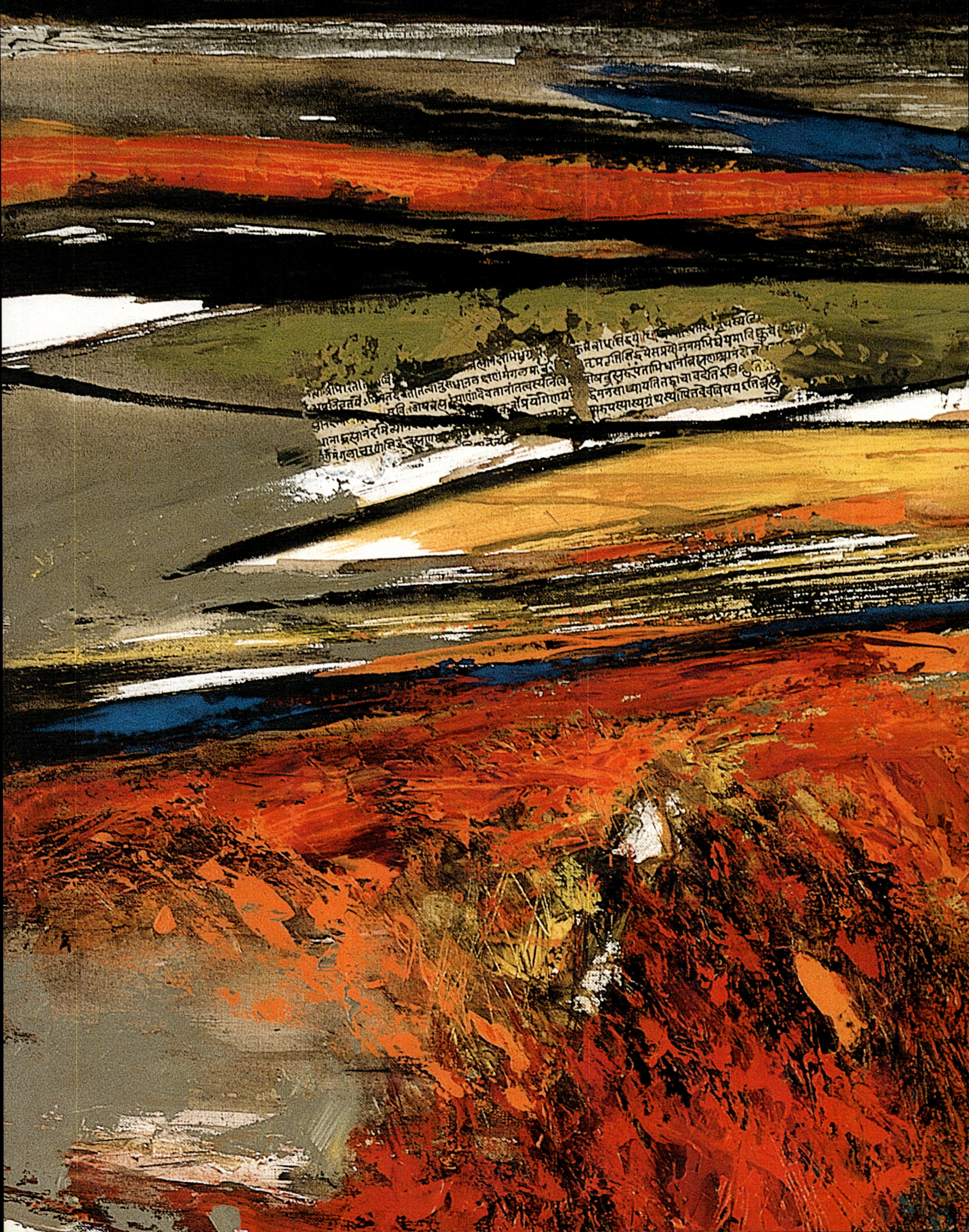

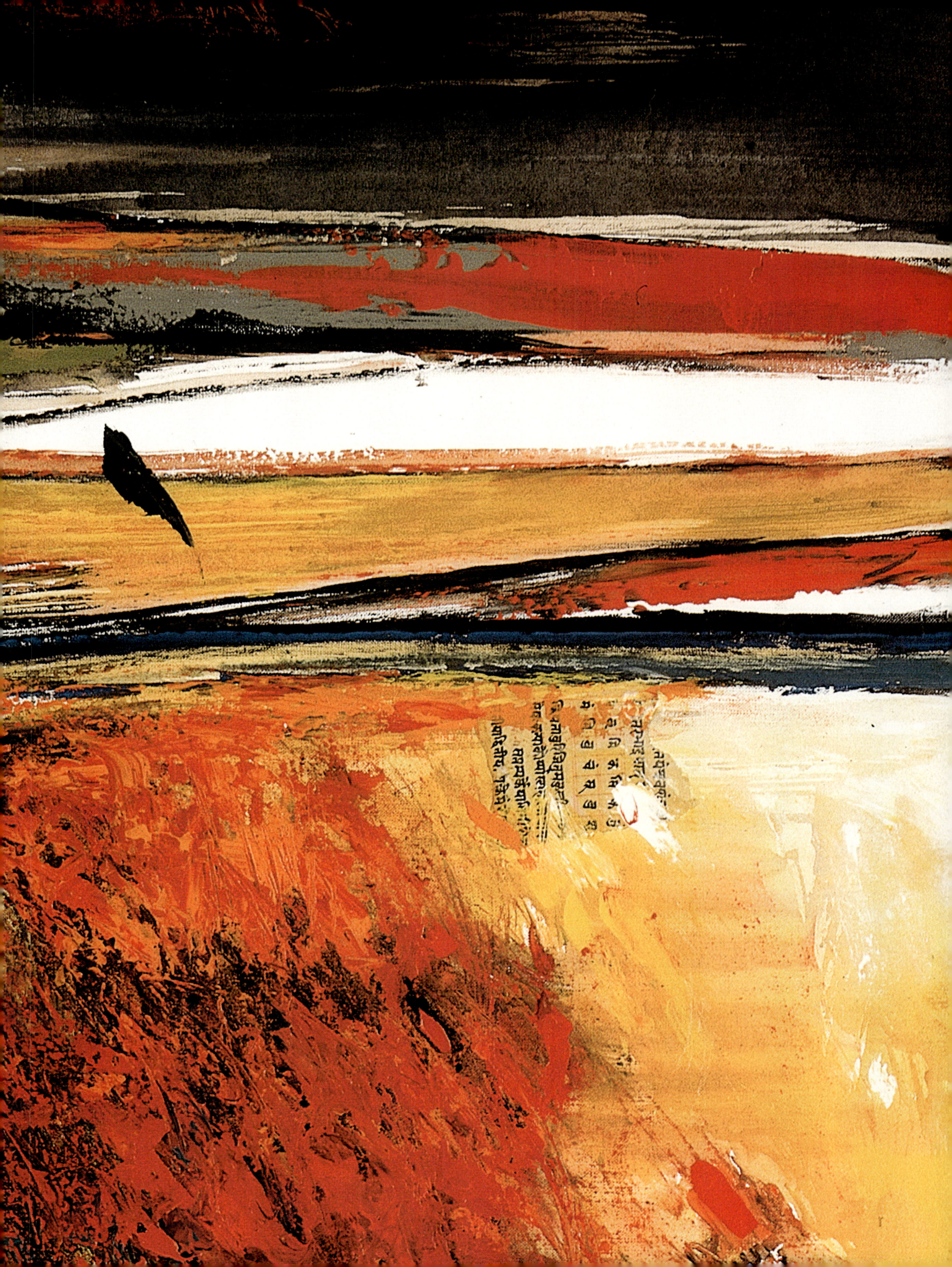

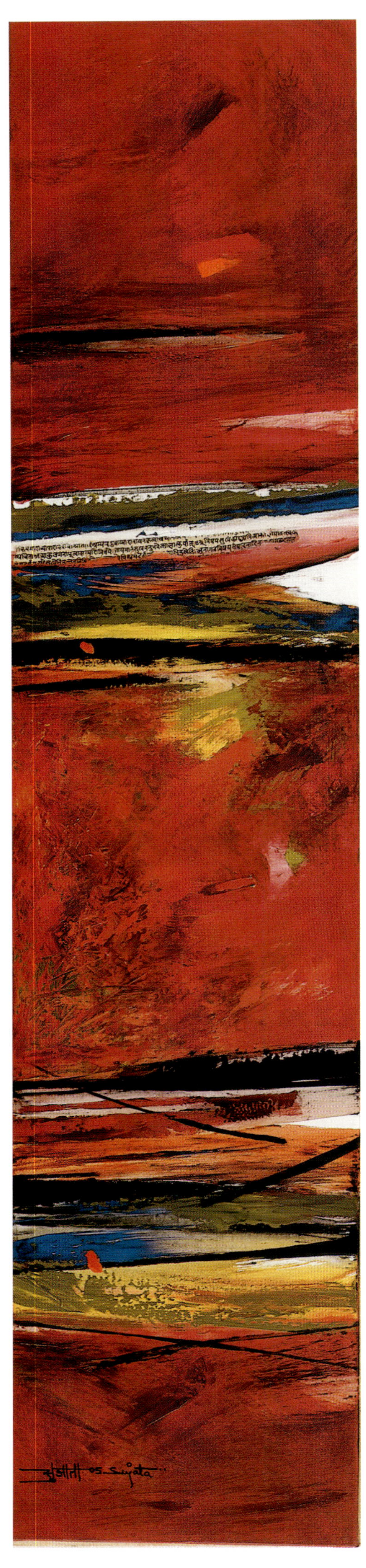

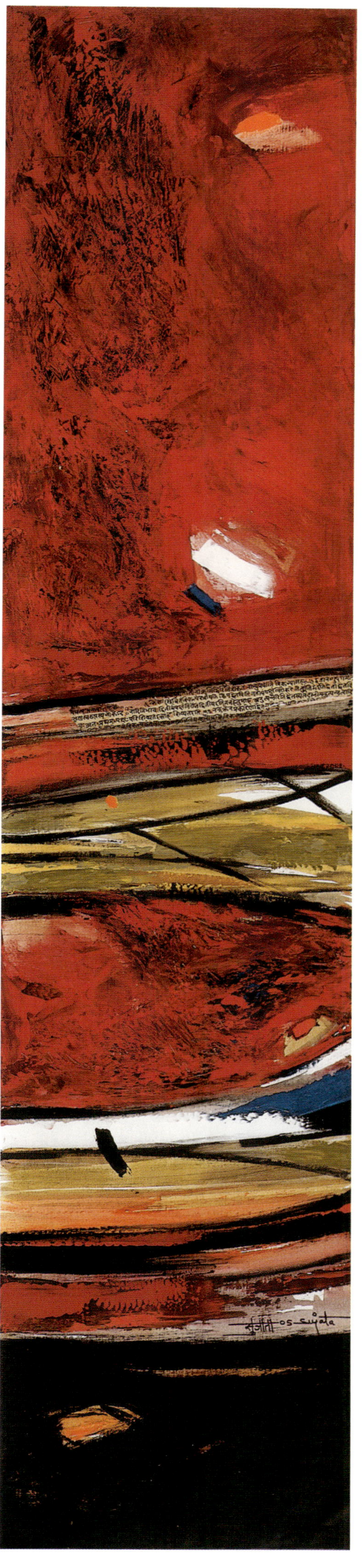

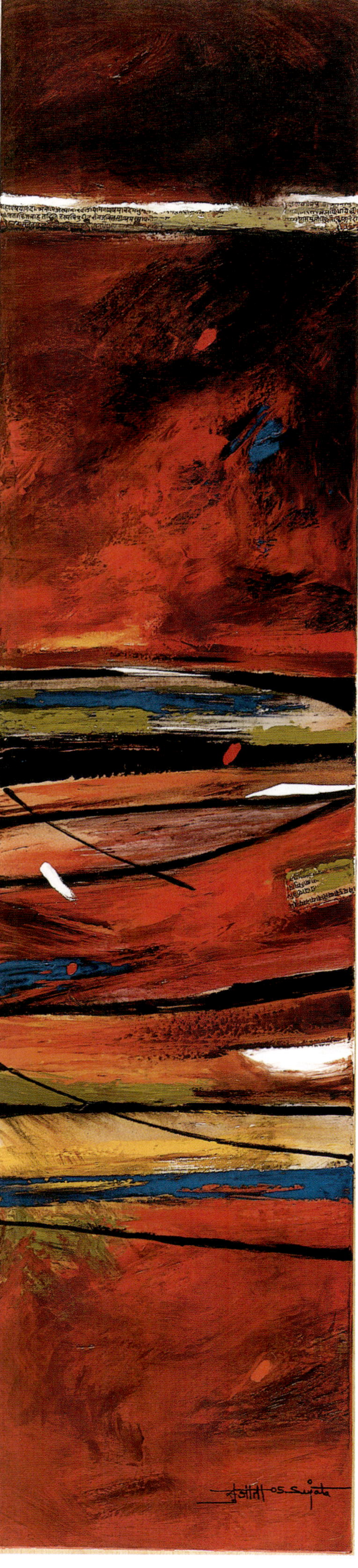

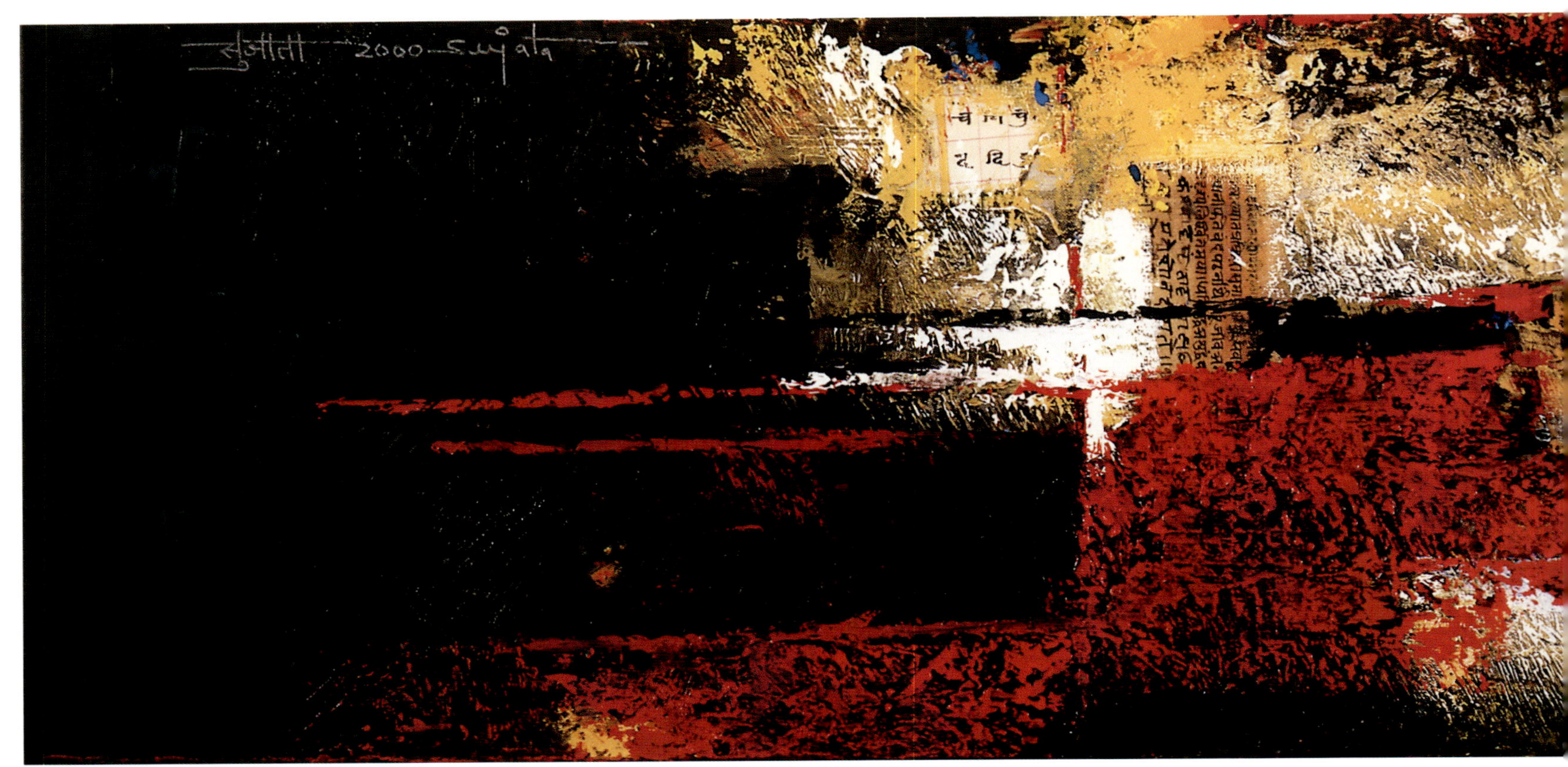

I say that death is negligence, that it is ignorance, that vigilance is immortality. Death is like a tiger hidden in the grass. We create children for death. But death does not devour the man who has shaken off its dust, it can do nothing against eternity. Wind and life come from infinity, the moon drinks the breath of life, the sun drinks the moon and infinity drinks the sun.

The wise man takes flight in the middle of worlds. When his body is destroyed, when no trace of him remains, it is death itself which is destroyed, and he contemplates infinity. I bid myself adieu and I see myself in all beings, I am all that has yet to become, I am the ancestor, I am space, the cause of my birth, I am the limit of everything, indefatigable, imperishable.

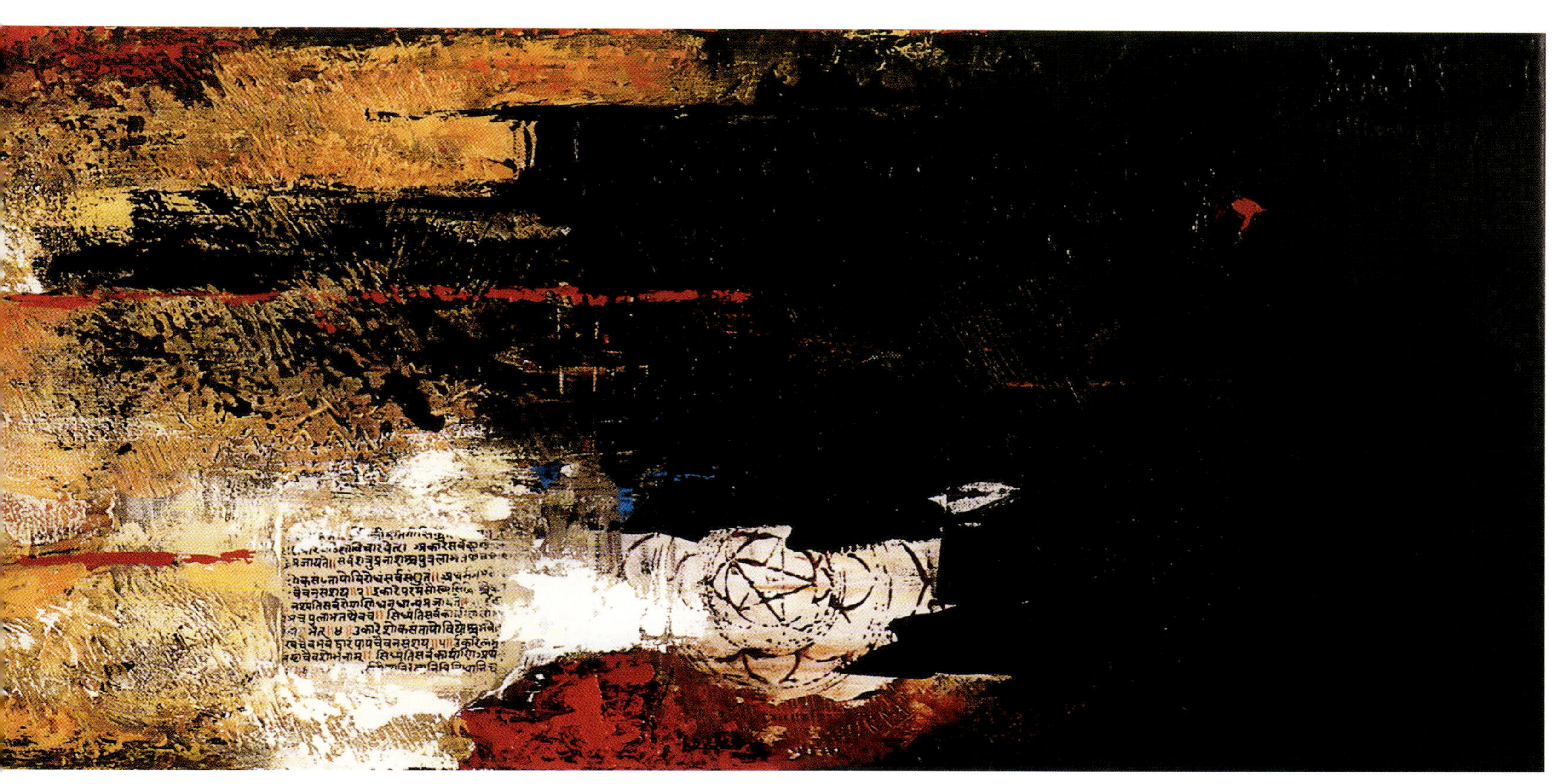

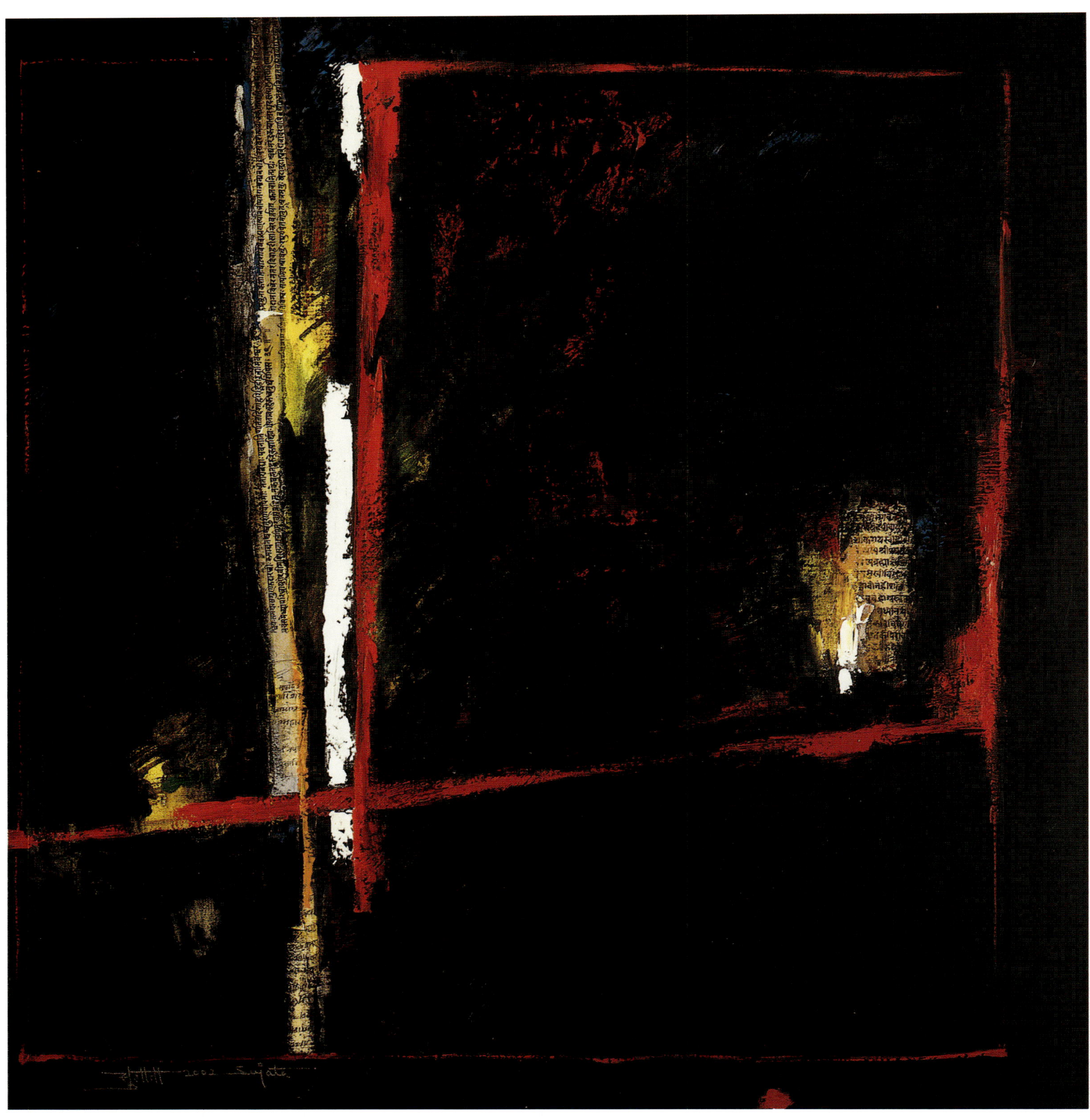

Long ago, all creatures had perished.
This world was nothing but sea, a grey, foggy, cold swamp.
Only an old man remained, spared by the destruction.
He was called Markandeya.

He walked in the glaucous water, exhausted. Nowhere could he find shelter or a living being; his spirit despaired and his throat was full of anguish. Suddenly, without knowing why, he turned around and saw a tree, a fig tree, looming in the marshy land, and at the foot of the tree was a beautiful, smiling child. Markandeya stopped, breathless, unsteady, not comprehending the presence of this child.

And the child said to him: "I see you are seeking repose, enter my body." And all of a sudden, the old man felt a great disdain for a long human life. As the child opened its mouth, a strong wind, an irresistible gale, rose, and Markandeya felt himself being drawn towards this mouth. Despite himself, his entire body entered it and he fell into the child's stomach.
Once inside, he looked around him and saw a brook, trees, a herd of cattle, he saw women carrying water, a city, streets, crowds, rivers; yes, in the child's stomach he saw the whole earth, beautiful and tranquil, he saw the ocean, the limitless sky.
He walked for a long time – for more than one hundred years without ever reaching the end of this body; then the wind rose again, he felt himself being sucked upwards, he emerged from the mouth of the child and saw him, once again, under the fig tree.

The child looked at him and smiled and said:
"I hope you are rested now".

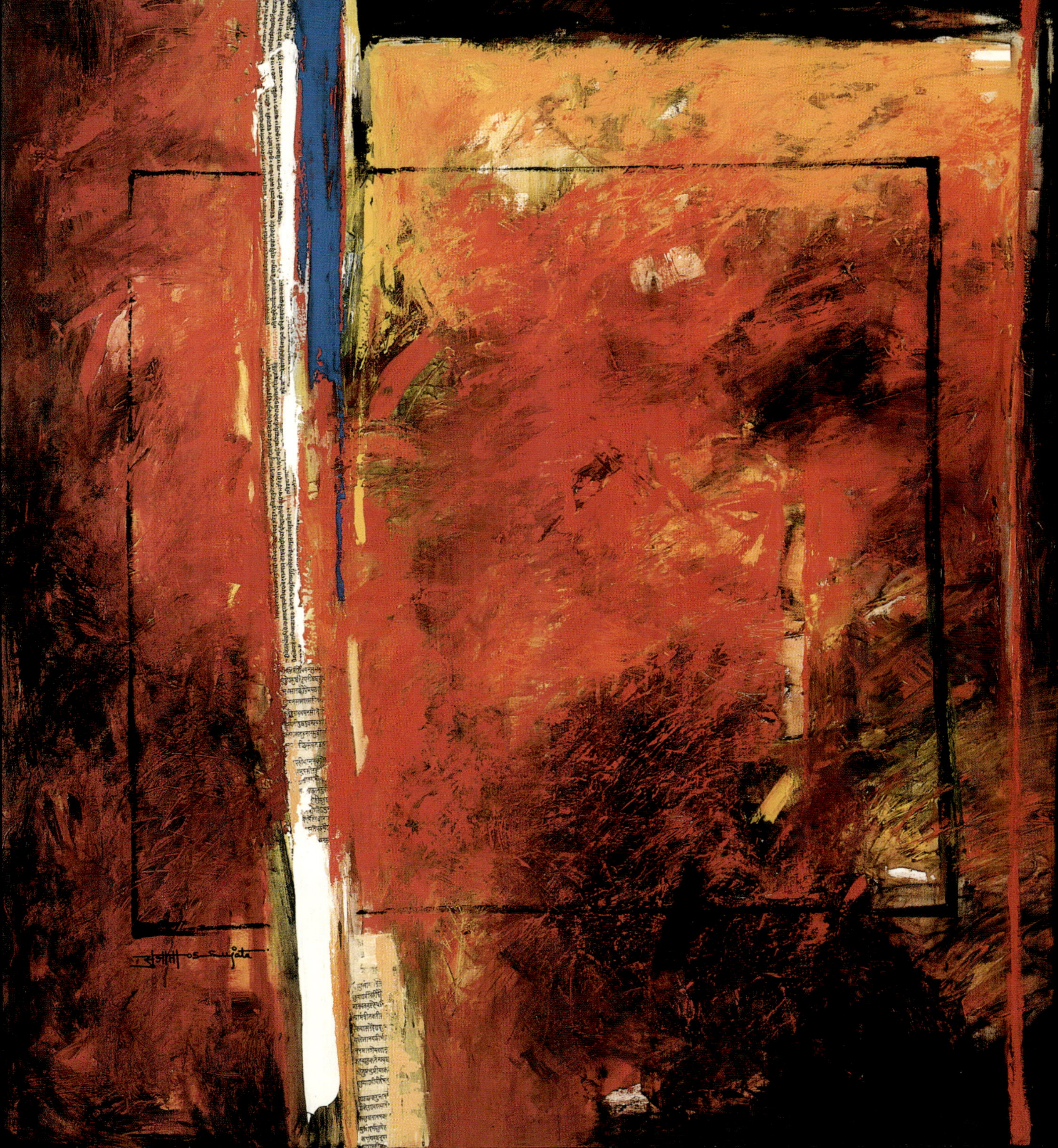

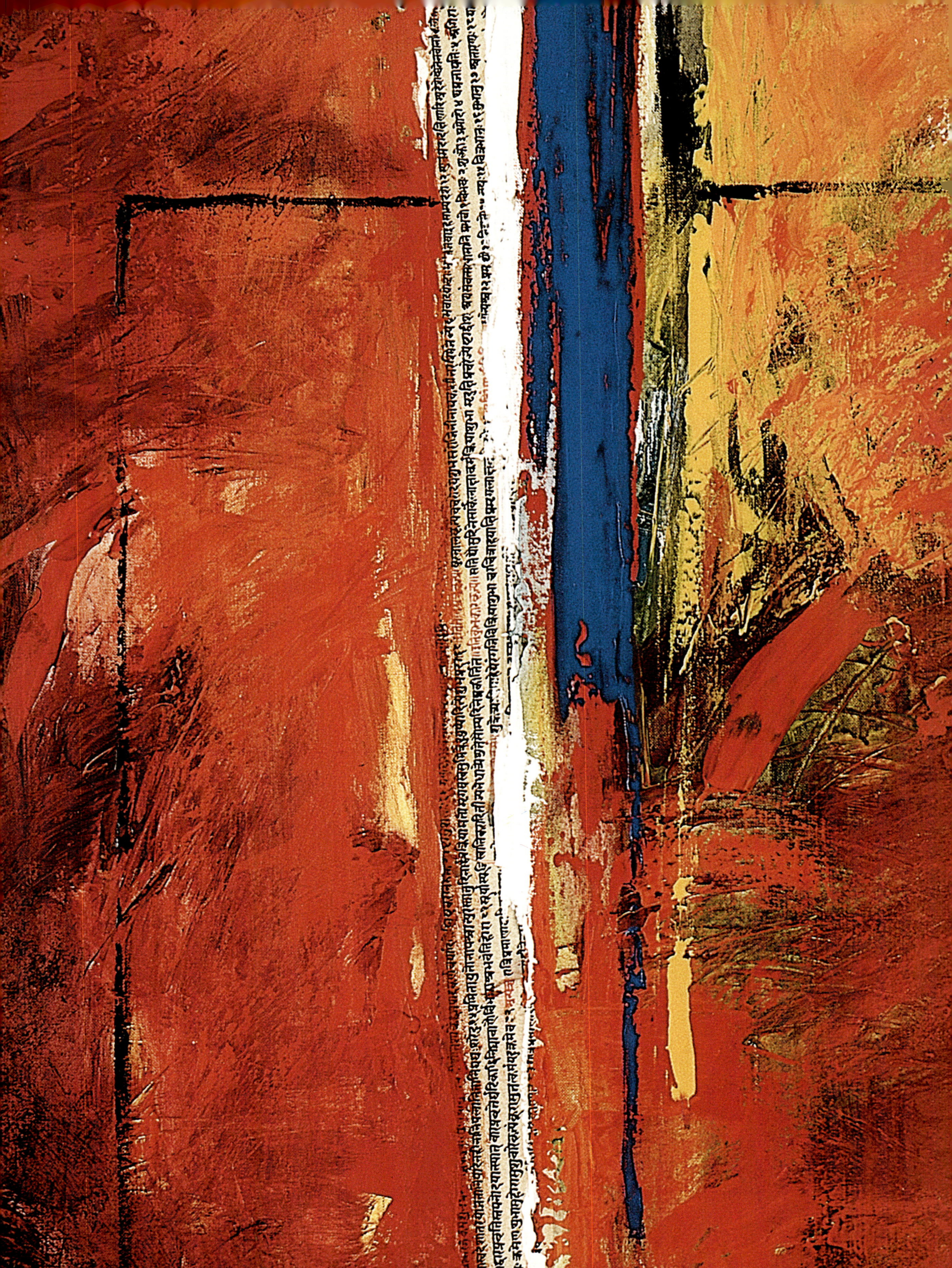

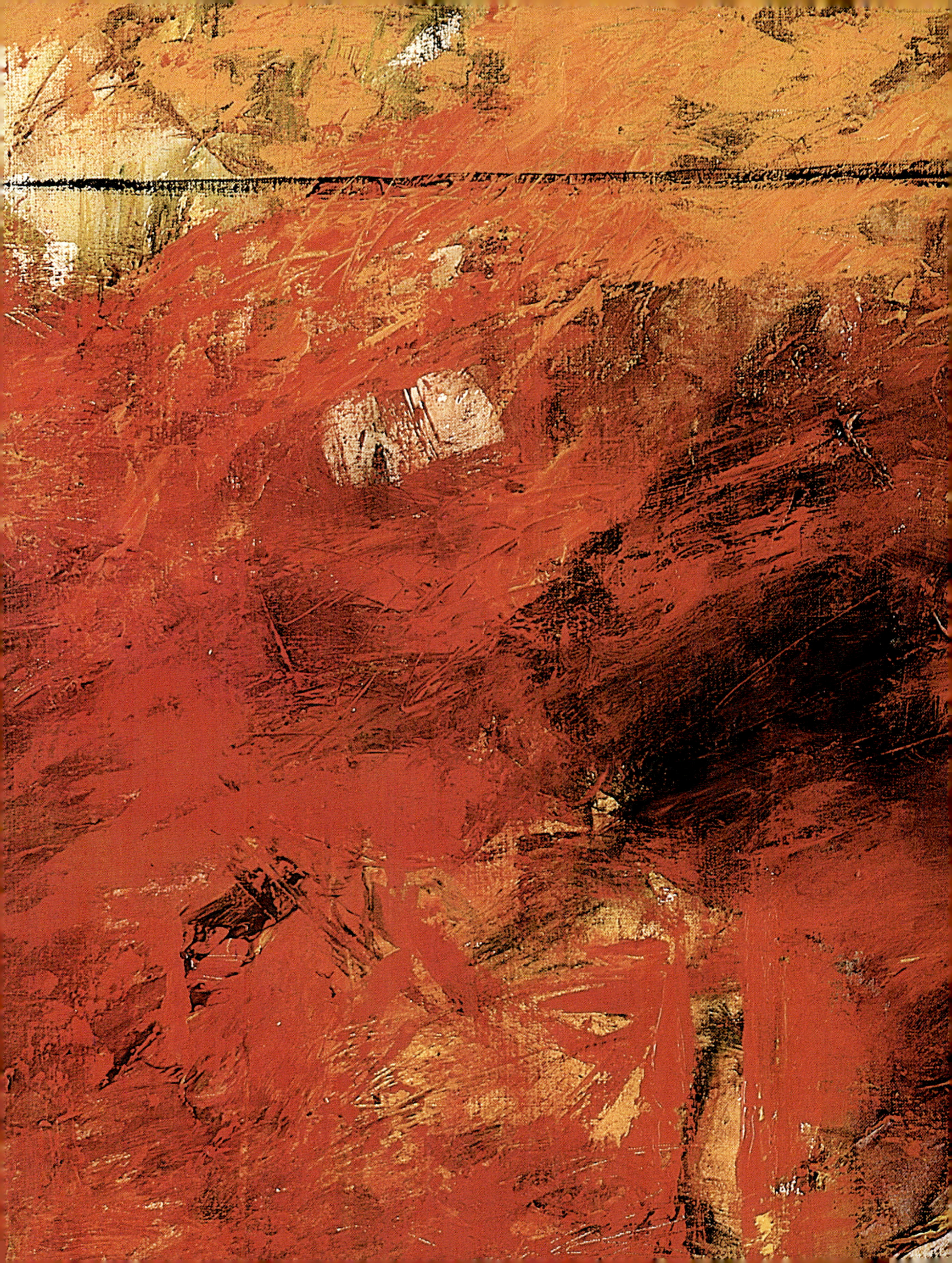

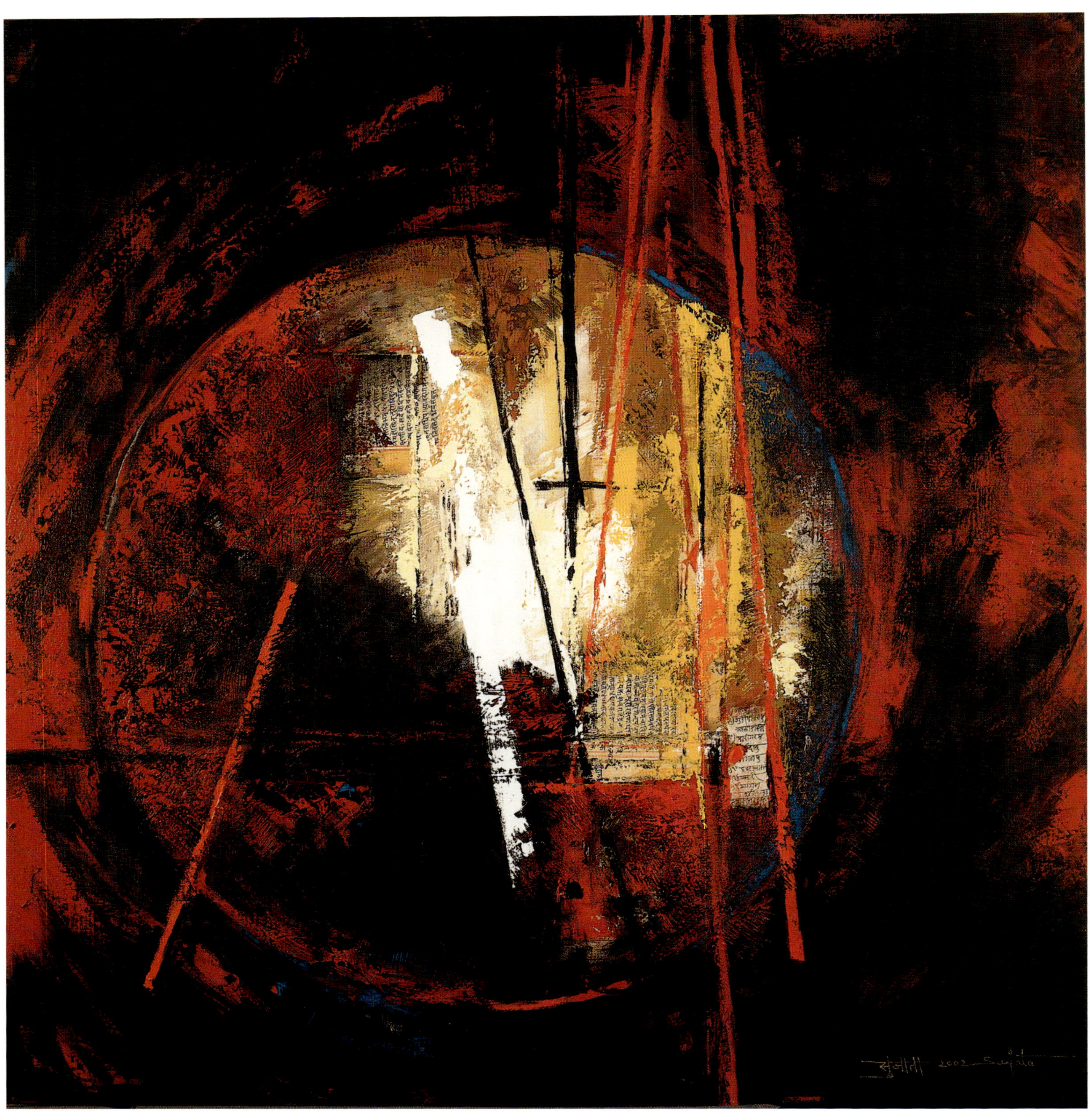

– What is inevitable for each one of us?
– Happiness.

सुजाता or Sujata.

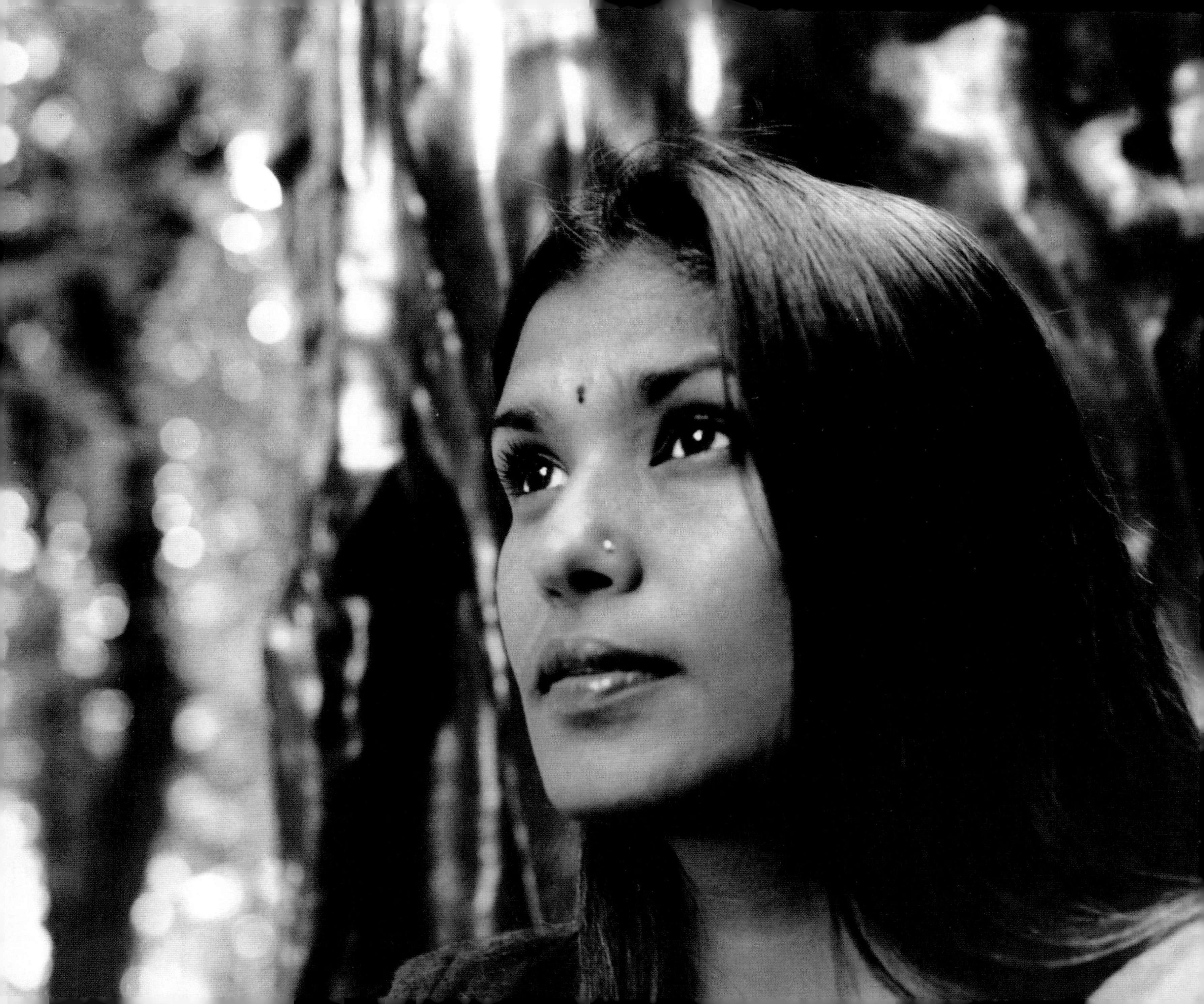

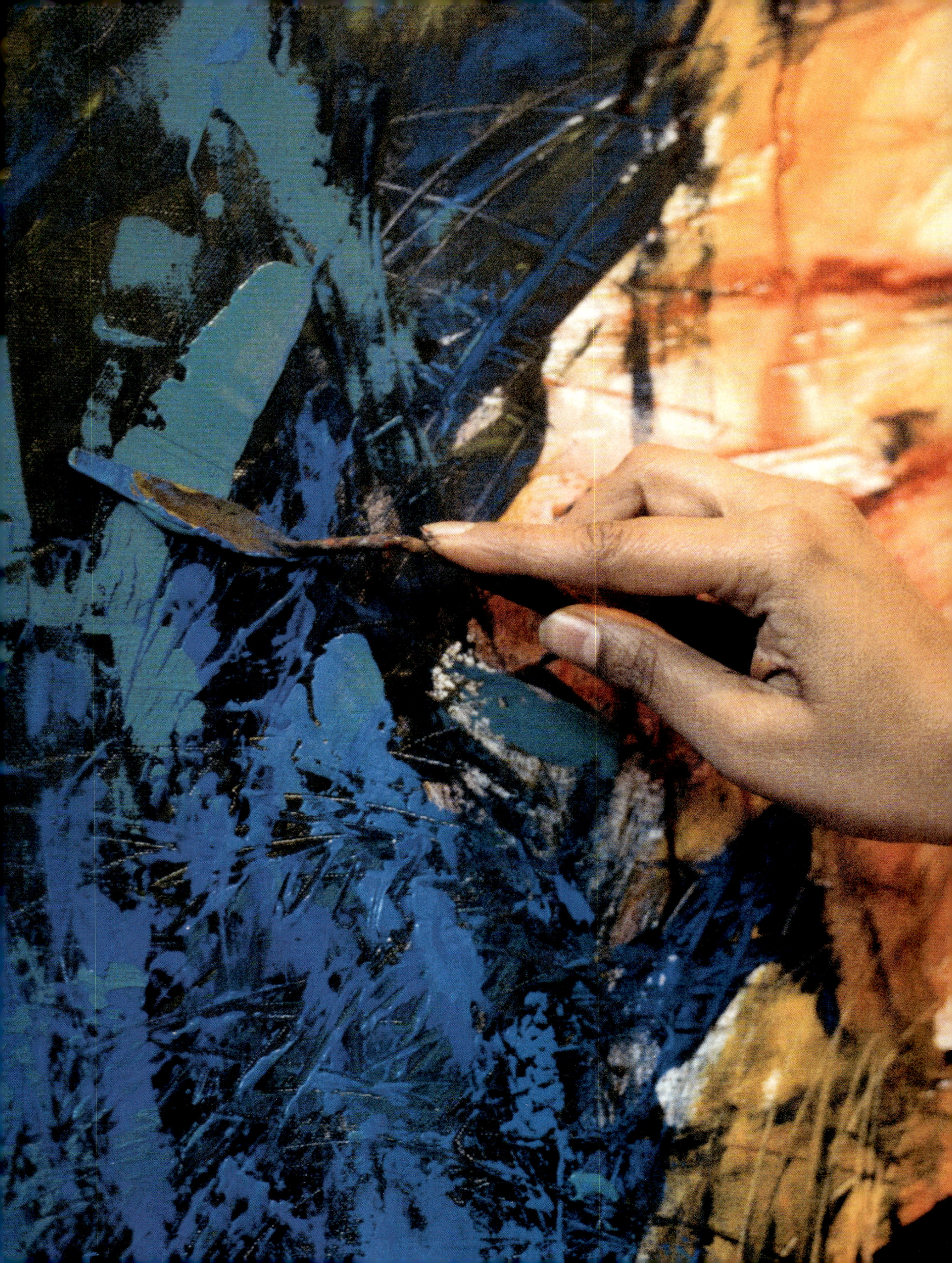

Sujata, an Explosion of Energy*

by *Lorette Nobécourt*

I remember having learnt at school a long time ago – but was it really all that long ago, and was it really in school? – that the whole is greater than the sum of its parts. A human being is much more than an accretion of events that makes up his or her life: birth, encounters, marriage, childbirth, sorrow, death. What, then, is a life? For long hours, I listened to Sujata Bajaj speak about her own. I learned of the events that have marked her. And yet, if it hadn't been for her paintings, what would I have known of her? Perhaps her paintings and her presence. Her presence, which speaks – as if in retreat, and in silence – of the passion and the quest that inhabits her; her presence, which speaks of what burns within her, and she seeks through colour – that which all of us seek with varying sets of tools. Sujata is connected to colour as if to an exceptional substance, she is nourished and enlivened by it. I understood this the last time I met her. I was about to leave when she said, with a touch of anxiety in her voice, "A colour must come alive, or else..." It seemed to convey to me, *in extremis*, the reason and the essence of her quest, as if she were suddenly afraid that all those hours spent in discussions came to nothing, because it is not all this – not all these biographical details and these events – that *really* make up her life. No. What lies at the root of her being is this need: "that colour must come alive, or else..." How clear was the urgency beneath these words, the hidden abyss behind "or else..." Or else, Sujata's life loses its *raison d'être*, is denuded of meaning; or else, life itself dies, emptied of substance. For Sujata, when a colour comes alive, life itself comes alive, yes, and the world is then a matrix of light and energy as reflected in her painting. Living colour is the freedom that spills over the frame of her canvas, the multiplicity that returns to the One; it is water making love to fire, the marriage of light and darkness, greater than all the sums of all the parts. For then, there is Being. And Sujata Bajaj is seeking just that.

"that colour must come alive, or else..."

An Indian Childhood

Is it because she comes from sacred India where the movement of Being is more manifest than elsewhere? Undoubtedly so. Sujata was born in Jaipur, the capital of Rajasthan, in 1958. Jaipur, the pink city that perhaps predestined Sujata to fuse with colour. Although she moved to Paris and spent five years in Stavanger in Norway, she never really separated from India. She has kept that millenial culture of service to others.

She is an Indian by the clothes she wears, the food she eats and by the way she paints, seated cross-legged on the floor. Through her window she sees the treetops and the sky. "It is a way of conserving a link to the earth," she says. It is also a way of meditating. "I forget everything." Isn't that the very principle of meditation – to move inwards, towards our core, towards Being? In all this, Sujata is quintessentially Indian, but she is even more so because of her childhood. Her father, Radhakrishna Bajaj, was close to Mahatma Gandhi. As someone committed to the cause from the very start, he – like Sujata's mother Anasuya – had renounced the idea of starting a family in order to better serve his country. It was Gandhi himself who noticed the two young people and brought them together.

She is an Indian by the clothes she wears, the food she eats and by the way she paints, seated cross-legged on the floor.

This is what he wrote to Sujata's mother on 25 January 1936:
"My dear Anasuya, I will not be present at your wedding. It will be impossible and I regret it deeply, but am helpless. Be an ideal wife; honour your religion and enhance the prestige of your country. Be assured that for you Radhakrishna is the best husband.
Blessings from Bapu[1]."

The same day he wrote to Radhakrishna Bajaj.
"My dear Radhakrishna, I will not be in Wardha for your wedding. It makes me very sad. It must be God's will. We can do nothing. The wishes I have sent Anasuya are meant for you as well. You cannot find a better wife than Anasuya. My faith tells me this. I have placed high hopes in your union, and you must realise them. With this letter I am sending you garlands[2] that I have blessed and woven with my own hands. Use them during the ceremony. I wish you a long life.
Blessings from Bapu."

An impressive collection of letters from Gandhi still lies in the drawers in Sujata's parents' home. Today, aged 101[3] and 88, they have spent their lives in the service of the country, defending its values of rigour, honesty and devotion, and transmitting them to their daughter. When Sujata's mother met Vinoba Bhave, the wise man who was to become the couple's spiritual guru, she was five years old.

Vinoba Bhave asked her why she was wearing such a colourful dress. Overnight, the little girl decided to wear only white as an expression of simplicity and continued to do so for the next 83 years, weaving her garments herself year after year. It is this kind of will-power that drives the Bajaj family.

"I didn't understand then how extraordinary my childhood was," says Sujata. "But yes, I had the feeling that I was receiving a lot. My parents moved around with the most unusual people. I remember in particular the philosopher Kakasaheb Kalelkar and many others. Whenever he came to our house, he would sit next to me and, before joining the others, would tell me a story. It was, in a way, his entry ticket, a little ritual between us; he had to tell me a story when he came in and when he left. My parents were incredibly open-minded. There was no question of any talk of caste in our house. All castes, all religions were welcome. I could as easily meet the Dalai Lama as eat at the home of my maid who was an untouchable. For us, the caste distinctions, which bog India down, did not exist. I did not have many toys or clothes. My life was very simple but very rich. I received a great deal from all those people."

And particularly so, since Sujata was the youngest among five siblings – sixteen years younger than her sister and twenty-one years younger than the eldest in the family. Surrounded by a swarm of relatives, hers was a special status, akin to being an only child. They have all contributed significantly, says Sujata, to what she has become.

"In India you often have to choose between freedom and emotional security, and I had the good fortune to enjoy both. My sister was like a second mother, and this gave me great strength."

"the one born under a lucky star"

Sujata was the name of the young girl who offered a bowl of milk and rice to the one who, upon awakening under the fig tree, became the Buddha, the enlightened one. "The one born under a lucky star" is what the name means. And indeed...

By the time Sujata was born, the bad memories linked to the family's political past were already fading. Her father had been to jail several times. He had even been condemned to death by the British authorities in the early 1940s in a case of false testimony. The intent was to destabilise Gandhi by attacking a close confidant. The execution was stayed at the eleventh hour, but Radhakrishna did serve a three-year term in jail. Those years were difficult for Sujata's mother, too.

She had to leave her marital house – which the authorities placed under seal – and move with her four children to her parents' home. And yet, Sujata does not recall any unpleasant word ever being uttered against the British by either of her parents. Her childhood was different from that of her brothers and sisters. *Ma* would often say to me: "when you were born we had electricity and fans at home; when you were born, all was well." *Ma.* You have to hear Sujata utter the word to understand how much the love and strength of her mother have helped to carry her forward and make her what she is today. It was her mother who noticed Sujata's love of drawing when her daughter was just three or four years old; it was she who encouraged Sujata to leave India and discover Paris and the museums of Europe. "Sujata, if your roots are solid, you can live anywhere," she would say. "Don't start comparing; take whatever is good wherever you are." And, again, it was she who accepted her daughter's independence in a country where women have often to submit to their fathers, then to their husbands and finally to their sons. "I couldn't think of getting married for social or financial reasons. For me, my husband also had to be a friend I could wholeheartedly count on. I wanted an equal relationship, in deed, not just in words." My mother said to me: "It will be difficult to find such a man." A few years later, when Sujata announced to her parents that she was going to marry Rune, a Norwegian, her father asked her just one question: "Are you sure of your love for him?" and her mother added: "Don't forget, life is like an artist's palette, it has all the colours."
But it is not only the sense of freedom that Sujata has inherited from her mother; she also has her father's stubbornness: a father she followed to the villages when he went there to serve the people. This man, who worked till he was 98, set an example for his daughter. Like him, she gave herself wholly to her art. "When you are strong from within," he would tell her, "when you believe in what you are doing, everything is possible, you can achieve anything."

"if your roots are solid, you can live anywhere"

The Discipline of Art

After completing her high school, Sujata left home to study fine arts in Pune, and received a gold medal upon finishing her first degree. She lived with her brother's family, and would continue to be with them for the next twelve years, dedicating herself to her passion and working up to eighteen hours a day.

When she did a portrait and was not satisfied with the result, she would compel herself to draw a head every day, refusing to eat until it was done. It is with the same resolve that she took to eating only grapes for ten days in September every year. "I don't like grapes, but this shapes my will."

In 1975, she was noticed by M.R. Kelkar, an artist and a professor of fine arts. Kelkar decided to help her. "He came with a thousand large-sized sheets of paper and six pencils, and said to me: 'You will draw vertical and horizontal lines till they are as straight as a ruler. I will come back in one month, and if they are not straight you will start all over again.' It took me three months, but I did it. It gave me freedom in my strokes." He was also the first to have *seen,* supported and encouraged her. "Sometimes, he would come at midnight to see my work, to know how I was progressing." After Sujata took the first prize in a University competition entitled "Composition with a folkloric symbol", Kelkar proposed to organise an exhibition of her works in one of the premier galleries of Pune. This was in 1978 and Sujata wasn't yet twenty. All those who had helped her were present at the opening. When the moment arrived for her to take the mike and speak, Sujata burst into tears of joy and emotion. That evening, tears and silence were her way of thanking life.

"in these tribes, art and life are so closely linked; they are integral to each other"

After obtaining a Masters in Fine Arts, Sujata decided to do a thesis in Indian tribal art – 'The Special Features of Indian Tribal Art and its Influence on Contemporary Trends of Art'. "I had followed my father to the villages. The pictures painted on the walls and floors fascinated me. Most of all, I loved to see how closely life and art mingled." For four years she travelled across India to study tribes, mainly the Madias-Murias of Bastar in Madhya Pradesh, the Bhils of Rajasthan, the Warlis of Maharashtra and the Saoras of Orissa. She followed their shamanistic rituals and discovered a different kind of rapport with the world. "I reached the first village after a 35-hour journey. They asked me what I was doing there. I told them I had come to study their art, but they replied that they didn't have any art. For a moment I thought I had come there for nothing. Then I entered a house to rest, and that's when I saw it! In these tribes, art and life are so closely linked; they are integral to each other. Birth, marriage, illness, death – all is linked. I saw people who lived with simplicity, without hypocrisy. I had to have a lot of patience, though; sometimes I needed four people to translate one simple sentence because their dialects are so difficult; but each moment of those four extraordinary years was enriching. I learned a great deal." The experience also gave her a taste for travel.

In order to analyse the influence of tribal art on contemporary art, she met several important artists. Among them was S.H. Raza who lives in Paris but visits India regularly. He was the second person after M.R. Kelkar to *see* the strength of her work. Sujata was then living in Pune. Raza pushed her to leave India and made her apply for a French Government scholarship. She applied, and obtained one in 1988. When she settled down in the International Cité Universitaire and enrolled in fine arts, Sujata was in love with Paris. It was Raza who met her at the Gare du Nord station and took her to Parisian cafés where the two discussed life and art for hours on end. "Raza played a very big role, he was like my guardian angel. Without him, I wouldn't ever have dreamt of going to Paris. When I arrived here, I didn't speak French, and yet I immediately felt at home. Paris was my city."

"Paris was my city"

The European Hour

Rune is as European as his wife is Indian. In 1988, when he was thirty-four, he was posted in Paris as the Director of the Maison de Norvège in the Cité Universitaire, and as the Cultural Attaché. Through his window, he would watch the Indians coming and going to the Maison de l'Inde located right in front. It was a country that baffled him, he was wary of it.

When he went to see an exhibition of seven international artists residing in the Cité Universitaire in June 1989, he did it more from a sense of duty than interest. To be sure, he liked painting, but he had never thought of buying a work. And yet, that's exactly what he did that day. As he entered the exhibition hall, he fell in love with one painting and with one painter. The painting was called *Struggle'* and the painter, Sujata Bajaj. He bought it instantly. "And I got the artist, too, for free!" he says. "She was magnificent, with her sari and her colours." Two years later, they got married in Paris, in the town-hall of the 14th district, with Raza as a witness. A short while later, the couple left for India to celebrate the event in the traditional way. Sujata's father wove garlands for the couple, just as Gandhi had done for him. "Sujata has remained very Indian. She wouldn't dream of living anywhere other than in her own country, and I couldn't see myself tearing

"it's enough to change your outlook on reality to transform it."

her away from it," says Rune. "So I married her country along with her." But the couple finally decided to live in France. Sujata continued her work; she discovered new techniques, especially the monotype with Claude Visieux at the studio Tanguy Garric workshop, which exposed her to new modes of expression.

In 1990 she was walking in the Marais neighbourhood with a friend. The two had emerged from a beautiful Parisian gallery on Rue Charlot, and Sujata was dreaming of just such a place to exhibit her work. She had already held exhibitions across India, but how should she go about it here, she wondered. At that moment, a woman came out of the gallery and accosted her on the sidewalk. Are you an artist? Yes, replied Sujata. Can I see your paintings? Of course. A few months later, Christine Marquet de Vasselot inaugurated a solo exhibition of Sujata in her gallery. Later, she presented her work in the Salon Découverte of the Grand Palais and in galleries outside France. Surely this was a lucky star shining on her, as her name suggests.

In 1994, even as Rune's diplomatic assignment came to an end, Sujata was pregnant. "I had always wanted a daughter, perhaps because of the close ties I had with my mother. I try to transmit what I have received. Helena has never hampered my work. On the contrary, she has given me plenty of energy. Becoming a mother nourished and inspired me. My daughter has always respected my hours of work and my space, even when she was small. She knows she mustn't disturb me when I am painting. She has an uncommon sense of colour. As a child she would tell me that blue and yellow go well together because they are like the sky and the sun." The little girl was born in July 1995. Rune had to return to Norway to continue with his work as a grammarian, and Sujata, despite her love for Paris and India, followed him.

The Norwegian years were lonely and harsh. "I am a vegetarian. I don't smoke, I don't drink. All the qualities which evoke admiration in India were misunderstood there. I found myself terribly isolated and alone. But I held on, thanks to the Indian in me. When you marry someone, you take what comes. And then, I have always believed in destiny. Without this faith, I wouldn't have succeeded in living there." She decided to snap out of her solitude by giving classes in vegetarian cooking. "It's enough to change your outlook on reality to transform it." And destiny followed. This rather cold country finally welcomed Sujata – both the woman and her work – in a way that quite exceeded her expectations.

"The beginning was difficult, but success did come." She held her first exhibition in 1993. Thereafter, her paintings were sold within the first hour of the opening of every exhibition. Norway's "Protestant and reserved" people – as Rune himself calls them – were enchanted by Sujata's energy and zeal. "I made a large number of friends. Now I go to Norway regularly where I have a studio and a gallery. I work there with as much pleasure as I do in Paris or India."
Thanks to some research work in 2001, Rune got an opportunity to spend another year in Paris. "Rune had a dream. He dreamed of living between Boulevard Montparnasse and the Luxembourg Gardens," says Sujata, "and I wanted to live in Paris too. This city fills me with an indescribable sense of happiness. I love almost everything here." Rune's contract was renewed year after year, till he finally had to return to Norway. The family, however, decided to settle in the French capital on Boulevard Raspail. Rune divides his time between Norway and France. Sujata flies regularly to Stavanger and Mumbai, and their daughter is growing up speaking French, English, Hindi and Norwegian.

It is autumn now, Sujata's favourite season. "Not only because of the colours, but because the simple fall of a leaf is reason enough to make a big painting." Sujata works every day, seated on the ground, in her white and sparse apartment that is in complete contrast to the colour and profusion of her canvases. Her white cat, Nicy, is at her side, even up to two in the morning. It never scratches or paws at the work in progress, but simply accompanies it. Sujata is preparing exhibitions around the world – in Paris, Mumbai, New Delhi, Tokyo, London and Hong Kong, working with acrylic "which allows for spontaneity," or with mixed technique on paper. At night she dreams of painting, of a stroke she needs to modify here or there, of harnessing – to use her husband's expression – this "overflow of energy" that fires her. She does, quite simply, what she has to do: to make colour come alive.

1. Gandhi was affectionately called Bapu in India.

2. During the marriage ceremony, the couple traditionally exchange garlands.

3. Sujata's father died on 15th May, 2007.

* Lorette Nobécourts' text was written after three interviews with Sujata Bajaj.

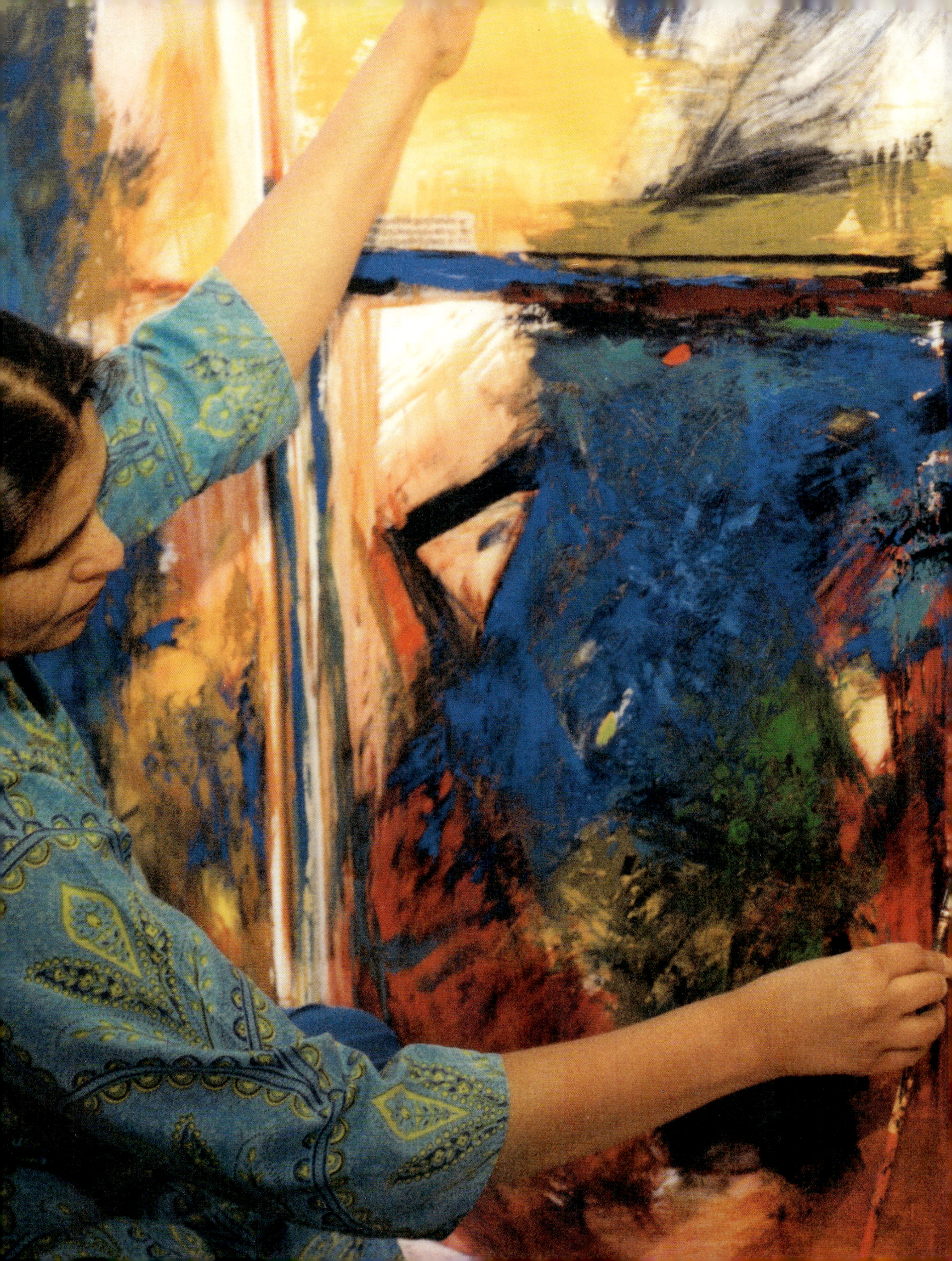

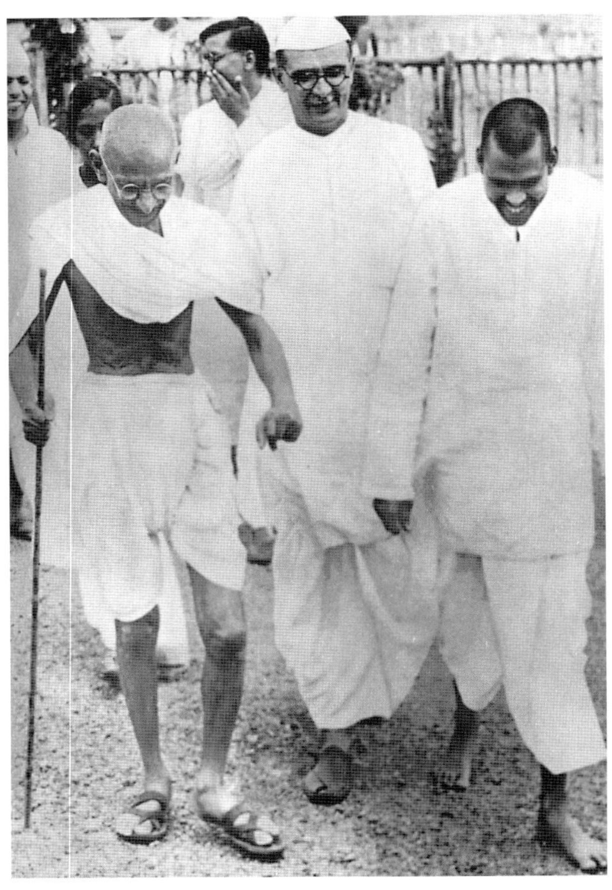

Mahatma Gandhi and Sujata Bajaj's father (on the right).

In the front row, from left to right:
Sujaja's father, Sujata sitting on Dhebar Bhai's lap, Jaiprakash Naryan and his wife, Sujata's mother.
Behind, from left to right:
Sujata's three brothers, Gautam, Ashok and Dileep, and her sister Nanda.

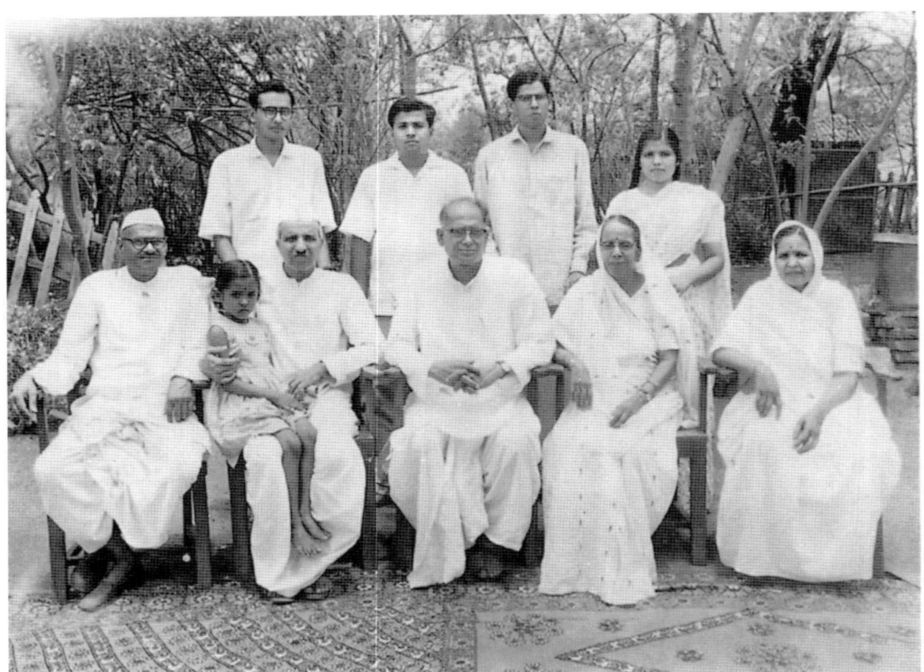

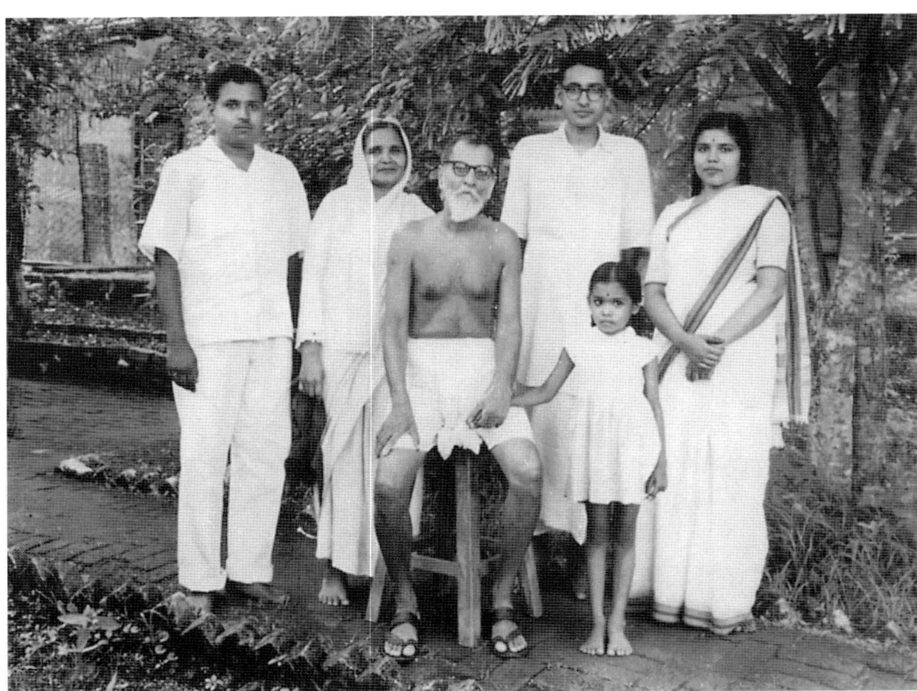

Ashok, Sujata's mother, Vinoba Bhave holding Sujata's hand, Gautam, Nanda.

Radhakrishna and Anasuya Bajaj, Sujata's parents.

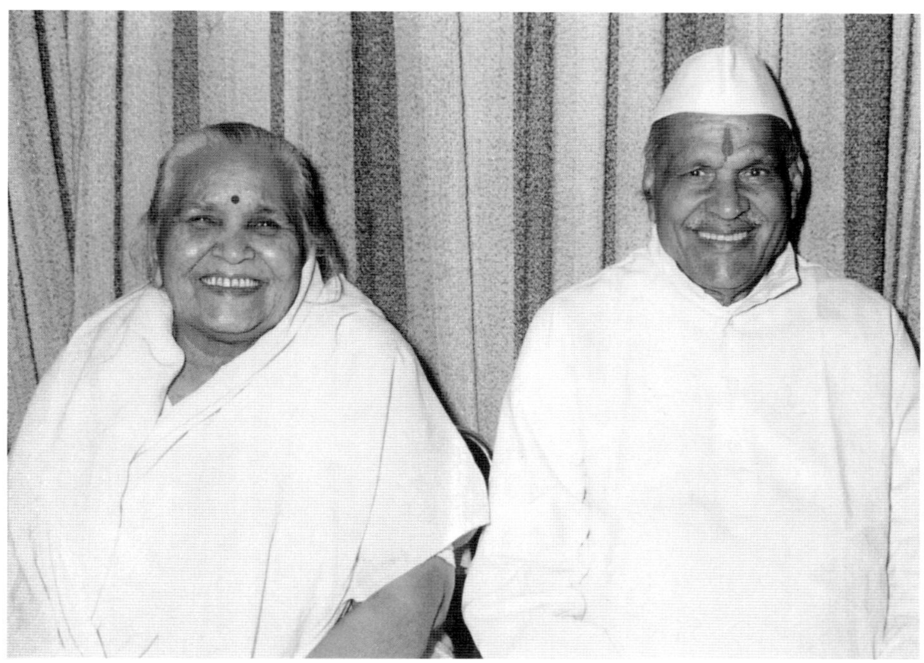

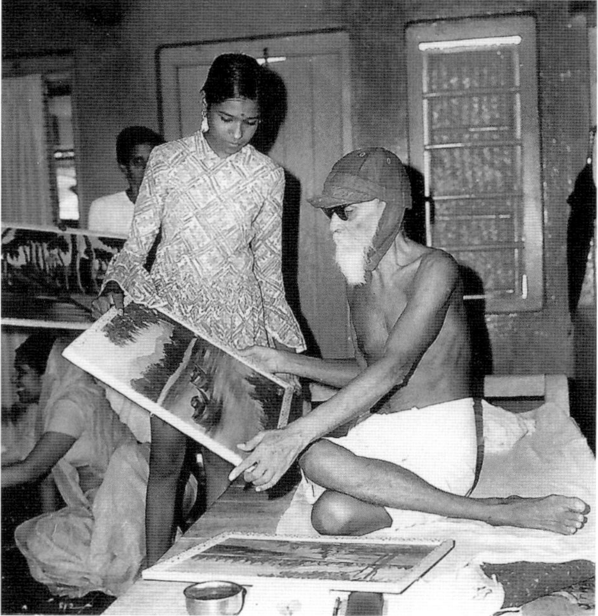

Sujata as a teenager: Vinoba Bhave admires one of her paintings.

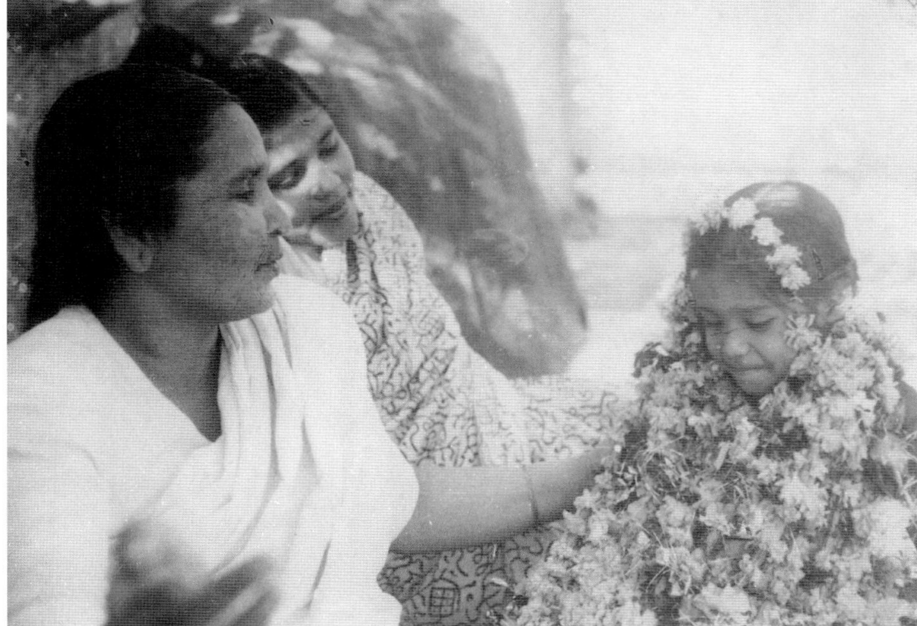

Sujata as a child, adorned with flowers from the garden, watched over lovingly by her mother and sister.

The artistic career of Sujata Bajaj

Awards

1979 Chancellor's Award, S.N.D.T. University, Mumbai.
1979, 1984 State Art Award, Maharashtra.
1982 Outstanding Young Person of Pune.
1983 Outstanding Young Person of Maharashtra.
1985 Painting selected for inclusion in the National Collection.
1986 Best painting award, Nasik Kala Niketan.
Selected for International Youth in Achievement, Cambridge.
1991 Bombay Art Society Award.
2003 "Raza Award".

International solo exhibitions

1988 Commonwealth Art Gallery, Edinburgh, U.K.
Mac-Robert Art Centre, University of Stirling, U.K.
American Cultural Society; Washington, USA.
1989 Centre d'accueil des étudiants du Proche-Orient, Paris, France.
Galerie Jean-Louis Voisin, Pourville-sur-Mer, France.
Galerie Bernanos, Ministère de l'Éducation nationale, Paris, France.
1991, 1994 Galerie Christine Marquet de Vasselot, Paris, France.
1992, 1993, 1995, Galerie Art & Data, Frankfurt, Germany.
1993 Maison de Norvège, Paris, France.
1993, 1997, 2000, 2003 Galleri Nordstrand, Oslo, Norway.
1994 Galerie Argile, Brussels, Belgium.
1998 Galerie Mohanjeet, Paris, France.
Galleri Akern, Kongsberg, Norway.
1999 Stavanger kunstforening, Norway.
Atlantic Gallery, New York, USA.
2000 Varatun Gard, Stavanger, Norway.
2001 Galleri Tendenes, Stavanger, Norway.
2002, 2004, 2005, 2006 Galleri Sult, Stavanger, Norway.
2004 Galerie Art & Littérature, Paris, France.
2007 Osborne Samuel-Berkeley Square Gallery, London, U.K.

Solo exhibitions in India

1978, 1980, 1982, 1984, 1985, 1987 Bal Gandharva Art Gallery, Pune.
1979, 1987 Kamalnayan Bajaj Art Gallery, Mumbai.
1979, 1980, 1984, 1989, 1992, 1996, 2000 Jehangir Art Gallery, Mumbai.
1982 Academy of Fine Arts, Calcutta.
1985, 1995, 2002 Triveni Kala Sangam, New Delhi.
1986 Taj Art Gallery, Mumbai.
1987 Karnataka Chitra Kala Parishath, Bangalore.
1988 Sarala's Art Centre, Chennai.
1991 Birla Academy, Calcutta.
1991, 1993, 1995, 2002 Apparao Gallery, Chennai.
2005 Chemould Art Gallery, "Fire and Water", Mumbai.
2006 Gallery Art Musing, "Transcendence", Mumbai.
2007 Gallery Art & Soul, "Sublimation", ceramic creations, Mumbai.
Palette Art Gallery, New Dehli.
Tao Art Gallery, Mumbai.

Selected for international Exhibitions

1988 L'Exposition de Peinture Contemporaine Indienne, Tarbes, France.
1989 Galerie de la Maison des Beaux-Arts, Paris, France.
Galerie du Cygne, "Artistes indiens à Paris", Paris, France.
1989, 1990, 1991 "Salon Art en Bray", Neufchâtel-en-Bray, France.
1989 Galerie Bernanos, "La Société Plurielle Égalitaire", Paris, France.
C.I.U.P, "Neuf Artistes de la Cité Universitaire", Paris, France.
"Salon de mai", Grand Palais, Paris, France.
1991 New York Art Fair, USA.
Salon des Indépendants Normands, France.
1992 Galleri Bryggen, Bergen, Norway.
Galerie Christine Marquet de Vasselot, Paris, France.
University of Frankfurt, Germany.
Salon "Découvertes", Grand Palais, Paris, France.
1993 "Contemporaines", Grand Palais, Paris, France.

1994 Ausstellung Indische Kunst, Frankfurt, Germany.
1995 UNESCO, Paris, France.
1996 Within the Frame Visual Art Centre, Hong-Kong.
1998 "50 years of independence", Hong-Kong.
"Indian Spring", Hong-Kong.
2001 "Indian Contemporary Fine Art", Los Angeles, USA.
2002 "Art Singapore 2002", Singapore.
"Cinq peintres indiens en France", Boulogne-Billancourt, France.
2003 UNESCO, "L'eau", Paris, France.
2004 Espace Auteuil, Comparaisons, Paris, France.
"Regard sur la peinture indienne contemporaine", Gorbio, France.
2005, 2006, 2007 Art Miami, Art Palm Beach, Florida, USA.
2005 Gallery ArtsIndia, "S.H. Raza and Sujata Bajaj", New York, USA.
Gallery ArtsIndia, "S.H. Raza and Sujata Bajaj", Palo Alto, CA, USA.
2005, 2006, 2007 Tate Britian, "Event Show", London, U.K.
2006 Art Space, Dubai, Hong-Kong.
Bodhi Art Gallery, "Roop Adhyatma", Singapore.
2007 "The Power of Peace", United Nations in Bali, Indonesia.
The Ueno Royal Museum of Modern Art, Tokyo, Japan.
London Art Fair, U.K.

Selected for Exhibitions in India

1978 to 1988 Lalit Kala Akademi, Bombay Art Society, Nasik Kala Niketan, State Art Exhibitions, Hyderabad Art Society, All India Exhibitions of Fine Art.
1989 Lalit Kala Galleries, "Indian Eclectics", New Delhi.
1993 Lalit Kala Galleries, "Souvenirs d'en France", New Delhi.
1998-1999 "White on White", New Delhi and Mumbai.
1999 Gallery Seven, "S.H. Raza and Sujata Bajaj", Mumbai.
2003 "Book 7", Bangalore, Chennai, New Delhi and Mumbai.
Tao Art Gallery, "Peace", Mumbai.
Gallery Guild, "S.H. Raza and Sujata Bajaj", Mumbai.
Apparao Gallery, "Tie Exhibition", Bangalore, Calcutta, Chennai, New Delhi and Mumbai.
"Torsormative Texture", Mumbai.
2003-2004 Gallery Art Musing, Mumbai.
2004 Gallery 88, Calcutta.
Saffronart and the Guild, "Generation", Mumbai.
Apparao Gallery, Chennai, Delhi and Mumbai.
Tao Art Gallery, "Sacred Space", Mumbai.
The Fine Art Resource, "Anticipations", Mumbai.
2005 Visual Arts Gallery, Habitat Centre, "Papermark", New Delhi.
Tao Art Gallery, "Roop Adhyatma", Mumbai.
Gallery Art Alive, "Roop Vidhan", New Delhi.
2006 Palette Art Gallery, "Roop Adhyatma", New Delhi.
Galleria, "Sensuality", New Delhi.
2007 Sanskriti art Gallery, "Tale of two Cities", Calcutta.
Tao Art Gallery, "Power of Peace", Mumbai.

Talks on Tribal Art

1988 George Washington University, Washington DC, USA.
Princeton University, Princeton, USA.
American Cultural Society, Washington, USA.
London and Hartland, U.K.
Commonwealth Centre, Edinburgh, U.K.
1989 Centre d'accueil des étudiants du Proche-Orient, Paris, France.
1990 Mandapa, Paris, France.
Ulster University, Belfast, U.K.
1991 École nationale des Beaux-Arts, Paris, France.

Table of reproductions

Mixed Media

pages 82-83
Water, 2006, 50 x 100 cm
(detail from page 84)

pages 84-85
Water, 2006, 50 x 100 cm

page 87
Water, 2005, 47 x 47 cm

pages 88-89
Water, 2005, 47 x 47 cm
(detail from page 87)

page 90
Energy, 2002, 46 x 46 cm

pages 92-93
Energy, 2002, 46 x 46 cm
(detail from page 90)

page 94
Energy, 2003, 75 x 30 cm

page 95
Energy, 2003, 75 x 30 cm

page 96
Water, 2004, 100 x 50 cm

page 97
Water, 2004, 100 x 50 cm

pages 98-99
Water, 2004, 100 x 50 cm
(detail from page 96)

page 101
Water, 2004, 32 x 30 cm

page 102
Water, 2004, 75 x 30 cm

page 103
Water, 2004, 75 x 30 cm

page 104
Water, 2004, 100 x 50 cm

page 106
Energy, 2002, 75 x 30 cm

page 107
Rain Drop (*Goutte d'eau, Boond*), 2003,
30 x 32 cm

page 108-109
Energy, 2002, 75 x 30 cm
(detail from page 106)

page 111
Energy, 2003, 71 x 71 cm

page 112
Space, 2003, 75 x 15 cm (détail)

Second fold-out page
Space, 2003, 75 x 15 cm
Celebration, 2006, 80 x 280 cm

Acrylics on canvas

page 113
Songe, 2006, 130 x 130 cm

pages 114-115
Songe, 2006, 130 x 130 cm (detail)

page 116
Ascent, 2006, 150 x 35 cm

pages 118-119
Éclat, 2007, 100 x 100 cm (detail)

page 120
Éclat, 2007, 100 x 100 cm

pages 122-123
Noces du clair et de l'obscur,
2005, 100 x 130 cm

pages 124-125
Horizon, 2006, 80 x 280 cm

page 127
Eruption, 2004, 120 x 120 cm

pages 128-129
Radiance, 2005, 50 x 50 cm (detail)

page 131
Radiance, 2005, 50 x 50 cm

pages 132-133
Enigma, 2007, 100 x 200 cm

page 135
Désir, 2006, 130 x 130 cm

page 136
Beyond, 2006, 100 x 100 cm

pages 138-139
Beyond, 2006, 100 x 100 cm (detail)

page 141
Esperance, 2006, 100 x 100 cm

page 143
Joie de vivre, 2006, 100 x 100 cm

pages 144-145
Joie de vivre, 2006, 100 x 100 cm (detail)

page 146
Ascent, 2005, 150 x 35 cm

page 147
Ascent, 2005, 150 x 35 cm (detail)

page 148
Enigma, 2006, 100 x 100 cm

page 151
Songe, 2006, 130 x 130 cm

pages 152-153
Traversées, 2006, 80 x 150 cm

page 154
Ange gardien, 2006, 150 x 35 cm (detail)

page 155
Ange gardien, 2006, 150 x 35 cm

page 156
Espérance, 2005, 100 x 100 cm

page 159
The last Bird, 2005, 200 x 100 cm

pages 160-161
The last Bird, 2005, 200 x 100 cm (detail)

page 162
Joie de vivre, 2005, 150 x 35 cm

page 163
right; *Joie de vivre*, 2005, 150 x 35 cm
left: *Joie de vivre*, 2005, 150 x 35 cm

pages164-165
Memories, 2000, 35 x 150 cm

page 166
Memories, 2000, 100 x 100 cm

page 169
Sublimation, 2005, 150 x 150 cm

pages 170-171
Sublimation, 2005, 150 x 150 cm (detail)

page 172
L'Ordre du monde? 2002, 130 x 130 cm

The publishers wish to thank Rune Larsen for his precious collaboration.

Photographs:
Jacques Faujour, Paris, pages 10 - 172
Serge David, Paris, pages 8, 175, 176, 185
Sujata Bajaj, Paris, pages 186, 187

Published under the direction of Jean Mouttapa and Valérie Menanteau
Graphic design lunapark-attractions graphiques, Bianca Gumbrecht
Production Véronique Ovaldé
Photogravure Bussière
Printing and binding Imago
Translation (from French into English) Latika Padgaonkar

First published in France in November 2007 by
Éditions Albin Michel
22, rue Huyghens, 75014 Paris
www.albin-michel.fr
ISBN 978-2-226-18404-7

Printed in Malaysia